FROM MY HOME TO YOURS

Our spectacular cycling journey from France to Vietnam

THIBAULT CLEMENCEAU

Copyright © 2021 Thibault Clemenceau

All rights reserved. No part of this publication may be reproduced, distributed or transmitted in any form or any means, electronic, mechanical, photocopying, recording or otherwise, without the prior permission of the author.

ISBN (Printed Version): 9782957725526

Pictures by Thibault Clemenceau

Maps by Trân Nguyen Khanh Nguyen

For more information and pictures from the author and Non La Project, please visit:

www.instagram.com/nonlaproject

DEDICATION

This book is for my mother, my dad and my four grandparents.

FOREWORD

This book is a true story. Names may have been altered in some cases to protect people's privacy.

Due to printing costs and some layout constraints, both eBook and printed copies of the text have a limited number of pictures. In the printed copy, pictures are in black & white, to cut printing costs.

We then strongly advise readers to have a look at the full HD photographs, which are uploaded on the following *Flickr* page:

bit.ly/myhometoyours

As you go through the chapters you can have a glimpse through the different albums available via the link. That way, you can have an enhanced experience of our book!

Cycling together from my home to yours, Georgia

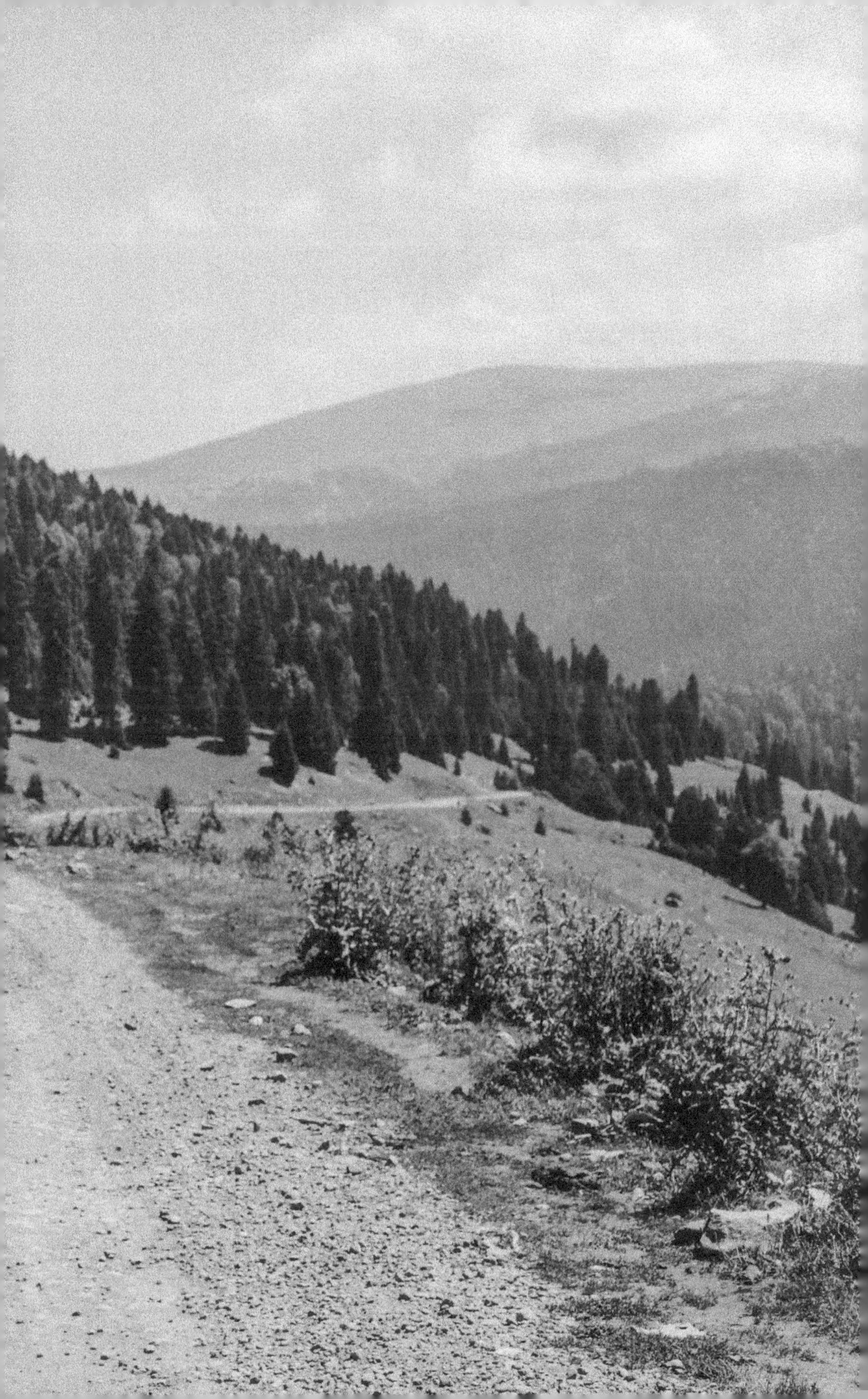

Tank, Thibault, Khanh Nguyen and Monster.

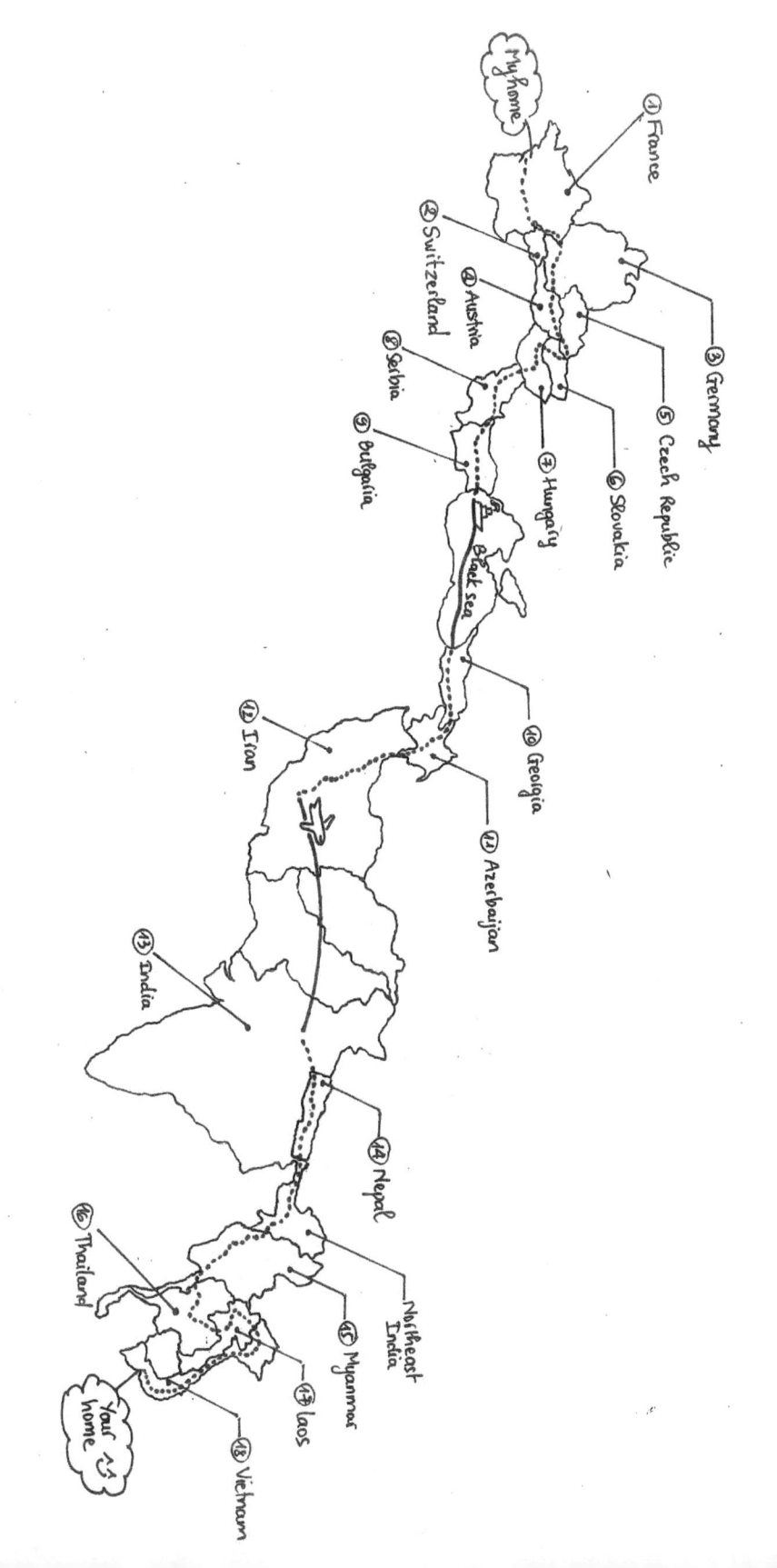

Our journey from France to Vietnam

- My home
- ① France
- ③ Germany
- ⑤ Czech Republic
- ⑥ Slovakia
- ⑦ Hungary
- ④ Austria
- ② Switzerland
- ⑧ Serbia
- ⑨ Bulgaria
- Black sea
- ⑩ Georgia
- ⑪ Azerbaijan
- ⑫ Iran
- ⑬ India
- ⑭ Nepal
- Northeast India
- ⑰ Myanmar
- ⑯ Thailand
- ⑮ Laos
- ⑱ Vietnam
- Your home

TABLE OF CONTENT

Introduction 15

Chapter 1
Childhood Pantheon 19

Chapter 2
Saigon Beginnings 23

Chapter 3
The Right Bike 27

Chapter 4
France & Switzerland: First love 35

Chapter 5
Germany & Austria: Monotony 47

Chapter 6
Eastern Europe: its vestiges of the Iron Curtain and the Divine Maria
.... 57

Chapter 7
Serbia: meeting with the fabulous Rusyns 69

Chapter 8
Bulgaria: last European pedal strokes 81

Chapter 9
Luminous meeting on the Black Sea 93

Chapter 10
Georgia: true freedom 99

Chapter 11
Azerbaijan, "Salam!" and Watermelons 111

Chapter 12
Iran: Discovering a New World 119

Chapter 13
Kalashnikov for me, Sexual Harassment for her 135

Chapter 14
In the land of Taarof 143

Chapter 15
From Qom to Abyaneh: Iran in all its diversity 157

Chapter 16
Leyla and Mustafa 173

Chapter 17
The province of Fars and the Qashqai.. 183

Chapter 18
Persepolis and Shiraz: finishing Iran in style 203

Chapter 19
Northern India: teleportation to a new civilization 213

Chapter 20
Nepal: between the Himalayas, the tigers and Buddha 231

Chapter 21
Northeast India: hugs and food poisoning 255

Chapter 22
Myanmar: Cat and Mouse with the local police 277

Chapter 23
Thailand & Laos: so close and so far from the goal 305

Chapter 24
Northern Vietnam: back among the rice fields and Covid-19 329

Chapter 25
Central & South Vietnam: the end, what end?.............................. 349

EPILOGUE 359

The Non La Project gear list 365

Introduction

How far would you be prepared to cycle for someone you love? Even the most respectable romantic would grimace at the prospect of 16,000km (10,000 miles), but Khanh Nguyen didn't. She was determined to make the last drops of our youth count. A few months after she accepted my proposal, she agreed to travel across continents, from my home to hers, from France to Vietnam.

I'd first left France for Saigon, Vietnam, in 2015. I'd landed a job as a business development manager. A mutual friend set up the first date I had with my future wife, and our relationship blossomed until we married in 2018. We spent four happy years together until I was given a promotion. I'd need to leave Vietnam for France again. If I took the promotion, my wife and I would've chosen to start a family, settle down and grow old. However, I knew there was still so much that I wanted to discover before then. So I turned the promotion down, following my heart with my wife instead.

Embarking on such madness would admittedly be less taxing for me than her. With a 4,000km (2,500 miles) journey with my brother across Europe already under my belt, I knew my limits. Khanh Nguyen could ride a bike but wasn't an endurance athlete. No one would've expected her to successfully cycle through desert sands and blistering snow by the end of the year. Yet she did. For Khanh Nguyen's family, just cycling to the market was cause for worry! A sharp contrast to mine who would encourage me to see such dangers as the opportunities of growth and the lack thereof to be far more dangerous.

I didn't want this rather special honeymoon only to impact our lives. After living for four magnificent years in the bustling Saigon, I had got to know an association: *Poussières de Vie*[1]. This association provides free schooling to underprivileged children and works to broaden their prospects. My wife and I's involvement had grown over the years with *Poussières de Vie* to the point of sponsoring three sisters taking part in the program: Diem, Duyen, and Trang. It, therefore, became natural to fuse our adventure towards enabling the advancement of Poussières de Vie. For every kilometer we cycled, we'd aim to collect a dollar. The total 16,000km (10,000 miles) would enable us to raise 16,000USD for their new school. After a year cycling the roads of the world, would we have successfully achieved this humanitarian goal? Could we convince enough donors along the way?

We decided to call our project *Non-La;* the Vietnamese term for the conical hats commonly seen in Vietnam. They symbolize Vietnamese culture and all the values of the peasants, plowmen of the ground, and planters of coffee seeds and rubber trees: arduous work, endurance, mutual help, and especially a good mood! But then came the tougher challenge of figuring out what we were truly letting ourselves in for. What would crossing continents be like? Who would we meet? How would we be received? And, most importantly, would our marriage survive the adventure?

According to the philosopher Nietzsche, we depend on the conditions under which we write. A book, even if it wants to be *objective*, is only the confession of its author. I am currently writing these reflections in a silence disturbed only by the occasional boisterous clucks of a rooster. It's two in the afternoon; the blue sky stretched above me, the heat made palatable by the cooling embrace of the wind. Khanh Nguyen and her parents are resting in the house behind me, visible through the window. The current Covid-19 pandemic almost cut this family reunion short.

---

[1] Dust of life in English

Chapter 1

Childhood Pantheon

Pedaling down an Iranian gorge chased by wild dogs on my honeymoon is something I can always thank my family for. They inspired our yearlong trip cycling half-way across the world; they gave me the name printed in a passport now bursting with multi-colored stamps. I see myself as the product of their influence, so to start this book, I want to start with them.

In the same family home where my great-great-great-grandfather had his childhood, I had a part of mine. Georges Clemenceau was the President of the Council of France during WWI and an ardent traveler. His resilient character and profound curiosity served as powerful examples to me. To race down our creaky set of stairs for the dinner call was to follow in his footsteps. It had a powerful impact on me.

His great-grandson was my grandfather, nicknamed Pouffy. A bohemian to the bone, he traveled the world with his camera, capturing everywhere from Japan to Central America. Sitting with us on the oversized couches he kept in his art studio, he'd give into our demands for more stories, recounting the tales with sparkling eyes.

My other grandfather, Bon Papa, hunted for volcanos throughout China and South America, snapping photographs along the way. When he came back to France, he'd carefully catalog them into heavy albums. Taking them from his shelves, I'd turn their pages with wide eyes, staring at the new landscapes and peoples I was discovering. For my adventures, I made sure not to leave my camera behind either, and my photographs are paced throughout this book to illustrate my stories.

My mom was the one who gave me my taste for nature, getting lost with me on endless horseback rides among the trees and streams. At the same time, my dad got me on a bicycle for the first time. For many years we spent our Sunday mornings cycling around the French countryside by bike until one day I went off alone and I haven't stopped pedaling since then!

"First you have to know what you want, then you have to have the courage to say it, then you have to have the energy to do it."

— **Georges Clemenceau**

Chapter 2

Saigon Beginnings

We began our training in sunny Saigon, Vietnam, hardly a cyclist's mecca. Good quality cycling shops were almost impossible to find. But, since my new wife and I had met and lived in the city, it became our default training ground. Before we could fly to our starting point in France, we would have to make do.

We realized there was some escape from the frenetic traffic to the coconut tree-lined south of the city, so we promptly moved there together. The owner of our apartment had an old bike he had no use for, and Khanh Nguyen's sister - Khoi Nguyen - had a bike collecting dust in her basement, so we had our wheels!

Two to three times a week, we woke up before five in the morning when the city is at its coolest and sleepiest. The first few days we made short distances: fifteen kilometers (9 miles) then twenty (12.5 miles) then twenty-five (15.5 miles). Our ritual motivation was that after every session we could stop at a street corner for a hearty bowl of Pho[1] ,Banh Cuon[2] , or a Banh Mi[3] always accompanied by a coconut!

Saigon is perfectly flat, and so it was impossible to train in climbing reliefs... except a few bridges! With a departure date fast approaching, we still had

---

[1] Vietnamese noodle soup with beef
[2] Vietnamese rice cakes
[3] Local Vietnamese sandwich

so little to be certain of, other than that our bodies were still young and would adapt.

The fan blew our hair slowly from right to left as we frantically researched the ample information to be found on blogs and discussion forums. We quickly realized we had our biases. While commonly portrayed in the media as war ridden and full of unpleasant characters, Iran was praised in the blogs of travelers as a fabulous country to visit, with an intricate history and enigmatic local population. We wanted to fight against our prejudices because I knew through my previous travels that a political decision isn't necessarily the general population's.

The time then came to say goodbye to Vietnam and our first training wheels. Khanh Nguyen's family took us to the airport for the morning flight by car. With anxiety wrought on their faces they told us repeatedly through the rear-view mirror not to take any risks. We could only nod our heads to calm them, knowing keeping such promises would be impossible.

The flight to France gave us our first tangible impression of the scale of the journey we were about to embark on. What would take a little over 13 hours by plane would take a year by bike. We flew over Oman then Iran, with impeccable visibility of the landscape below. I wondered how we were going to survive down there on the arid ground. For the first time, my confidence took a beating. I squeezed Khanh Nguyen's hand a little harder, and she turned and smiled at me.

The big Airbus landed softly at Charles de Gaulle. French March temperatures are so cold compared to those of Vietnam. We took our second flight to Nantes over the plush green countryside to where Dad was waiting for us beaming.

Chapter 3

The Right Bike

We had six weeks before the big departure and considering all that we still had to do, it wasn't that much time. We hadn't even found the right bikes, and a lot of our equipment was still missing. We also needed to start communicating on social networks about our adventure. Without a good website and effective communication on social networks, it would be difficult for us to collect many donations.

Despite the cool temperatures below 10°C (50°F), we had to start training. The two bikes used with my brother, Amaury, five years earlier for our trip through Europe were still snoozing under a dusty sheet at the bottom of the old barn around the back of our house: "No more early retirement guys! Let's get back to work." I was excited to show Khanh Nguyen my beautiful Vendée countryside woven with groves and small paths. The first training sessions went well: about twenty kilometers (12.5 miles) then quickly about forty (25 miles) every two or three days.

Between two training sessions, we spent precious time with our people. However, it was still impossible for us to find our mounts to cross Eurasia... What we found was either too expensive or not up to the experience we expected! Luckily, I came across an ad on the Internet that proposed a long-distance bike in Khanh Nguyen's size. The ad was super detailed, and the bike was well equipped. The person who wrote the ad, Manu, seemed passionate about long-distance travel. I gave him a call: we talked at length about the bike's characteristics: it was a 1997 Giant steel frame on which he worked endless hours to add all the necessary elements for a great trip. Each component of the bike had to be robust; designed to withstand thousands of kilometers. Being on the Kazakh steppes would all be well and good, but where would we be able to repair our bikes? Manu worked in a store located in Brantôme, two hundred kilometers (124 miles) away. His experience and prices made the long round trip by a car worth it.

A few days before meeting Manu and purchasing Khanh Nguyen's future steed, we had the opportunity to decide on my own! A customer had just dropped off a bike at Manu's that he wanted to resell. It was my size. The bike was almost brand new, just over a thousand kilometers (620 miles) ridden and fully equipped for the long ride (casket, transmission, pedals, steel luggage rack). There were a few elements to adjust or change, but nothing too difficult. It was a bike from the German brand *Patria*: perfect for the long course at more than a reasonable price. When we took the car that crisp March day to Manu's, Khanh Nguyen and I were extremely excited. Manu stood waiting for us in the doorway of his shop. The bicycles were there. They were magnificent! They gave a real impression of strength and robustness and it was like love at first sight for both of us.

Khanh Nguyen nicknamed hers "Monster": with its multiple extensions on the handlebars, it had a real monster's head which was not so scary when you faced it. I called mine "Tank". With its steel racks and structure, it looked like a siege weapon. We were going to be family for the coming year!

～

The last few weeks went by quickly, too quickly. We had been able to buy and gather almost all of our equipment for a year: luggage, the two-person tent, sleeping bags, the stove, repair & first aid equipment... We always had to compromise between strength, weight, and price when deciding on them. I particularly liked that mental exercise, as it made me realize the excess

Khanh Nguyen meeting Monster

utility we often don't need. Tank weighed more than 42 kilograms (93 pounds) with all the equipment packed on, not counting the water and food I would have to carry. Monster's weight was a clear 36 kilograms (79 pounds) that Khanh Nguyen would have to push all the way to Vietnam! Please refer to the end of the book for our full gear list.

Our training was now done with Monster and Tank, so we left with them in search of places to practice setting up camp in the middle of the forest. The installation of it wasn't second nature yet, and our nights were far from peaceful. Every animal that passed made us open our eyes. Sometimes it was a roe deer or a hedgehog, sometimes a huge beetle. We had to do this several times before we could really enjoy a long, restful sleep.

Our website was ready, and *Poussières de Vie*, the association we supported, had just launched the online donation platform. From the very first days, we had received more than three thousand dollars in donations, which increased our motivation tenfold and emboldened our little hearts.

Then one day, it was the day before our departure. It had all happened so fast. Were we ready? Not really. We had everything we needed on the bike and equipment side, but our bodies would need to adapt. As Charles de Gaulle[1] said, "the stewardship will follow" On the eve of our departure, the roof of Notre-Dame de Paris burned down. Continuous news channels relayed the terrible images in loops. Could this be a bad sign? I was leaving the television to join Khanh Nguyen. In the living room, we prepared our luggage like schoolchildren serious at the prospect of school. We weighed the bikes and equipment for the 200th time. We fell asleep for the last time "at home", under our roof.

The next day, we prepared the bikes, then pedaled to La Réorthe town hall (the official start point). The local TV waited for us and the local cyclist's association, and once we arrived, the mayor made a speech. Amaury, a friend and witness at our wedding, was there too. He'd came specially from Nantes that morning to wish us the best. My siblings, Linda

---

[1] Major French politician during the 20th century

Departure Day

- my stepmother -, Mami - my grandfather's second wife, and our dear neighbors were there too. Even Didi, our Jack Russell, was there! But my father was missing from the picture: a professional obligation. We had said our goodbyes a few days before, in our contained sincere way.

Khanh Nguyen and I kissed each other, hugging tightly. We realized that this was no longer a joke: we were there. We couldn't turn back now. A group of about twenty cyclists and Tara - my younger sister - and Enguerrand - one of my four brothers - joined us. We formed a merry bunch over fifteen kilometers (9 miles). Our bikes seemed so heavy compared to theirs: they flew, while we dragged ourselves along the Vendée asphalt.

Our little troop split at the next village. Before leaving, my little sister Tara threw an "If you die, Thibault, I'll kill you" my way, which dad often said before I made a long journey. But this time, it resonated. It was very possible. After she had cycled off, we were alone, facing our sixteen thousand kilometers (10,000 miles) to cover.

I felt like I was at the beginning of the novel Journey to the End of the Night by Céline. Bardamu, the narrator of the Journey, enters on a whim with one of his comrades in the French army during the First World War. Their newly formed troop leaves the city whose clamor from the windows and alleys exalts and carries the soldiers. And then they left the city, and then nothing, no more cheering. Bardamu leading at the front then said to himself: 'we're done for".

Chapter 4

France & Switzerland: First love

Mileage Meter: 0km to 1,242km (0 to 771 miles)

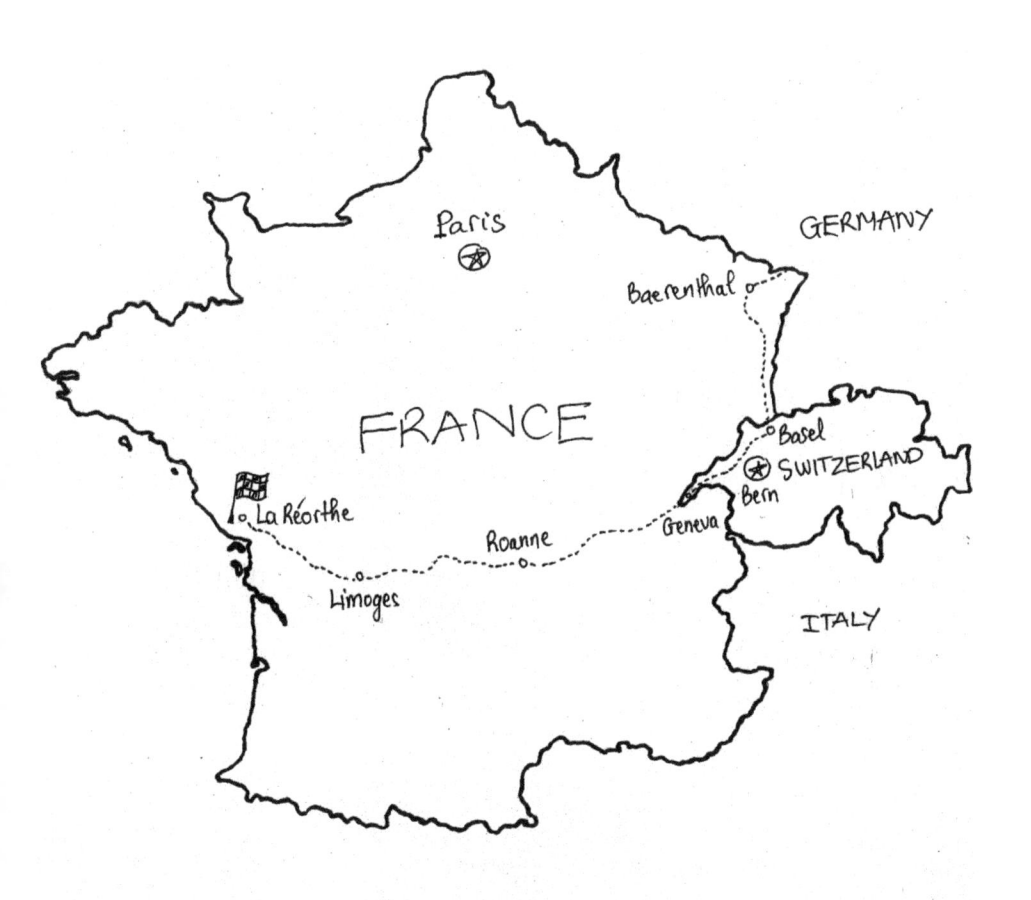

The repetitive and circular movement of our pedals, the intensity of the days, and our encounters gradually undermined our fragile representations of space and time. After a year on the road, I often felt like I had been away for at least ten years, if not a lifetime.

Our first challenge was to cross from the Centre of France to Switzerland and Geneva. It was the time of first discoveries where our bodies needed to adapt and find their own rhythm. France in April was magnificent to cross: the milder temperatures gave us a glimpse of fauna and flora that were gradually regaining their full intensity. France lacks Veloroutes[1] compared to Germany or the Netherlands, but its secondary network is exceptional. Its small roads were generally in superb condition and some days we hardly met anyone. There were endless opportunities to stop near a lake or a river.

We spent days at more than seventy kilometers (43 miles) through the center of France: Creuse, Puy-de-Dôme, Loire, Rhône, Ain, and Jura. Our leather saddles were starting to hurt our butts. From the British brand *Brooks*, it talked about a thousand kilometers (620 miles) to finally start to mold to our delicate bottoms. The end of the day was therefore often painful and accompanied by soreness. Khanh Nguyen suffered particularly badly, especially as soon as difficulties arose: hills, stony roads, muddy tracks … But, nonetheless, she kept going. I did everything I could to support her, encourage her, and push her to continue. She needed to keep her motivation intact and for as long as possible if we wanted to go far.

Where did we spend our first nights? Apart from staying once in a tent in Creuse, we were inside every night. Our first three nights were with three different hosts from the *Warmshowers* community. I have to explain what *Warmshowers* is because it's quite fabulous: it's a website where

---

[1] Special roads designed for bicycles

cyclists from all over the world welcome other cyclists to stay with them for free. There are thousands of members all over the world. Just send them a message to introduce yourself and your possible arrival dates. Replies are usually quick and quite often positive. Our Warmshowers hosts mostly welcomed us as longtime friends.

Our first hosts were called Etienne, Binh Duc, and Stephen, and they offered us dinner while leaving a room just for us at their home. And then there was the shower, always hot! This community isn't called *Warmshowers* for nothing! Binh Duc, for example, was of Vietnamese origin - you couldn't make that up - but he didn't speak Vietnamese. He welcomed us near Niort with his family, who prepared a superb dinner for us. For Khanh Nguyen, it was a true small revolution. Vietnamese people are generally distrustful of others and it's often unthinkable for them to invite someone they don't know into their home unless a family member or a friend has introduced them. This trip was already giving her a glimpse into new ways of behaving and reshaping her representations.

Binh Duc had taken a long solo bike ride around the world. He had a lot of stories to tell and wanted to hear ours. These kind of moments were priceless as they allowed you to unwind after a long day on the bike. But keep in mind not to spend too many nights with *Warmshowers* hosts! It can quickly set up tiredness that I would describe as "relational". Meeting new people every day can take up a lot of energy. You have to know how to balance meeting new people with your own time in a tent or a youth hostel.

Khanh Nguyen and I once spent an Easter weekend at my family's home on my mother's side in Creuse. Bon Papa and my grandmother, Maman Zouzou, were there and many of my cousins and their kids. My grandparents weren't in particularly good shape. Sickness and old age were weakening them by the day. It became difficult to really communicate with them, but being with them brought back the most beautiful childhood memories and felt good. I became afraid of being thousands of miles away in the middle of this journey and not being able to return if Bon Papa or Maman Zouzou were to fall fatally ill. These are the familial risks one faces in long journeys away. The cousins, for their part, were impressed by Khanh Nguyen. After two short nights, it was already time to leave. We hugged all the cousins and had a few precious minutes with my grandparents before leaving on Tank and Monster..

The kilometers followed one another through the countryside. We arrived in Roanne in the department of the Loire. Our hosts for those few days were special: Sylvie and her family were part of an association, le *Sourire Levant*, which volunteers to welcome young Vietnamese people in France to train them for jobs. This year, it was four girls: Ly Ba, Tru, Jami, and Duom, who also went through *Poussières de Vie*, the association we supported through our adventure. Different families hosted them. Ly Ba, for example, was practicing her hairdressing. She gave us an offer we couldn't refuse, to do Khanh Nguyen and I's hair for free! A real family spirit emerged between all those families: the Vietnamese girls had created a real dynamic with all these Roannais. Some arrived at the others' homes, inviting each other to dinner, to have an appetizer, or to go for a walk. Sylvie also organized an interview on the radio and then in the press. After two days, we left full of new energy. Traveling by bike allowed us to access great people: in the sharing and the gift of self, far from small calculations and ego.

―――

The first real difficulties came with the Jura and the Swiss mountains. The incline gradients started to become difficult, and the weight of the bikes felt. Khanh Nguyen had little experience in the mountains, and it soon showed. One day, she was struggling to climb a hill, and I took the lead. Behind me, I heard her burst into tears, tears that came from deep within her. I hurried back to her and hugged her with all my strength. Her beautiful little head was against my chest, and hot tears soaked my T-shirt. After regaining some composure, she explained to me that they were just tears of tiredness. Her mind wanted to reach the top of the hill, but her body was screaming for her to stop. We sat for ten minutes on a small wooden bench lined with foam, drank a little water, swallowing two or three cakes. Then Khanh Nguyen was ready to try again: a real warrior.

Two weeks passed before we approached our first border. It was Switzerland! The day before the border crossing, we spent the night at Régine and Michel's house. They were two retirees, also members of the *Warmshowers* network. In their chalet perched in the mountains and among the cows, they told us about their past and future trips. At more than sixty-five years old, they impressed us by having crossed the Andes [1] by bike. We said to ourselves that we still had beautiful days ahead of us on our bicycles.

The next day as we crossed the border, we saw a flagpole with the Swiss flag flying valiantly in the fresh air at the top. We were very proud to take our picture at the base. Switzerland is like a painting. I see it as the "The European Japan": as everything was as finely tuned and functional as a pocket-watch. The landscape was painted like a masterpiece. Blades of grass were carefully cut to match the height of the others. Nothing moved. It was easy to move around with an enormous network of bike routes, and we quickly arrived in Geneva, where Emmanuel and his family were waiting for us. Emmanuel was one of our best men at our wedding: our friend and my former manager in Vietnam. His parents spoiled us as if we were their grandchildren.

We took advantage of our few days in Geneva to have Monster inspected. Its derailleur had a problem, and we couldn't fix it. If Switzerland and Geneva did have a problem, it was their prices! Everything was horribly expensive. Hot chocolate could cost eight euros (US $9.50). So, when we arrived at the bike store, we were already worry about the bill that would await us. We entered the store and met Fred. Fred had a real cyclist's body and a frank smile. We explained to him our problem, but also our adventure. We left him a business card with our website. Before leaving the store, I asked Fred:

---

[1] Mountain range in South America

French countryside landscapes

"And in terms of price, how much do you think this will cost us?"

"Oh, for a standard inspection, I'd say about a hundred and fifty euros (US $180) per bike."

I wanted to shout "NO!" and run straight out of the shop, but naturally, politeness, shyness, and necessity prevailed and I accepted. Those three hundred euros for two bikes were going to hurt. As we returned to Emmanuel's parent's home, I felt embarrassed not to have at least negotiated a bit! But that afternoon, I received a call: it was Fred!:

"Hello, Thibault? It's fine, we were able to fix the problem with the "Giant" bicycle. We went on your website, and we decided to do the maintenance and cleaning of your bikes for free; to support you and your association".

I can't tell you how much adrenaline and joy that brought me! We headed back to the store to pick up Tank and Monster. Fred stood smiling, and we thanked him warmly for his gesture. We took advantage to discuss more with him during his work break. He was a former professional rider who'd won races and participated in the Tour de France! He had retired to spend more time with his family. Unbelievable: A former Tour de France racer had fixed tank and Monster!

We set off again on the beautiful Swiss roads along Lake Geneva and then climbed up to Lausanne, where a cousin, Stanislas, and his wife, Sophie, and their two children waited for us. It was cold at the beginning of May. So cold that I looked at the weather forecast for the next day they predicted snow during the night. Snow in the middle of May! We settled down around a beautiful fondue[1] for dinner when Khanh Nguyen exclaimed,"Thibault, look! Look! Snow!". It was the first time in her life that she'd seen snowfall. A thick white blanket of it gently settled on the frozen ground. Her reaction made me realize that the wonder of nature had become routine for me. Her passion reignited mine. Both of us curled up under our thick comforter. The next morning Stanislas told us to stay, the snow was thick, but we

---

[1] Melted cheese mixed with white wine

decided to go anyway. Our bikes slid and fused on the asphalt, which traced the road through the white scenery. We even took advantage of a golf course immaculate with snow to take pictures by ourselves lost in the middle of an ocean of white. We were equipped for low temperatures but not really for winter temperatures. Our coats didn't protect us from the humidity, and my gloves didn't protect me from the cold at all. So much so that I had to cover each of my hands with one of my socks! Style had to take a back seat. We came across a cow and her calf, prisoners of the snow, then took a long descent which made us lose altitude. The temperature became progressively more bearable. We arrived tired and trembling in the only coffee shop open that Sunday. The hot chocolate at eight euros (US $9.50) was really welcome this time!

After the city of Basel, we made a small detour through the East of France. We went up the Rhone-Rhine canal to Strasbourg and then to Baerenthal. There, special hosts were waiting for us: Laure & Fabien Mengus. They were both owners of the Arnsbourg: a restaurant with a Michelin star and a five-star hotel. Laure & Fabien welcomed three young Vietnamese women from the region of Kontum in the center of Vietnam who, like our friends from Roanne, went through *Poussières de Vie*. They had completed a six-month training program of their choice (hotel business, service, or cooking) in that prestigious setting. That morning in May, we had to arrive by eleven o'clock.

A local TV crew was waiting for us as well as the whole Arnsbourg team. A few kilometers before reaching our destination, we went up along the channel when I heard the cry of Khanh Nguyen calling for help. She had just been stung above the eyebrow by a bee that had gotten stuck in her sunglasses. We rode as fast as we could to the nearest pharmacy to invest in an *Aspivenin* We had to avoid the swelling for television! Just outside of the pharmacy,

The Swiss snow, Lausanne

I positioned the *Aspivenin*[1] on Khanh Nguyen's sting. But I put the plastic tip in the wrong direction, doubling her pain! What an idiot... I apologized and this time I sucked the bee's venom in the right way. Khanh Nguyen was fortunately not allergic and her face did not swell.

We arrived at the Arnsbourg in good time. We were superbly welcomed by Thuy, Hao, and Nung and the whole team of the Arnsbourg. Laure, the host, even offered us the privilege to stay in a hotel room for two nights and enjoy dinner that evening in their starred restaurant. Fabien was the chef who'd earned the Michelin star for that restaurant. We were overwhelmed by their generosity. We were only at the beginning of the trip and hadn't done much yet after all.

Of the three Vietnamese apprentices, Hao stood out with her smile and aura. She behaved like a true professional and seemed so comfortable walking around the hotel. Thuy, in the service, and Nung in the kitchen of the starred restaurant also brought a real dynamic to the whole team. By their smiles and attitudes, we perceived that the team worked well together and were glad to see them doing so well!

The time had come to continue to cycle to Germany, which wasn't far away. In the morning, Laure prepared another surprise for us: a huge check both in size and amount for our collection of donations for *Poussières de Vie* as well as loaves of bread and pastries generously donated by the local craftsman. We left laden with the memories and flavors they gave for the border of Germany; our third country!

---

[1] Medical tool to remove the venom

Chapter 5

Germany & Austria: Monotony

Mileage Meter: 1,242km to 2,178km (771 to 1,353 miles)

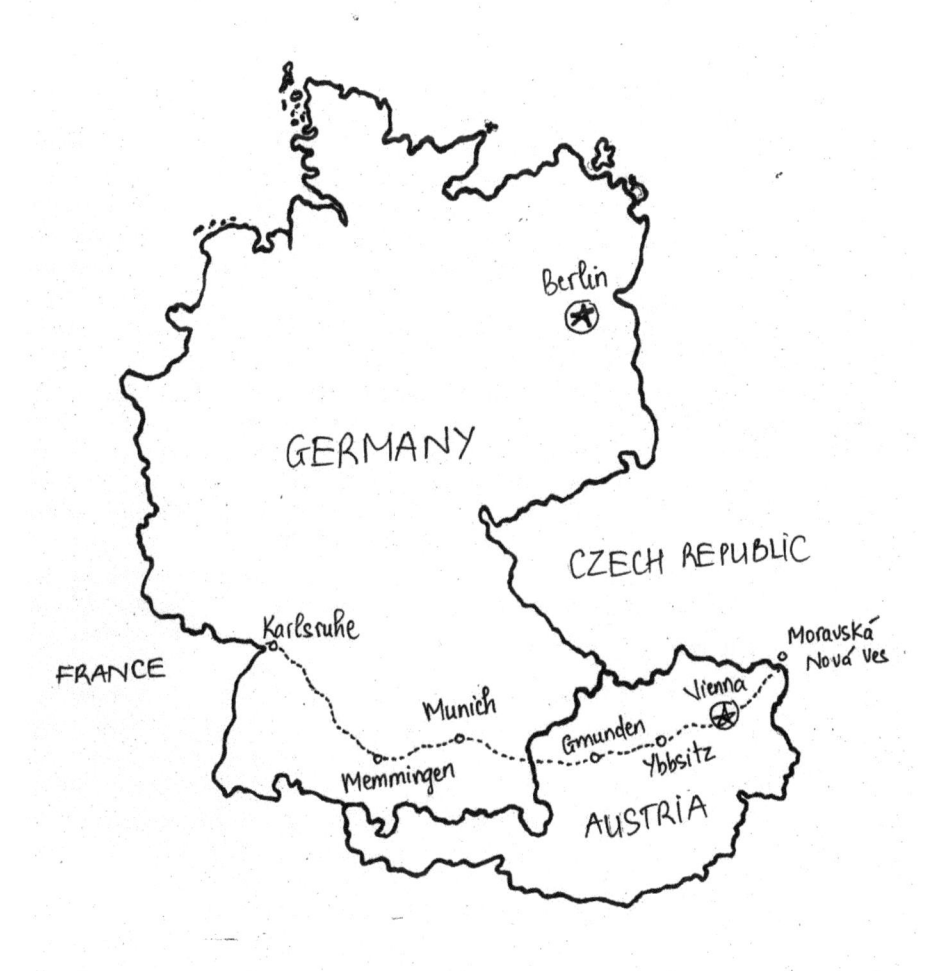

I have few vivid memories of Germany and Austria. Despite spending almost three weeks there, only the monotony we suffered comes to mind. West Germany from the French border to Munich has little to offer the frequent traveler. Potato fields galore and unwelcoming people who never greet you and hardly answer when you say hello. It was cold and wet. Our joy in experiencing this land eventually matched theirs.

And then, before passing through Bavaria, we met Roman. He was a tall Czech man more than sixty years old who had come to Germany to start a family. He belonged to the *Warmshowers* community and welcomed us for a night at his home. His English was in its infancy, but he made us both laugh a lot. He lived with his wife, his two sons, and his daughter. His two sons, both over 18 years old, pouted at our presence and barely said hello. Roman tried to stir their interest:

"Michel, greet Thibault and Khanh Nguyen. He's French and she's Vietnamese!"

"Hello Michel. How are you doing? We are traveling from France to Vietnam for one year and sixteen thousand kilometers (10,000 miles), I said"

"Ha..." Michel cut me short with indifference and fixed his attention back on his iPhone.

With Michel preoccupied in his own world, we spent the evening with Roman. Roman had made it a personal goal to provide for his own needs. He did everything by himself: brewing his own beer, even raising his own ducks and rabbits to eat. The dinner he had cooked for us was hearty. He was a bodybuilder and seemed perfectly built to endure the endless winters on the German plains. Roman was a cyclist too who had made trips to the Czech Republic through Germany. He was a character. In front of his house, he had installed a funny mannequin made of junk with his bike at the foot. He had hung a sign from it that he had scrawled in English *"free water for cyclists"*. The next day, after a peaceful and refreshing night, the three of us posed in front of the house for a farewell photo.

The route to Munich was smooth and with a detour through the town of Kissing. I spotted it a few days ago on the map, and I proposed to Khanh Nguyen to add forty kilometers (25 miles) to our day just to pose for a kiss in front of the city sign. We got there quickly: the city of Kissing has absolutely nothing to offer except a small church perched on a daunting-looking hill. So, we installed Tank and Monster in front of the yellow sign with "Kissing," written in black. I placed my camera and its tripod on the safety railing: switched on the timer and ran towards Khanh Nguyen for a big fiery kiss. The result you can see below: a kiss in Kissing. Not a bad memory for a young couple!

Near Munich, we were hosted by Albert and Sylvia. He was a psychologist; she was an art teacher. They were the parents of a friend of mine, Chris, whom I had met during a university exchange in Taiwan. During those five days we spent together, through our stories, our energy, and the countries that awaited us, we gave them the desire for the delights of travel again. We took the opportunity to be tourists in Munich during that beautiful month of May. The city center, built during the Nazi period, was a bit scary with its main streets and Nuremberg-style buildings. But life now seemed sweet in the large parks where you could lie on the grass, surf in a canal with a strong current, or drink a huge mug in a Biergarten. It's also the time of mutual discoveries. That of white beer, sausages, and pretzels for breakfast for Khanh Nguyen and me. We liked the originality of the experience, but we didn't want to repeat it! Khanh Nguyen then took advantage of the arrival of my friend Chris, and his girlfriend, Franzie, to cook for the whole family some Nems and bowls of Bun Bo Huê[1]. We had spotted an Asian restaurant run by Vietnamese people that offered everything Khanh Nguyen needed to cook. The owner even gave us a ten percent discount: a perfect example of the solidarity amongst compatriots.

---

[1] Vietnamese vermicelli soup with beef, vegetables and lemongrass

That Vietnamese interlude and last dinner all together became a great success. After five days, it was time to set off again for Austria. This is the hard part for long-distance travelers: when we begin to get attached to the people we meet, it's unfortunately often the time to leave again

⌒〜⌒

As we crossed Bavaria the landscape became noticeably more pleasant. Lakes nestling in and around forests knotted together in an endless dance. The temperatures were also ideal for cycling. We stopped wherever we wanted among the flowering fields. Every now and then we checked the online platform for donations for *Poussières de Vie*. We were on time: 1,700 kilometers (1,056 miles) covered, and more than 4,500 dollars collected so far. Everything was going well.

The border crossing with Austria, our fourth largest country, went smoothly. We felt our little legs getting stronger. So, we decided to explore the relief of southern Austria through Gmunden, Ybbsitz and finally reached the Danube before Vienna. A pedal ride took a lot of time, but we hung on. We sweated a lot and the arrival at the very top was always a source of great satisfaction: the descent was all the more appreciated. Nature is beautiful in this part of Austria. It was easy for us to camp among does, deer, and roe deers. Traveling by bike allowed us to move almost silently. Our forest friends usually spotted us only at the last moment and left as fast as their hooves could take them; their little white hairy buttocks bouncing into the distance. Whenever it happened, Khanh Nguyen was overcome with laughter.

Our guests from the *Warmshowers* community went after one another here and there. We were always amazed by their incredible sense of hospitality. Among them, Herbert and Hertha left us with particularly vivid memories. Both retired, they lived in Gmunden on the beautiful Lake Traunsee. They welcomed us for a night in their beautiful little house. Herbert impressed

Kiss in Kissing, Germany

us with his physical strength despite his seventy years. He was an epicurean who enjoyed his walks in the mountains, playing the guitar, and cooking. Herbert and Hertha weren't cyclists by any stretch of the imagination, but through the *Warmshowers* community, they wanted to welcome the world into their home and travel through the stories of their hosts. Herbert and Hertha made a dinner worthy of a great restaurant. Starter, main course, cheeses, and desserts made with local products. The wine also, from the Donau region, went perfectly with all our dishes. We roamed from one subject to another. What a joy to be able to make friends with two people we didn't know at all a few hours before. To close the evening, Herbert grabbed his acoustic guitar and played a Beatles song: *When I'm 64*. The rhythm was catchy, and we started to sing along with him. Herbert's and Hertha's eyes sparkle, ours too, as if by resonance. We went to bed with the melody and their smiles echoing through our senses. The next morning, once again, we had to say goodbye. A few days later, we consulted the page of donations for *Poussières de Vie*. Among the recent donations, one stood out: a hundred dollars from... Hertha and Herbert...

Vienna came where we rested for a few days at a friend's of Khanh Nguyen's family. Chi Anh Ngoc moved there more than twenty years ago. Anh Ngoc lived in a small apartment in the Karl-Marx Hof complex with one of her tenants, also Vietnamese, who was studying medicine. It was a social housing complex built in the thirties and was more than a kilometer (0.6 miles) long, imposing in both size and symmetry. Anh Ngoc, by the look of her kitchen and forthright attitudes, reminded us of the good Vietnam that seemed so far away. She projected on us her fears and warned us like a good Vietnamese mother: "Be careful when you camp; it's so dangerous! Take care Khanh Nguyen of your skin. Beware of the sun too!" It must be said that Anh Ngoc was allergic to many things and in particular to pollen and contact with plants. Just sitting in the green grass was completely unbearable for her. She, therefore, saw our journey as a world of imminent and multiple dangers. Taking advantage of this Vietnamese time capsule with Anh Ngoc was also an opportunity for Khanh Nguyen to wear the Áo

Night under the tent, Austria

Dài - the traditional Vietnamese long silk dress. Khanh Nguyen chose to carry in her luggage a magnificent yellow Áo Dài with floral patterns. As if to celebrate the time spent together, Anh Ngoc, her tenant, and Khanh Nguyen all decided to put on their Áo Dài. It was such a beautiful moment as they recognized the beauty of their culture, so far away from their homeland, that I had to immortalize it with my camera.

The German-Austrian duo offered us some nice encounters, but we didn't really have the sense of adventure and excitement that we were looking for. The weather certainly played its role: often rain, cold, and wind. But the cities and the landscapes we crossed; the people who live there remained almost indifferent to us as we remained indifferent to them. I know that these feelings are part of the long journey, but fortunately, they are often the fertile ground for future and unsuspected emotions and exaltations. In my heart of hearts, I hoped that the Czech Republic, Slovakia, and Hungary would provide us with so-called adventures. As we pedaled through our last Austrian kilometers, I turned around and caught Khanh Nguyen's gaze. I smiled at her, and she smiled back at me.

Chapter 6

Eastern Europe: its vestiges of the Iron Curtain and the Divine Maria

Mileage Meter: 2,178km to 3,584km (1,353 to 2,226 miles)

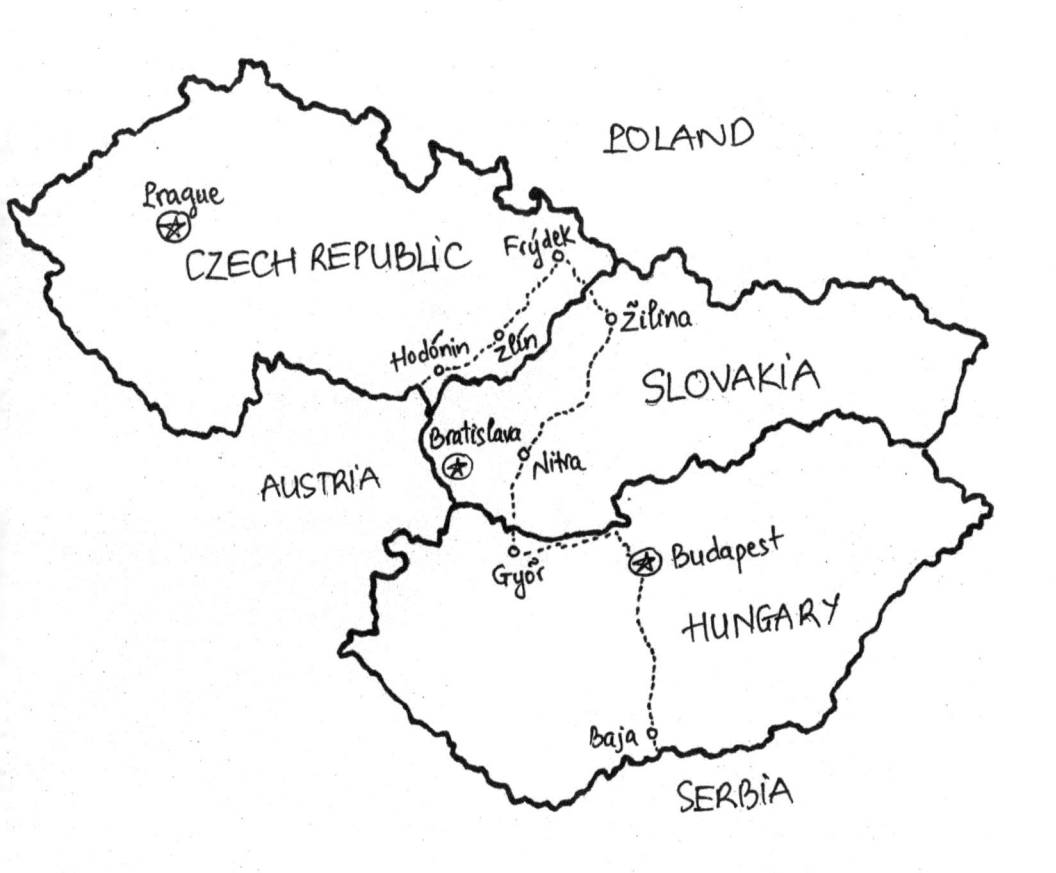

Vienna and its violins were moving away. We walked along the former Iron Curtain that separated the communist world from the capitalist world. While the Iron Curtain no longer exists the former border still forms the branch that splits Europe's cultural history. The area of the Iron Curtain that we crossed was infected with mosquitoes. It meandered between Austria, the Czech Republic, and Slovakia. We resigned ourselves to not stop: a stop was synonymous with dozens of bites from our voracious friends.

Once you enter the Czech Republic, the difference with Austria is quite clear. The infrastructure was less maintained, old houses or factories rusted in the open air. For the first time, we found carts pulled by donkeys or horses. We felt that the Czech Republic was still recovering from the communist trauma, especially from the Prague coup of 1968. This impression was confirmed with what remains one of our most beautiful moments of this trip.

Again, we contacted Michal via the *Warmshowers* website to spend a night at his home in the small town of Moravská Nová Ves in the southern Moravian region. Michal wasn't there but his parents, Maria and Vojtech, generously offered to receive us. A small message was waiting for us on their front door: "Thibault and Khanh Nguyen: welcome! Come through the garden gate". We pushed the gate and threw a cheerful Dobry' Den[1]. First, we met Vojtech, Michal's father. A thin gangly man with a big tuft of hair, Vojtech didn't speak a word of English. His smile however served as the most beautiful of welcomes. Maria, his wife, walked through the door leading from the kitchen to his garden. She spoke impeccable English. She explained that she was a retired English teacher but continued to give lessons to children in the village

---

[1] "Hello" in Czech language

Maria and Vojtech's home was like traveling back in time. It was an old house from before the fall of communism with a soul, a real one. With its wallpaper, its furniture, and the accumulation of its objects, it wanted to tell us a story, its history. We were told by Maria as she unfolded the old sofa bed that we would sleep in their living room. I took the opportunity to look at the paintings and pictures around us: Christ, Pope John Paul II and Pope Francis had prime wall space. There were also black and white portraits of Michal, Maria and Vojtech. They were both beautiful, our guests for the evening. Maria then told us a little more about some of her little students: "They are Vietnamese! Their families have settled in Moravská Nová Ves and run two small supermarkets that supply the whole neighborhood".

Khanh Nguyen and I immediately proposed to meet them. Maria, for her age, was in great shape. She wobbled down the road on her old red bike and we followed her with Tank and Monster. After three hundred meters (1000 feet), we stopped at the first supermarket held by a first family. The son was at the cash register, the mother, Vân, wandered around in her shelves full of all the things we need in life. We introduced ourselves; I placed a few words in Vietnamese. Vân couldn't believe it.

"From France to Vietnam? But for how long? That's great! And you speak Vietnamese? You're amazing! What do you want? Take what you want from the store!"

With Khanh Nguyen, we declined one by one the various treats that Vân offers us: chocolate, cookies, chips, vanilla ice cream, and even... perfume! In front of our resistance, Vân hastened to put everything in a big bag and gave it to Maria. We all laughed at the absurdity of it!

"Let's go see the second family now," Maria said. The dynamic Vân accompanied us to the front of her store. We all took a picture together and then Vân wanted to give us money: Czech koruna! We refused, she insisted. We refused again, she insisted even more! No choice. We accepted, but on one condition: the money she gave us would be donated to the pool in favor of *Poussières de Vie*. That compromise seemed to suit her! We then left each other full of wholesome energy.

The other convenience store run by a Vietnamese family was a minute away by bike. The reception we got was the same, and the proposals too. This time it was Ngoan, a mother from northern Vietnam, and the boss at the helm. The ecstasy was so great for these Vietnamese who were so far from home to meet Khanh Nguyen and in this context. Nevertheless, we felt discomfort from one family concerning the other: from one supermarket for the other. Being the two local supermarkets, they were doomed to be rivals. It was such a shame... both families were so wonderful and welcoming. They seemed to ignore and even despise each other.

The two Vietnamese families invited us for dinner at their homes many times. Vân even harassed Maria on the phone, wanting her to let us stay at her house that night. Maria answered abruptly: "tonight, they are having dinner at my house". End of discussion!

Back at Maria and Vojtech's house, we both rested in the small living room. The married couple left the two newlyweds for an hour to go tomass. We took the opportunity for me to sort out the photos of the day, and for Khanh Nguyen to write her diary. We had two different approaches. Khanh Nguyen preferred to write down all the details in her little notebook: the cities, the number of kilometers, the names of the people we met... Me, I focused on my photos. I let my little memory take care of the rest. It doesn't do so badly, my memory!

Our hour, just the two of us, with the Pope hanging on the wall and the other cardinals, passed quickly. Vojtech and Maria were finally back! Vojtech was there, always so smiling. We were so happy to have him back. Maria asked us to settle down around the table in the kitchen. While preparing the dinner, she made sure she was translating between her great husband and us.

Our discussions became more and more personal as the trust between the four of us grew. Maria and Vojtech graduated just before the Russians arrived. She as an English teacher; him as an engineer. They had a difficult life as sons and daughters of landowners who refused to submit to collectivization, but also as devout Catholics. Vojtech told us about the difficult moments and those few moments of short joy here and there. Then came the collapse of the USSR in 1991: the end of a long sentence that had been

Vân, her husband and the divine Maria

Maria & Vojtech on their wedding day

Dinner for the four of us

stretched too far and of resistance against the occupier that had finally paid off. The dial of the clock already indicated ten o'clock. It was time to go to bed. We fell asleep leaning against each other with a special feeling that we'd lived a unique and beautiful day.

The next morning, Maria was there, the perfect mother hen. Vojtech had already left for the day. We swallowed a few slices of bread with a bowl of milk. We had everything but the desire to leave those two special people, but we had to go on. Maria kissed us both, blessed us, and gave us two small medals where the Virgin Mary was engraved. I squeezed the virgin very tightly between my little fingers, got on Tank, and pushed my pedals round. Little by little, she grew progressively smaller in perspective as we moved towards the horizon.

The Czech Republic, at the start only a little hilly, had reserved a mountain range for us on the journey to Slovakia: the Beskides Massif. The small passes followed one another, and tiredness accumulated, especially for Khanh Nguyen. One day, she was hungry. She had no energy and her legs weren't responding as a result. The last ten kilometers (6 miles) of our long day ended in pain, so much so that we decided to take a rest day the next day. Khanh Nguyen was in pain, but she held on. I gave all the energy I had to cheer her up and support her in those difficult moments.

The border crossing Slovakia, our sixth country, was at the top of a long climb where the wind blew and swept the flowers of the fields. Slovakia was a beautiful country with its landscapes, forests, and mountains. Several times we swam in its crystal-clear rivers. Camping was also easy thanks to the generally low population densities. The pleasure and satisfaction of being among nature were unbeatable: swimming in rivers, cooking at sunset, and then falling asleep together in a tent to the nightly sounds of the dense forests; who could ask for more? We often found beautiful tracks that passed through imposing forests and meadows where countless horses lived peacefully. We regretted only spending a few days in Slovakia before going on to Hungary.

On the last day before crossing the Hungarian border, we had our first encounter with police officers. We had just said goodbye to Igor and his family, the previous evening's hosts in the small town of Lipové and were on the open road without our helmets. Our hair free to flutter in the wind, a police car pulled in front of our path. The two policemen had just stopped two older men on their bikes also without helmets a little up the road. One of the policemen, sporting an impressive Danny Zuko quiff, asked us to wait for our turn. I immediately called Igor to come to our aid. I saw the two little old men getting angry with the policemen. One of them threw a "Rusko" at them. I interpreted this as a desire on the part of the little old man to make it clear to the policeman that he thought they were corrupt. They finally paid a ten-euro bill each, then left grumbling. Now it was our turn. I gave our passports to Danny Zuko, whose brow furrowed at Khanh Nguyen's Vietnamese passport. It was certainly the first one he had seen! Igor arrived from behind us in the meantime and tried to defuse the situation. He explained to them, with the right words, about our trip. Danny Zuko found it hard to believe that we were going to pedal all the way to Vietnam. Then he asked for details about our route, which was a good sign. We explained our route, and he relaxed more and more until he finally let us leave, finishing with a:
"Put on your helmets! And understand that we had to stop you... otherwise, the two little old men would never have paid the fine. They would never have accepted that we let you go while you were riding without helmets!"

After crossing a long bridge over the Danube, I quickly realized Hungary wasn't for me. Maybe we were pedaling in the wrong season, but I found it difficult to form a connection with locals, and with rotting garbage and animals lining the roads baking in the midday sun a series of unpleasant smells accompanied us along the exceedingly flat landscape.

We were in the middle of the heatwave in Europe, and the conditions near the Danube River favor the proliferation of millions of mosquitoes. When we followed the course of the Danube towards Budapest, it was impossible to stop for more than ten seconds without swarms of mosquitoes attacking us. They even bit through our clothes, the little bastards! We followed a semi-bike route that wasn't really finished... I felt that the budgets of the European Union had been spent there and that a lot of money had been lost in corruption... The path disappeared very quickly to leave only high grass. We decided to go on anyway, and the GPS indicated that the main road wasn't very far anymore. We shortly arrived at an abandoned factory and a long wall topped by barbed wire. Impossible to pass. The mosquitoes started to rush on us. They were hungry, and their multitude seemed to increase their excitement tenfold. The stings came in their dozens, and we both started to go a little crazy. They stung us everywhere: on our legs, on our back, on our face... We sprayed ourselves with all the mosquito repellent we had without much effect... We had to get out of this hell! We turned back to get out of the disused factory and took a small road which was supposed to bring us back to the main road. The mosquitoes continued chasing us despite our speed. The path passed through a kind of open-air dump where shady guys were roaming around looking for something. Our survival instincts kicked in, and we pedaled with all our strength. We finally saw the road. We were safe. We arrived without any strength left to a municipal camping lot, paid for the night, and looked for a good spot. Mosquitoes continued to swarm. I installed our tent as fast as I could. We rushed inside without daring to go out again: receiving any further bites was a completely unbearable prospect for us. We took off our clothes and started to inspect our war wounds: 76 stings for me and 120 for Khanh Nguyen. We spent an awful night tossing and turning and scratching all over our bodies.

We spent about ten days in Hungary, punctuated by our meals, the rain, and naturally the mosquitoes. The day's main activity was to pedal, trying to do an average of one hundred kilometers (62 miles) a day so as not to spend too much time in this country.

Our last day in Hungary had one last surprise in store for us. On the map, I spotted a border post that allowed us to avoid the main road to reach Serbia. It seemed a good idea. We drove on a very quiet road before arriving at the border post. The policeman inspected our passports and gave them back to us immediately:

"This border post can only process European passports. For you, Madam, with your Vietnamese passport, you can only pass through the main border post."

Now we either had to turn around and ride another thirty kilometers (19 miles) on the road or ride along the border on a five-kilometer (3miles) dirt road to get to the main border post. The choice was quickly made. We followed this dirt road which went along an impressive barrier made of barbed wire with heavily equipped police officers with their dogs. We saw for ourselves all the efforts made by Viktor Orban's Hungary to stop illegal immigration.

We finally arrived at the border post. Everything went well. It was clearly the first time since the beginning of the trip that we were relieved to leave a country. One thing was for certain: we would never set foot back in it, let alone our tires!

Summits to conquer, Czech Republic

Crossing the Slovakian border

Relaxing next to a small river, Slovakia

Night on the banks of the Danube with thousands of mosquitoes, Hungary

Chapter 7

Serbia: meeting with the fabulous Rusyns

Mileage Meter: 3,584 to 4,074km (2,226 to 2,531 miles)

It's amazing how a border crossing can change everything! From the first pedal strokes in Serbia, we felt immediately more comfortable. Serbia doesn't belong to the European Union: we had just left the Schengen area. We finally had our first stamp on our passports!

Some passers-by greeted us, the villages were well maintained, the grass freshly cut, and flowers bloomed in the gardens. We quickly split the thick protective shell we had built up in Hungary. We crossed the town of Sombor with its pleasant pedestrian streets. Rather than following all along road number 12 to Novi Sad, we decided to take a path that passed through fields. From my bike, I turned to Khanh Nguyen and said:

"How about knocking on someone's door tonight? We'll see what happens!"

"Ok, but you're the one who knocks and asks!"

"Of course! I'll show you how to do it and next time it's your turn!"

During one of our many breaks, I prepared a small text that I translated into Serbian using *Google Translate*:

"Hello, we are Thibault and Khanh Nguyen. We are husband and wife. We are currently cycling from France-Vietnam by bike for one year and 16,000km (10.000 miles). Would it be possible to install our tent in your garden? We will leave early tomorrow morning. Thank you very much!"

We continued riding under the sun for a good hour until we saw a beautiful little white church with a blue edging at the bottom. A large green lawn surrounded it. It seemed to be the perfect place to set up camp. I left Khanh Nguyen, Monster, and Tank outside and knocked on the wooden door of a two-story house next door. No answer. I knocked again. I heard a noise. Someone was approaching! The door opened, and a rather corpulent woman appeared, with short dyed hair. She was dressed in a long black

T-shirt dotted with white butterflies. She didn't look easy-going at first glance. I gave her my best smile and hastened to show her the message on my phone. She read it, seemed to understand, and then told me to wait. "I hope she says yes..." A minute later, she was back with the beginnings of a smile on her face! That was good! She waved to us to come inside and led us to the kitchen, where another woman was waiting for us. She had the same build as the one in black, with a similar haircut. She was wearing jeans and an apple green top that let both of her arms hang freely. We asked them what their names were. The woman in black was called Efemija; the one in apple green was called Melanjia.

They both went over to the stove, warmed up some leftovers for us and offered us some local pear alcohol. What a welcome! We tried as best as we could to communicate via my phone. We understood that they didn't live there but that they took care of the house of a man (presumably a priest) called Janko, who oversaw the sanctuary. We were, in fact, in a place where the Virgin Mary had appeared. On the same holy day, we'd appeared years later! The current was going well with our two friends. Janko, on a walk in the village, had been warned. He came back on his bicycle with strawberry ice cream for us! A few minutes later, we learned that he had a flat tire on his old bike. I rushed to him on the stony road to help him. Janko was missing an arm and struggled to push his bike while holding the ice cream pot. I greeted him warmly and hurried to push his bike. We both came back to the sanctuary, and the five of us enjoyed a tasty strawberry ice cream! Janko turned out not to be a priest here but a layman who guarded the place. He generously welcomed us to sleep at his for the night.

Our Vietnamese hats intrigued our three guests of the day. Khanh Nguyen hastened to make them try them on and the result made us all laugh hard. They then showed us around the small chapel so pleasantly decorated and built. A good hour later, a car arrived. A sister who spoke...and it was the French language that graces our ears. Her name was Martine-Agnès, but everyone in the village called her "Sestra Martina": Sister Martina. She had lived there for more than twenty or thirty years... I don't remember exactly. Sister Martina said to me then:

"It's your lucky day. Tonight is the annual festival of the Rusyn community!"

"Who are the Rusyns?" I eagerly replied.

"A community that has its own language and traditions. They are scattered all over Serbia, Slovakia, and also in Ukraine. Tonight is their big festival with their songs and dances. Would you like to go there with me?"

We hastened to answer her with a big "Yes". We had traveled by bike for this kind of moment: to access people and moments we couldn't possibly imagine. We left Janko, Efemija, and Melanjia behind and jumped into Sister Martina's car. She wanted to show us her house and a little chapel. We met Sister Christina, Sister Martina's superior, and discovered a splendid confidential place of worship. Under Tito's dictatorship from 1953 to 1983, some Christians were marginalized. Especially the Catholics who wanted to remain dependent of Rome, which Tito refused, wanting a Catholic Church of Yugoslavia. So, they had to hide, to do things confidentially. Sisters Christina and Martina participated in their resistance to the regime in place. The place was all the more beautiful and sacred because of its confidentiality.

We got back in Sister Martina's car to go to the festival. The music and dancing had already started. The public clapped their hands and sang with contented hearts. Wonderful traditional costumes were displayed on stage one after the other. A group of men formed on the left side of the stage while a group of women sang on the right. Then, the two groups merged, and each one found its ephemeral partner. I passed rather incognito in the crowd among all these faces, but Khanh Nguyen really didn't go unnoticed with her features being so different from theirs! The locals greeted us warmly and even offered us a beer.

Then came the turn of a young group coming straight from Ukraine! About twenty Rusyn children, all blonder than each other, danced in their beautiful white, green, and orange costumes. We even had the opportunity to take a picture with the whole group after their superb performance! Martina told us that it was time to go. We said goodbye to our joyful hosts for that evening. Back at the sanctuary, all asleep, our two friends, Efemija and Melanjia, had gone home. There was still Janko, waiting for us outside. Letting us sleep outside in our tent was apparently out of the question. We would be sleeping in the living room of his home. We decided we would wake up early the next morning to say goodbye to Sister Cristina. We fell asleep at the sanctuary with our eyes bathed in stars and of the memories of the colorful dances we'd so gratefully witnessed.

Early the next morning, Janko blessed us with the sign of the cross on our forehead and wished us all the best for the rest of our trip. We had just lived a rare moment with the Rusyn community, one of those experiences you never search for but finds you and leaves you in bliss.

We were still in the middle of the heatwave in Europe. The midday sun was beating down so hard. We took regular breaks to hydrate ourselves and took advantage of the shade when available. Day after day, we got closer to the famous Iron Gates. Shortly after leaving the country's capital, Belgrade, we experienced our first mechanical glitch. The rear derailleur cable had broken down. I had made the mistake of not changing Tank's cables when I bought it. I had a spare cable in my repair kit, but it was too hot. We were near the village of Pancevo, and I spotted a bike repair shop on Google Maps. "Let's go!" In two minutes, we were there. It was a very small store with a few bikes lying around. With a faded green front, "Pedala" was written. A lanky man was smoking a cigarette in the shade: "Hello guys! I am Vladimir. Sorry my English not very good". Vladimir's eyes sparkled with wary humor. Our Non-La hats amused him, and quickly he decided he wanted to pose with one. While he was busy changing Tank's cable, I took the opportunity to have a chat with him. Pancevo was gloomy to spend time in. Before the war in Kosovo, Vladimir had lived well. He had sold bicycles almost every day: everything had been fine for him. And then came the war, a dirty war. The United States and NATO intervened; Milosevic surrendered. And since then, everything had frozen, time, buildings, people. And people who are frozen no longer buy bicycles.

After a few minutes, Vladimir changed Tank's cable. I walked towards him and was about to pay him. He insisted on offering us the repair. Despite several exchanges between him and me where I insisted on giving him a bill, it was impossible for me to win. So with Khanh Nguyen, we decided to go to the local supermarket to buy some beers. We returned loaded up with bottles back to Vladimir's workshop. The three of us sipped our beer in the shade. We continued to exchange about the trip, about Vietnam. We felt really good beside Vladimir and his humor. Our beers finished; we left. I thanked Vladimir again. The Iron Gates were waiting for us!

We continued to follow the Danube, which was getting narrower and narrower. The road gradually became astonishingly beautiful. Mountains now surrounded us in this canyon. On the other side of the Danube was Romania. We had to find a place to camp that night, but the mountains rose so steeply that there wasn't really a flat place where we could pitch. It was only a little before sunset that we eventually found a kind of vacant ground where trucks came during the day to collect sand or stones and hid from the main road behind a mound of sand. It wasn't ideal, but it would do for that night. I set up the tent; Khanh Nguyen prepared the dinner. On the evening menu: fresh pasta and vegetables, bread and omelet. With a full belly, we fell asleep quickly. Late in the night, we were woken up by the sound of stones:

"What is it?" Khanh Nguyen whispered to me.

"Do you think someone is coming?"

I slowly opened the zip of our tent and took a look outside. Nothing moved. Then I heard stones roll again. I glanced up and saw goats moving like tightrope walkers along the rocks. Some of their missteps triggered the fall of a stone or two. Their white fur was bathed in the light of the full moon. Their nocturnal movement was poetic and gentle. It was a magnificent sight. I reassured Khanh Nguyen, and we went back to sleep.

The next day, early in the morning, we attacked the slopes of the Iron Gates.

Vladimir the repairman, Pancevo, Serbia

The tunnels followed one after another and were getting longer and longer. It was never a pleasant moment to cross a tunnel: they were usually dark, oppressive, and gave the impression that the vehicles would never see you on a bike regardless of any investment in a yellow vest. The worst was when a heavy truck rumbled through. It was like in Zola's[1] book *Germinal*! All the walls of the tunnel shook, and the monster's overpowering headlights radiated light. In moments like that I became a believer in moments like that, praying that I wouldn't be crushed as easily as a fork turns a potato to mash. The return to the open air was always met with a sigh of relief. After we escaped the tunnel, we arrived at the highest point of the Iron Gates with a lot of effort and sweat. The view on the canyon was breathtaking. We felt like kings of the world: The Prince and Princess of the Iron Gates!

After many days making buddy-buddy with the Danube, we resigned ourselves to leave it to get closer to Bulgaria and the region of Vidin. In the morning before crossing the border, we rode quietly: me in front and Khanh Nguyen behind. A stray dog came out of nowhere, snarling and barking at us with all his strength. I braked a bit too quickly, and Khanh Nguyen immediately hit me from behind. She fell, and my rear bags fell too. Other dogs arrived as equally hostile as the first. They were aggressive but fearful and therefore didn't get too close to us. Fortunately, Khanh Nguyen was fine. As for my back bags, one end was broken, but it was easily repairable. We were soon back in our saddles again. Soon we were clear of the group of dogs still barking in the distance, clearly happy to have had some fun today and to have managed to bring down these strange travelers.

The border was coming! We got our exit stamp and approached the Bulgarian border post. A man in uniform with a square head, heavy brow, and steely jaw asked us for our passports through the window of the small place where he was seated. My passport got its stamp without any problems, but I saw right away that he had trouble with Khanh Nguyen's Vietnamese passport. He meticulously inspected each page, going back and forth between them all. "Do you have hotel reservations? Do you have sufficient

---

[1] French writer

The Iron Gates, Serbia

resources to travel to Bulgaria? How long will you stay in Bulgaria? Where are you going afterward?"

We had no hotel reservations or statements, so I played other cards I had in my hand: our marriage certificate and the insurances that covered us in Bulgaria. We had to avoid anger and instead just show goodwill and respect for his job. He made some calls. We started to get restless as more than thirty minutes passed. He beckoned us with his index finger to come back to him. "Okay, normally I can't let you in. But today I'm in a good mood, so I'll be okay this time. Next time you have to take all the necessary documents with you." He then stamped Khanh Nguyen's passport. That was good! We arrived on Bulgarian soil relieved to have finally been able to pass. We also remembered the lesson for the next time: to have more supporting documents (hotel reservation, bank statement, bus ticket to leave the territory, etc.) even if it was not clearly required.

Serbia had been a pleasant surprise for us. It was one of those countries that we talked so little about while planning but had so much to offer us in practice. We particularly appreciated the generous and humorous Serbs. The Iron Gates were also a great discovery with their magnificent views of the Danube. We would return to Serbia one day to visit our new friends again.

Chapter 8

Bulgaria: last European pedal strokes

Mileage Meter: 4,074 to 5,020km (2,531 to 3,119 miles)

The fact that we decided to go from my home to Khanh Nguyen's home by bike meant we went through places and regions where we never would have gone otherwise. This geographical constraint of a route from France to Vietnam reserved good surprises most of the time but, from time to time, the bad ones.

The region of Vidin was one such surprise. It was a very poor abandoned region. As for the first kilometers, we could feel a heavy atmosphere. The dilapidated villages went after one another, the stray and aggressive dogs too. Some locals looked at us out of the corner of their eyes, without kindness. There were many Roma people, absently wandering along the roads with their strollers and children. Our stomachs were in knots as we pedaled. Sofia, the capital, was two hundred kilometers (124 miles) away. It would take us two or three days to reach it. We promised ourselves that we wouldn't camp. It was too dangerous. Men, some of them quite dubious, roamed the fields and forests.

Then we witnessed the animosity of the "locals" towards the Roma community. We saw some Bulgarians who called themselves "purebred" sometimes violently chasing the Roma people with harsh words or kicks. We spent the first night next to a motel in our tent. The manager welcomed us for free. He had already welcomed other cyclists and wanted to help us out. We felt reassured by his hospitality, spending a peaceful night and finally taking a real shower.

The next day we headed on to the city of Montana. Same set, same actors, same atmosphere. The huge piles of trash stretching along the road. After an interminable day on the bikes, we really didn't know where to sleep for the night. We left the main road to reach a small village with a few houses that seemed to be inhabited. I rang the bell on one of them. Two men in swimming trunks with enormous bellies barreled out towards us. They welcomed us into their garden offering us soft drinks which tasted of pure sugar. The one with the biggest belly presented us with his German shepherd. He had nicknamed it "Robocop, the gypsy killer". While he told us this, the other looked at Khanh Nguyen in a way that didn't sit well with me, and an awkwardness set in. Khanh Nguyen discreetly asked me for my phone and then gave it back to me a few minutes later. She wrote on it

"I really don't feel good here. I don't trust this place. We have to leave."

I discreetly put my phone back in my pocket, smiling at the two men. A few tense minutes later, I pretended that our other cycling friends were waiting for us in the next town and that we had to go. They let us go. We rushed back in the saddle on Tank and Monster. We had a little less than one hour before sunset to find a place to sleep. There were no hotels around. No choice: we had to camp. We pedaled with all our force to find a suitable place in time. I spotted a hill nestled among the fields. A few trees here and there could hide us. We left the main road without anyone seeing us, and we sat down, well hidden.

A few Roma people and their sheep were moving in the distance, but they didn't come in our direction. The sun began to set. Its hues were a thousand shades of orange. We decided to start cooking and set up the tent when it got dark. Suddenly, the Roma and their sheep made a U-turn and headed straight towards us. It was impossible to pack up and leave. We then tried to act as if everything was normal. Two teenagers arrived by us with their herd. They were surprised to find us there and didn't speak a word of English. We offered them cakes and cookies that they firmly declined. The older of the two mimed us sleeping and then pointed out the place where our bikes were. I said "no" with my head and said "*Montana*" while pointing in the direction in which the city was located with my finger. Those two teenagers didn't scare me, but I was afraid that they would tell their evening encounter to a cousin or an ill-intentioned friend who would come to visit us during the night. The two companions left us with their sheep that formed a light cloud of dust and noise. We finished our dinner. The night was almost there. We took the opportunity to move all our burdock a few hundred meters further, well-hidden between the bushes. Luck was with us:

the weak light from the moon and numerous clouds hid us. After all that stress, we finally fell asleep without too many difficulties. The night went by calmly, and our sleep was only disturbed by a brief downpour of rain. We woke before daybreak putting everything back in our bags and leaving before someone could spot us..

Arriving in Sofia, the Bulgarian capital, was a real relief. We were fortunate that we would be hosted for the week by Gilbert who lived with his two sons. Gilbert was a French man who had moved to Sofia more than twenty years ago. He had heard about us through my aunt, Murielle, who was following our adventure on social networks. Sofia was a beautiful city with cobblestone streets, surrounding mountains, and a wonder of architecture: the Cathedral of St. Alexander Nevski.

We were also in Sofia to make our Iranian visa. We had to pass by the embassy that day to deposit our file. The news was starting to get hot in Iran: The United States of Trump had just withdrawn from the nuclear agreement and sanctions were raining down on the Mullahs' regime. A Franco-Iranian researcher had also been arrested. I received a message from my father:

"Are you sure you want to go to Iran? Do you have a plan B?"

"We will do the Iranian visa and then we will see how the situation evolves. If the situation worsens, we will cross the Caspian Sea from Azerbaijan to Kazakhstan."

"Be careful. Kisses."

Iran provokes so many negative reactions in modern European society, but we resolved to bite the bullet through this fabulous country with an open mind. To acquire an Iranian visa, you have to have a kind of invitation letter that they call an "e-visa". For about thirty US dollars each, we got it through an online agency. It was also necessary to prove that we had

Bulgarian sunset, Bulgaria

insurance that would cover us in Iran, which we had with all our documents secured tightly under our arm. We cycled the road to the embassy. A lady wearing a *hijab*[1] welcomed us, consulting our file, which she then passed to her Director, who we heard grumble a thank you from his office. She came back to us and asked us for additional documents: bank statements and a marriage certificate. We gave her these documents. At no time did we mention that we were traveling by bicycle. We simply stated that we were on a long trip for our honeymoon and entering Iran by land from Azerbaijan. The grumpy Director finally accepted our application. After paying the visa fee, the lady in the *hijab* gave us a big smile and asked us to come back at the end of the week..

We took real pleasure in strolling through the streets of Sofia during those few days of waiting. We never got tired of walking past the Nevski Cathedral and delighted in a delicious *tarator*[2] and a *shopska*[3]. Those few days were also an opportunity to rest and recharge our batteries. Cycling on Tank and Monster all day often draining our mental and physical resources. During that welcome break I felt that my body was grateful for the opportunity to recover. I started to appreciate that long-lasting effort requires a long-lasting rest. Having negated that I had risked injury. I had to listen to my body. I was as much at its service as it was at mine.

We also took the opportunity to have Monster and Tank inspected in a bike store on the outskirts of Sofia: nothing to report; they were in great shape after more than 4,500 kilometers (2,800 miles)! The mechanic even told us that they were made to make it to the end of the trip.

At the end of the week, we returned feverishly to the Iranian embassy. We worried Iran would refuse us entry into its territory and that recent geopolitical events were going to prevent us from crossing the border. Fear and doubts suddenly regained the upper hand. The same lady in the *hijab* handed us our passports and our files, and that was it! We both had an Iranian visa! Our trip could continue!

---

[1] Islamic clothing covering the hair and neck, leaving the face unobstructed
[2] Cucumber soup
[3] Salad with cow's milk cheese

Well rested after a week in Sofia, we were ready to leave again. Tank and Monster were as good as new and wanted to hit the road as much as we did! We had about 400 kilometers (248 miles) which separated us from the Black Sea. We chose to take a mountainous secondary road that passed by the city of Karlovo to enjoy wilder landscapes. Bulgaria and its mountains offered us beautiful wild camping opportunities. Thanks to its multiple streams, it was easy for us to camp, take a good shower, and do our daily laundry. A daily shower was essential for us, especially for Khanh Nguyen: we could go a maximum of two days without taking one. We wondered how some long-distance cyclists we'd researched had managed longer!

My method to find a place to camp was often the same: I located a place far from any human activity on *Google Maps* with a river nearby if possible. These were often the "greenest" places on the satellite map: a forest almost always guaranteeing a river too. I remember a particular night we spent in Bulgaria. After spending a day climbing up and down, we quickly moved away from the road without anyone seeing us. We followed a path along the side of the mountain. Opposite was a gigantic valley and its thousands of horses with free roam of the immense space at their disposal. The show was magnificent! Behind us were fir trees that were perfect for camouflage. We set up our tent and prepared dinner as the sun began to descend slowly. The horses began to gather for the night. I took Khanh Nguyen in my arms, and we contemplated that magnificent spectacle. Countless mares freely escorted their little foals around. Some of the foals seemed intrigued by our presence, but their cautious mothers prevented them from getting too close. A magnificent stallion arrived at the tail of the group to assess the situation. With its imposing black mane and its finely drawn muscles, it emanated power and assurance. We couldn't take our eyes off this little production life was performing for us. Time seemed suspended. The blackness of the night finally pushed us back to our tent, and we resigned ourselves to go to bed.

As soon as we got into our comforters, the thunder started to rumble. Louder and louder and closer and closer. Like kids, we counted the time gap between the detonation and the blinding light that arrived: three kilometers (1.8 miles), then two (1.2 miles), then... one (0.6 mile)! The wind was blowing with an alarming amount of power. So much so that we had to cramp the frame of our tent with all our strength. If we let go, we were convinced that we'd be fired to Mars! The thunder came down right next to us making us jump. The wind began to weaken but left in its place a wall of water that fell on us. The tent held on, and we stayed miraculously dry despite the liters and liters that poured furiously on us for so long. Eventually, the rain finally faded away. We collapsed from fatigue.

The next morning, I opened the zip of our tent. A little pond had formed around the tent because it had rained so much. We had done really well to set up our tent on a high point otherwise we'd have woken up swimming! The sheeting of the tent was completely soaked but we would dry it later in the sun. We took to the road again, towards Burgas which opened the doors of the Black Sea and where our boat was waiting for us.

Burgas was a seaside town of little note that overlooked the Black Sea. Above all, it marked 5,000 kilometers (3,106 miles) traveled. We had crossed all of Europe from West to East: from the Atlantic Ocean to the Black Sea! For us, that was already something quite incredible and unique. To have arrived there by the strength of our calves gave us a feeling of euphoria. In terms of donations for *Poussières de Vie*, we now had more than $7,000. We had continued to receive donations regularly, and each message of encouragement that accompanied them increased our motivation tenfold. We also realized that we were now so far from France, from home. Those three months on the road had already transformed us. We felt stronger, more self-confident, and so much better for it in our relationship together. We had the deep conviction that if we both stayed as we were in that moment, nothing could touch us. We had learned to live to the rhythm of the sun,

Camping in the middle of thousands of horses, Bulgaria

to find opportunities to grow and learn in our encounters. I was also taking pleasure in observing the slow metamorphosis of Khanh Nguyen into a true adventurer. She was taking confidence in herself, in her capacities, and her unsuspected resources. She often repeats to me still as she did that day:

"You have changed my life, Thibault. Without you, I would have had a dull and uninteresting life!"

I always answer her that our meeting was surely not due to chance. It had been determined. I also told her that she also made me grow in her own way and had changed my outlook on many things in a lasting and irreversible way. I kissed her on her forehead, in the hollow of her neck, and finally on her lips.

We spent three days in Burgas and then it was time to take our tickets to cross the Black Sea. Destination: Batumi, Georgia. I haven't yet explained to you why we couldn't go through Turkey before reaching Georgia. It was simple: a Vietnamese passport only gave us the right to thirty days in Turkey, which wasn't long enough for us to cross from West to East. A French passport allowed us to stay ninety days without paying a cent. The Turkish visa for Khanh Nguyen could only be obtained on arrival at an international airport, which implied that we'd have to dismantle our bikes and put them into cardboard boxes. The constraints were, therefore too great for thirty short days.

Late that afternoon, we reached the pier. We seemed tiny as the heavy goods vehicles circulated us, waiting to go through customs. Bulgarian, Georgian, and Turkish trucks followed one another. The boat which awaited us was huge! A big monster of three floors with an enormous chimney. The trucks rushed one by one into it. Besides them we felt insignificant. We left Monster and Tank on the lower floor where to our surprise, we discovered the bikes of two other long-distance cyclists!

We weren't the only ones on this crossing.

Chapter 9

Luminous meeting on the Black Sea

We laboriously brought all our bags and equipment to the upper deck. The cabins were distributed all around the refectory: on one side the Bulgarian, Georgian and Turkish truckers and their testosterone. On the other the travelers: by motorcycle, car, trailer, on foot and bicycles! We shared our four-person cabin with a Japanese woman, Kazumi, and a Swiss woman, Fanny. The cabin was tidy and clean. The sheets were white and spotless. Nothing to complain about!

We didn't know that our encounter with Fanny would become one of the most beautiful we'd experience on the trip. A few minutes before, we witnessed our last European sunset before reaching the far Caucasus. We were watching the trucks continue to climb with difficulty one by one in the ship's den when Fanny approached us:

"Hi! Are you the couple that goes from France to Vietnam? *Non-La Project, right?* I saw your photos on Facebook! I'm Fanny."

"Hello, Fanny! I'm Thibault and this is Khanh Nguyen. Yes, our project is called *Non-La Project*! We left France three months ago and we're going to Vietnam! What about you? "

"I left my home in Switzerland and I don't really know where I'm going... I still have three more weeks before I have to go back."

It was always a special pleasure to meet other long-distance cyclists like us. There was a fraternity, a *je-ne-sais-quoi*, that connected us. We often shared the same dreams, the same sorrows. In those moments, I felt like a knight in the 10th century who meets another knight on a small road through the Forest of Tronçais, or a cowboy on their mount who by chance meets another cowboy in the desert. The objects of discussion were often the same: the road we took before arriving here, anecdotes of our trip, the road we intended to take next, the characteristics of our bikes and our equipment.

Fanny was impressive in her good humor, her ability to break the ice and engage everyone in the discussion. In less than an hour, she knew almost everyone on the boat, both passengers and truckers. She was fully engaged in the discussion, living in it to the fullest. We could talk with her for hours without stopping because it was her because it was us. A bell rang, which meant it was time for dinner. Everyone gathered in the refectory and served themselves pasta, *shopska*, and some kind of powdered orange juice. Next to us sat the fourth cyclist of the ship: Richard. He was a New Zealander, a kiwi, in his fifties, traveling around the world on his bicycle. His accent was sometimes hard to understand, but I was hanging in there. My connection with him was much weaker than with Fanny, but that's the way socializing is sometimes; you can't force things.

All the occupants of the boat gradually went to bed. It was only very late at night that the ship finally got on its way. I opened my eyes for a few seconds to note with satisfaction that we were finally moving on to the Black Sea and went back to sleep immediately.

Two days then followed one another, punctuated by meals and waves. We took advantage of the good weather and the great sun on the upper deck. We looked far to the horizon and had endless discussions with Fanny. While we were discussing Bulgaria, I saw a kind of shiny material that appeared then disappeared in the distance. Getting closer to the railing, I realized they were dolphins! They were a small pod and were playing with the waves caused by our boat. The show was magnificent and so unexpected! I ran towards our room to find Khanh Nguyen. By the time I had dragged her outside, the superb mammals had already left us.

Truckers smoked to pass the time or otherwise drank *Rakkia*.[1] After two days of boredom, the Bulgarians started harassing the Turks, then the Turks bothered Georgians, and the Georgians then brought it back to the Bulgarians. Fortunately, there were few injuries. The following morning, we would finally arrive in Batumi, Georgia. Between two of the fights, I suggested to Fanny that the three of us take to the road together. She accepted with a huge smile. Richard, the kiwi, seemed more of a lone wolf and I didn't propose that he join us.

The early morning brought our first glimpses of Batumi. The boat started to sway severely. The weather was capricious, and the waves got higher and higher. In the refectory it was war. Plates, glasses, and pitchers smashed from the shelves onto the ground. Everyone tried to hold on to what they could. Some shouted while clinging onto a table. On the upper deck, it was even more impressive: Khanh Nguyen held tightly to the railing and didn't dare move. The truckers anxiously watched their trucks swaying from right to left. Gradually the sea calmed down slightly, but docking would be impossible. We would dock the next day. All the passengers lamented that they had to stay another day in this prison and still had to swallow the same pasta and the bland powdered orange juice.

The next day, the Black Sea was very calm. We could finally dock. The Georgian immigration service disembarked and checked our passports.

---

[1] Brandy made from fermented fruit juices

Our boat to cross the Black Sea and its sunsets

Khanh Nguyen's Vietnamese passport required, once again, more time before getting its stamp. She did have the Schengen visa, which opened the doors of Georgia to her. But the officer in front of a passport whose color he didn't see very often preferred not to take any risks and got the approval of his superior after a short phone call.

With that, we had finally landed in Georgia! Our legs itched after so many days of inactivity. They would get to achieve their dreams with the mountains waiting for us. We also had one more member on the team: Fanny.

Chapter 10

Georgia: true freedom

Mileage Meter: 5,020 to 5,590km (3,119 to 3,473miles)

Georgia is the kind of small country that isn't really on the radar of mass tourism. "Move along, nothing to see". Georgia is perfect for discovering with your bike, your tent, and your stove.

It's a true crossroad, Georgia. Many civilizations pass through it: Persians, Romans, Byzantines, Arabs, Mongols, Ottomans, and finally the Russians. The result is a great ethnic, culinary, and cultural diversity. Georgia also surprises by its language and writing. When I look back at the trip, there are many similarities with Burmese characters. They both have rounded characters joined together to form beautiful word and phrases.

On the way from the boat with Fanny and Khanh Nguyen, we discovered a whole new world, very different from ours. We took advantage of the big city of Batumi to get some Lari - one euro was worth about 3.5 Lari- and made a sufficient stock of food for the coming days. The next few days were going to be really difficult. On the program: 257 kilometers (160 miles) with the Goderdzi pass on the menu, culminating at more than 2,000 meters (6,561 feet) before arriving at the Paravani lake. The Paravani Lake is one of the highest lakes in Georgia and is more than 2,073 meters high (6,801 feet). That was our first real mountain test. Spending the coming days with Fanny was therefore a source of relief to face the slopes that awaited us.

It didn't take us long to get out of the modern Batumi. We quickly found ourselves climbing the first laces of the Goderdzi pass. The nature and the reliefs were superb. We followed the limpid Acharistskali river, which flowed with force into the Black Sea. We passed old cars in ex-Soviet style and herds of goats that took up the whole width of the road. In turn, we formed a temporary duo (Khanh Nguyen-Fanny, Fanny-Thibault, then Thibault-Khanh Nguyen) driving side by side, discussing everything and nothing. Thus, pain and fatigue were less felt. We climbed the difficult incline gradients without really realizing it. After several hours and multiple stops to take pictures, we had to start looking for a place to sleep. I suggested to Khanh Nguyen and Fanny to try and knock on someone's house. We passed by a small village when two children called to us from the courtyard of their home: "Hello, Hello". Their house seemed to have a garden: perfect for our two tents.

I knocked, and a tough-looking man with a shock of white hair opened the door. I showed him our introductory message, this time translated into Georgian, and asked if we could spend the night there. He accepted immediately. I shouted to Khanh Nguyen and Fanny: "It's okay! They welcome us in their home". It was always an immense moment of joy for me when someone accepted strangers like us in their home. It was the happiness of the immediate encounter, of the unconditional welcome for a traveler in need. The old man was Okrobir: a former wrestler. His two grandchildren, Andréa and Amico, were the ones who had called us. Andréa spoke a little bit of English and was extremely excited to see three foreigners arriving at his house on strange bicycles. A little further away was their grandmother, Natela, who was cracking chestnuts. She was as hardy as Okrobir and smiled at all three of us with great kindness.

We proposed to help her to break her nuts. We all settled down around the basket to break chestnut after chestnut. It was a great moment of sharing. Nato, Andréa, and Amico's mother arrived with coffees for the three of us. Her brew was strong, with a thick ground layer that rested at the bottom of the glass! Andréa positively insisted that we discover everything to know about his home: it overlooked the Acharistskali river. He told us that he had seen a bear roaming once... He ran to show us his goats, his chickens, the fruits and vegetables, as well as the tobacco leaves left to dry. It was such a joy to following him on a wave of enthusiasm, and it caused me to completely forget my own fatigue.

Our Vietnamese Non-La hats were a success. Andréa, Amico, and Okrobir tried them on in turn. I particularly liked the photo I took of Okrobir. He did an impression of the Vietnamese revolutionary leader Ho Chi Minh, which he had probably seen in one of his schoolbooks dedicated to the *glorious* history of communism. Okrobir then made us understand that we wouldn't be sleeping outside in our tents but inside their house in a large room just for us. We were in heaven. We took a quick shower, and then dinner was ready! It was a beautiful evening that I find can often be neglected in our modern Western lifestyles: taking time to simply discover the lives and quirks of new people

The *chacha* glasses, the local alcohol, followed one after another, as did the topics of discussion! Andréa cranked up the TV to let us hear the local music. Kitschy music belted out and enveloped the room, which Andréa opportunistically used to show us his most beautiful dance steps and for Fanny to try to follow him!

The three of us quickly fell asleep in the double bed of our one-night room. It hadn't been a bad first day in Georgia!

A new team member: Fanny!

Okrobir and Andrea trying the Non La

The next morning: like Sisyphus of modern times, we redid our saddlebags and installed them on our bikes. After a hearty breakfast with the whole family, we exchanged addresses and Facebook accounts. I tried to give back in my gestures, looks, and smiles to the family that had offered us such priceless memories. But it was time to go; the top of the Goderdzi Pass was calling to us!

It would take us two more days to reach the summit. The road was in bad condition. The asphalt quickly gave way to gravel, holes, and mud which slowed us down. But we were carried by the energy of our small group and the Georgian atmosphere. Many drivers greeted and encouraged us.. For the first time on the trip, we had the impression we would be an attraction to the locals for the day. Children waved then curiously approached, speaking to us in Russian. Fortunately, Fanny spoke it a little bit. Several vans even proposed to take us wherever we needed to go. A driver put himself at my height and beckoned me by the window to put my bicycle on the back of the vehicle. It was tempting, but we weren't there for that. We wanted to reach the summit by ourselves, by our will and strength. Khanh Nguyen was impressive, by the way. She climbed with a hearty smile on her face. Cycling alongside Fanny was giving her extra motivation. .

After a night in a bed and breakfast, we arrived at the top of the Goderdzi pass. In winter it was normally a ski resort. That August, we pedaled along the chairlifts. One last effort and we arrived at the top. The wind was strong and fresh. Two big dogs, a male and a female, were playing with us. The feeling of ecstasy is difficult to explain. It came as our reward for such a long effort: a feeling of connection to the world. A small mountain restaurant was right next door. We took the opportunity to taste some delicious Georgian bread, as well as a kind of cow cheese fondue. With a full belly, we took advantage of a long descent with multiple waterfalls and rivers that became opportunities to swim and refresh ourselves.

Georgia was total freedom actualized. We were free to stop wherever we wanted and to set up our tent whenever we wanted. Landscapes and mountains paraded into the horizon. The road from the Goderdzi pass to

Tbilisi with its three hundred kilometers (186 miles) remained a week laden with happiness and simple joys. The road was grandiose, passing through canyons, valleys, and mountains. The Georgians were very kind to us. One evening, we were even invited to share a birthday dinner with a large family. The table was generously filled, and our hosts encouraged us to take from the endless supply of food as we pleased.

On the way, we would also see the Paravani Lake located not far from Turkey and Armenia. The region reminded us of those lands of Central Asia or Mongolia that stretched as far as the eye could see with their herds of thousands of cows and goats. In the town of Ninotsminda, a baker generously offered us huge and hot loaves of bread. We thanked him, tore huge bites out then crossed the road of a shepherd perched on a magnificent horse. We decided to camp on the edge of Lake Saghamo, which is about ten kilometers (6.2 miles) from Lake Paravani. We couldn't have felt wilder or more cut off from the world. We installed our small tents at the edge of the immense lake. Each one prepared its small dish to share it with the others. Happiness, the honest kind

The Paravani Lake that we discovered the next morning was just as glorious, with a small monastery called Saint-Nino standing proudly in front. Nature here was raw. Tourists passing by even offered us chicken and watermelons for lunch. What else could someone ask for? The road rose, still as beautiful as ever, to give way to a long descent to the valley below. Luck continued to smile on us: at the end of the day, a van pulled up to my height. The driver spoke to me in English but with a strong French accent:

"Hello! Do you know where to sleep tonight? I live in this village with my wife who is Georgian. I come from Savoy! Come to the house!"

Result! Without even having to search, we had found a roof for the night. The stars were aligned for us.

My wonder at the stars dancing in the night sky was brutally interrupted that evening as I heard my phone buzz. On my family *WhatsApp* group, my aunt told us that my grandmother, Maman Zouzou, was probably living her last days. It had been one of my greatest fears: being far from my

Moments of freedom, Georgia

relatives when they needed me. Without hesitation, I opened Google and booked a round trip from Tbilisi to Paris. In Azerbaijan or Iran, it would be too far, too late to return. It was now or never if I wanted to say a *last goodbye*.

We quickly traveled a hundred kilometers (62 miles) to reach the Georgian capital. Fanny and Khanh Nguyen would stay with Sam and Ia (pronounced "e-ah"): friends of friends who generously welcomed us into their apartment during our stay in Tbilisi. For the first time in four months of travel, I had left Khanh Nguyen.

I took an early morning plane with a connection to Bucharest. The plane passed over the Black Sea and then the next one along the Alps. I just wanted to find my grandmother, to tell her that I loved her one last time. My plane arrived on time in Paris. On the way between Charles de Gaulle airport and the Austerlitz train station, I got a call from my aunt. Maman Zouzou had died in the night, and her funeral would be that weekend in Creuse. I didn't move as a flurry of feelings washed over me. Immense sorrow gave way to a sudden strong will to be with my family. Once in Creuse, I was relieved to find my brothers and sisters, my cousins. My Bon Papa and my dad were there too. Bon papa was in very bad shape too. When I went to see him in his room, I had the feeling that I was saying goodbye to him. Maman Zouzou's funeral was beautiful. Everyone was there, the sky a stark blue. Briefly returning to the life I'd left behind in France had been a decision well made. As a salmon swimming back upstream to the place it was born, I had needed to go back home and say goodbye for the very last time to my ancestors. More than ever before, I felt that the journey I was on was about much more than just putting one pedal in front of the other: it was about the idea of what one can make of their life while they have it

I returned the next day to Georgia. I found my wife, Khanh Nguyen, whom I held in my arms as though I had never hugged her before. Fanny had taken good care of her as had Sam and Ia.

We also had to say goodbye to Fanny who had to return to Switzerland. Her bus for Istanbul was going to leave that morning. We accompanied her to the bus station. The three of us hugged knowingly, nodding to each other

Last kilometers before leaving the beautiful Georgia

about the moments we knew none of us would ever forget. We promised that we would see each other again.

Chapter 11

Azerbaijan, "Salam!" and Watermelons

Mileage Meter: 5,590 to 6,209km (3,473 to 3,858 miles)

To reach Azerbaijan, we decided to take the road a little further north of the country, passing through Shaki. Shaki is a mountain town located on the ancient Silk Road. Over its long history, thousands of horses, camels, spices, metals, and pigments had traversed past, and now both Tank and Monster.

Azerbaijan was my first real culture shock of the trip. After having crossed the border without difficulty, all the old Lada[1] that crossed our path made headlight flashes to say hello or yelled "Salam" out of their windows in jubilation at us. Azerbaijan is the first Muslim country we had crossed. A former Soviet territory, its population is mainly Shiite and less conservative concerning women, who aren't forced to wear the hijab by law.

In the first city we passed through, Balakan, we stopped at the first ATM we saw. In front, the men formed a line to the left, and the women formed a line on the right. Insistent glances from the queue landed on my legs, and before I got too disturbed, I realized I was the only one in shorts in the entire queue. All the men were in pants. After withdrawing some 'manat' and consulting a little more about Azeri manners on my phone, I read that wearing shorts is considered disrespectful, especially outside the rich capital: Baku. Some Azerbaijanis even consider wearing shorts to be reserved for the depraved. At the earliest opportunity, I bashfully put on my trousers. Pedaling in trousers under the sun was a minimal price to pay.

We took to the road again for Shaki. Azerbaijan was a man's world. In the streets, the shops, the cafes: men. From time to time, I saw a woman stealthily closing the gate of her house, but nothing more. On our first night in Azerbaijan: those men invited us to have tea. They were really welcoming and the presence of Khanh Nguyen didn't pose any problem. "She is a

---

[1] Russian car brand which met a great success in all Eastern Europe

traveler and travels with her husband. Her features are Indo-Chinese and so different from the women here that we will tolerate her with us." they seemed to think. Fifty men drinking *Cay*[1] and laughing heartily sat around Khanh Nguyen and me. Several handfuls of sugar sweetened the cups of black tea. Men were all around us, yet we both felt comfortable. The boss even invited us for dinner and to sleep at his place for the night. We looked at each other and accepted with big smiles and our tea in-between our hands.

During the entire crossing of Azerbaijan, we were regularly stopped by passers-by and cars. Our Non-La conical hats were a real success. Everybody wanted to try them on and take a selfie! We met Hussein who ran a small supermarket. He called out to us from the end of the sidewalk and pointed at our hats with excitement. Khanh Nguyen made him try hers. Hussein was the owner of a small convenience store. He had an elongated face and a splendid mustache. I took advantage of the opportunity to do our daily shop inside. When it was time to pay, Hussein put all my daily purchases into a plastic bag. I handed him my manats, but he refused to take them. I insisted, he still refused. He wanted to offer us everything for free! I offered him my manats again, but he refused. Aghast, I began to put some of the items back on the shelves. He plucked them back, put them back in the plastic bag, and prevented me from doing it again. I realized refusing his generosity wasn't an option and expressed my deep gratitude to him. Our bikes left laden with Hussein's beautiful gifts.

    As it turned out, his generosity was instilled in every Azerbaijani, and we came across it daily. It must be said we were being offered impractical gifts, though. At regular stops, heavy melons and watermelons were eagerly thrown into our hands. We gorged them gratefully on the spot and cut the remainders to keep them for the rest of the day. One day, we stopped in the shade for lunch. A brand-new police car, glowing under the sun, passed in front of us. Khanh Nguyen said to me, "do you think they will ask us to leave?" Then the car made a U-turn and stopped in front of a young boy

---

[1] Local tea

selling (you guessed it!) watermelons. The police car left, and the young boy advanced towards us with an enormous watermelon in his arms. It was from the police officer!

Shaki finally stood before us. It was a mostly Sunnite city because it was close to Russian Dagestan. But above all, it was an ancient stopover on the Silk Road. We took advantage of the two days to have a well-deserved break. We explored its small sloped paved streets. In the middle, a discreet stream flowed. The Khan Palace, built without a single nail in the 18th century, was refinement epitomized. We strolled as lovers through the streets of Shaki. It felt good to have that kind of moment to ourselves, just the two of us. On the road and with all the encounters we were making, intimacy hadn't been as accessible! Shaki was a beautiful parenthesis for both of us: we put our most beautiful clothes on, which waited for us at the bottom of our saddlebags and strolled hand in hand while the sun played hide and seek behind the tops of the surrounding mountains.

We also tried the local cuisine with its *baklavas* and *pitis*. The piti is a traditional dish consisting of sheep, chickpeas, vegetables and saffron. It was a treat for me but less for Khanh Nguyen who couldn't stand the strong smell of the sheep. So I finished her portion of piti to the sound of the muezzin praying in the distance, voice echoing across the mountains.

After Shaki, we took the road south to Iran. The road was of little interest as we drove along a pipeline going to the Caspian Sea. The Azeri economy revolves around oil and its capital, Baku. We took a big highway where I saw a white light crackle in front of me. I first though it was a worker doing welding on a metal railing, but it was actually a bicycle lit by its front generator. It was three loaded bikers like us: Cédric, Chummany, and Mickael! They had left Orleans in France and were aiming to reach Thailand. We quickly got acquainted and decided to camp together for that evening.

They were a bit traumatized by the previous night. They had been evicted several times by the local police in the middle of the night because they had settled too close to the big pipeline. They wanted to be more careful this time.

The five of us left in search of a quiet and well-hidden place. After a long search, we found a field. The bushes made us invisible from the main road. It was a pleasure for me to be able to meet fellow countrymen so far from home and express myself in my native language again! To talk in French with my fellow citizens was thus a truly jubilant moment for me as I could express my experiences and my feeling with meaningful and tangible words. It would be our only night together. They had to go east to Baku to take their boat to Kazakhstan. For Khanh Nguyen and I, we needed to head south to Astara and Iran. The night would be calm and without any sudden police evictions.

The next morning the road split, heading towards our separate destinations. We wished them well and followed our road. We found it hard to believe we were almost in Iran!

The last days before Iran were tough. The road we took, which passed through Bilasuvar, was under construction for more than a hundred kilometers (62 miles). We quickly got tired of avoiding potholes, holes, and incessant irregularities. Hundreds of trucks threw up dense dust that made the air unbreathable. Some stray dogs were unusually aggressive, and it took us some time to lose them snapping at our back wheels. After a rather gloomy night on the terrace of a restaurant along the road, we continued to fight on that bumpy road. It was now mind over matter. Otherwise, we would suffer even more. I did my best to stay positive and to motivate Khanh Nguyen. However, I could see on her face that she was at the end of her tether and might break down soon. I pulled my breaks, took her in my arms, and promised her that our hell would be temporary. Words have a placebo power. She got motivated again and held out.

Then it began to rain. We decided to take shelter in front of a house

The policeman's gift: a watermelon!

Daily talks with locals, Azerbaijan

with a metal sheet roof rusted by years of weathering. It seemed abandoned but a few moments later the door opened. A man came out with a cigarette butt hanging on his lips. He proposed we should have some tea inside. Kitschy decorations adorned a strange room. He made us sit down and served us some *Cay*. The first woman we saw entered the room to watch TV scantily clad. We suddenly realized we were in a brothel! I pressed Khanh Nguyen to quickly finish her tea, curtly thanked the manager, and we got out into the open air once again. The rain had stopped. What kind of purgatory had we just left! The road stretched out in front of us, worsened now by ample mud. After about forty kilometers (25 miles) of struggling, the works disappeared to give way to a perfectly asphalted road.

We spent our last night in the north of Astara, located on the Caspian Sea, which spans Azerbaijan and Iran. I was happy to have crossed a country like Azerbaijan. Our cycling adventure was an opportunity to pass through places that are often overlooked and discover the richness of their culture and population. Several signals had nevertheless alerted me that I had to be careful with Khanh Nguyen. In a man's world with such a small public female presence, it was advisable not to leave her alone.

We would be in Iran by tomorrow! I couldn't believe it; it all felt like a joke. Had we really gotten there by bike? From my home in provincial Vendée to the home of ancient Persepolis? Really? Iran wasn't the end of the trip, but it represented for us the summit, the goal: the adventure in its strongest sense. We would have to put aside all our fears and apprehensions and go for it.

Chapter 12

Iran: Discovering a New World

Mileage Meter: 6,209 to 6,547km (3,858 to 4,068 miles)

(Astara – Emamzadeh Hashem)

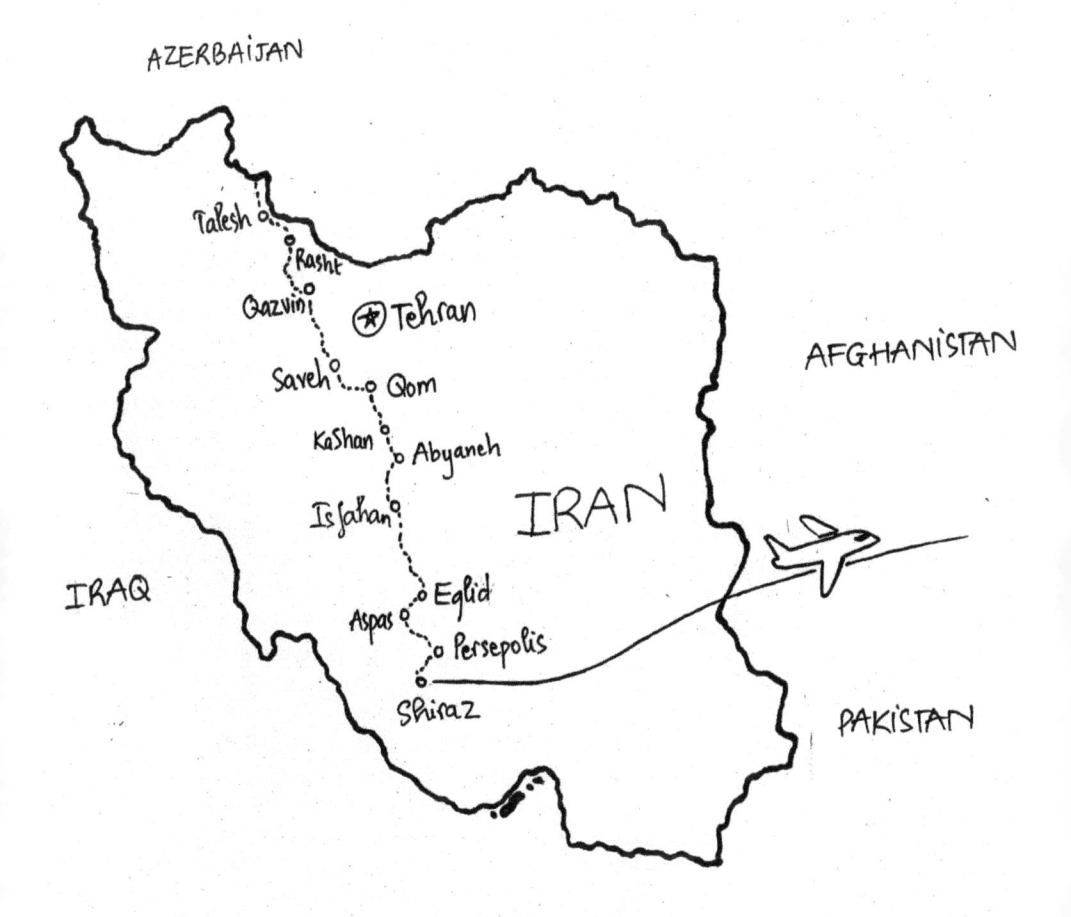

The day before crossing the border, we prepared as best we could. We checked that we had all of our papers while memorizing our route: "Astara - Isfahan - Shiraz - Bandar Abbas". We would have to repeat this like scouts to the immigration officers. Some constraints also applied for Khanh Nguyen: she had to follow Islamic law by covering her head and neck with a hijab. She also had to cover her hips with a loose piece of clothing. We made do with what we had: until we bought what was needed on the other side of the border. To cover her hips and head, she wore my large shirt and a scarf. It was a little difficult for me to see Khanh Nguyen like that, for she had been so free to the world before that. I felt then that it was my duty to make sure that she felt as happy as possible.

The good news was that our uncertainty ended with a phone call from an Iranian man, Amin. We regularly shared our adventure on social networks, especially Instagram, to promote the charity and fundraiser. Several Iranians were following us, and among them, Amin. Amin had spotted that we would go through Astara on the map of our route posted online and contacted us through Instagram. He then proposed to pick us up at the border so we could spend our first few nights in Iran at his place. We accepted immediately, trusting his generosity with open hearts.

The next day, we still had knots in our stomachs before we crossed the border. So many stories had been circulating about Iran before that point. We faced another constraint: because of the American sanctions, it was impossible to use our Visa or MasterCard in Iran. So, we had to take with us enough dollars to exchange for 'rials' on the spot. I withdrew seven hundred dollars for the two months, a little less than twelve dollars a day for both of us.

First days in Iran at Amin's family, Astara

We arrived at the border around 1 pm. The Azeri soldiers were on lunch break, and we lost a good hour while waiting for them to return. Once the exit stamps were obtained, we crossed the small bridge towards the Iranian checkpoint. An Iranian soldier leaning on the barrier asked me:

"Where are you from?"

"I'm French, and my wife is Vietnamese."

"Ha, French! Do you know Saman Goddos? He plays football in Amiens[1]!"

"Yes, I know him!"

The Iranian soldier immediately relaxed and gave me a broad smile. Football is a universal subject to break the ice. I would play that card many times throughout our trip. From there, it went smoothly. At no time did they check our phones, our computer, or our GPS. The officer stamped our two visas. Iran could finally open its arms to us!

As soon as we got out, a swarm of men with their black beards threw themselves on us to offer us their exchange services: "Dollar? Dollar for Rials, Sir. Good price, Sir". They were numerous, and it became intimidating. A man then appeared in front of us: it was Amin! He'd come with his bike and explained to the bearded people that we were his friends and that we didn't need their services. They walked away, muttering. Amin was in his thirties, with a kind face and salt and pepper hair. He made sure that everything went well for us and asked us to follow him through Astara to his parents' home

We crossed Astara for about five kilometers (3 miles). Black, red and green flags hung from grey and white Peugeot 405s as they swarmed the road. Women in black chadors[2] walked the pavements lined with copious mosques practically chained together. We felt like we'd just landed on another planet. Everything seemed so foreign to us. To have Amin as our guide and protector was a blessing. We followed him through a set of small streets. They led to a large boulevard in front of his home. We left Tank

---

[1] Northern France city which has a football club: Amiens Sporting Club
[2] An Islamic garment that covers everything but the face

and Monster on the first floor and went up to the second floor to Amin's parents' home.

Asshieh and Khalil were waiting for us impatiently and gave us a warm welcome. Asshieh was quite small with dyed blonde hair and glasses. She immediately put Khanh Nguyen at ease by telling her that she could take off her scarf and do what she wanted at home. Khalil was quite large and corpulent; he had a thick grayed beard three to four days old. He was a former civil servant. Amin also worked for the public administration (the Astara water department). The whole family had prepared a huge fruit platter for us, as well as lots of local cakes, all served with black tea. Amin and his parents really knew how to make us feel comfortable and welcomed. Amin then asked me:

"Thibault, tell me what you need for the next few days?"

"I need to change dollars, buy a sim card and I need pants for Iran. Khanh Nguyen needs to find a hijab and a cardigan. Ha, and both of us would like to get a haircut!"

After we snacked on some of the fruit, Amin offered to take me to the hairdresser. Khanh Nguyen couldn't join me: when it came to hairdressing, men and women needed to stay separated. We came back home a little later, Amin, me, and my new haircut. Amin had paid. I looked like a real Iranian now with my beard and a classic short back and sides!

Dinner time came. Asshieh and Khalil had cooked together and prepared the best they could offer. On the menu: white fish from the Capsian Sea, rice with saffron, and dishes made with nuts and vegetables. It was an absolute delight! Khanh Nguyen even encouraged them to open their own restaurant. To drink, we had "Coca-Cola", which we would find wherever we stayed. It surprised us to find it in Iran considering the American embargo until we realized it was probably counter-feinted. .

On the following days, Amin showed us around the city while we took care of our little to-do list. We exchanged two hundred of my US dollars in an exchange office: the rate was 110,000 rials for one dollar. I quickly found myself with a huge wad of bills as the rial had been devalued against the dollar. "You have to be careful," said Amin, "in Iran there are rials and tomans. A toman is 10 rials. The prices are generally displayed in toman. If you aren't sure, just ask!"

So, I exchanged 200 dollars and with that we had 500 dollars left. Why didn't you change it all at once, you might say? One, to protect us from a further devaluation of the rial against the dollar, and two, to avoid carrying the huge wads of bills. I'd exchange the remaining dollars when we needed them in the big cities we'd pass through.. Highway thieves were well aware that foreigners often traveled through Iran with a lot of cash as international credit cards weren't accepted. We had to be careful.

We then went to the Bazar of Astara to find our Iranian clothes. I quickly found some grey pants that were quite light and would be perfect for biking. Khanh Nguyen spent more time finding her hijab and cardigan. Her choice finally went to a rather colorful hijab and a navy-blue cardigan. By looking around a little, we realized that many women in Astara wore colorful clothes, their hijab placed just high enough on their heads to follow the rules, but low enough to let their luxurious hair flow out. Iran is a diverse country. From one region to another, from one city to another, and even within the same city, there is a lot of cultural variance. Some Iranians are very practical and rigorous, others more secular in their attitude and dress habits.

During those few days at Asshieh, Khalil, and Amin's, we particularly liked the breakfasts with the nuts, fresh cheese, and... *Sangak*: one of the best Iranian loaves of bread we sampled! *Sangak* is an Iranian delicacy baked in gigantic ovens with small, heated stones. The dough is put on those stones with the help of several wooden handles. Once baked, the loaves are placed on iron grids. It's up to the customers to remove any stones remaining in the *Sangak* after purchase!

Lunches and dinners, each as delicious and copious as the other, followed one another at Asshieh and Khalil's. Meanwhile, Khanh Nguyen was accompanied by Asshieh to the beauty salon to get a haircut. The result was perfect! I also took the opportunity to clean and maintain *Tank* and

Monster, which was necessary after more than 6,000 kilometers (3,728 miles). We also stopped by to buy a SIM card, which Amin, once again, paid for on our behalf. It was impossible to negotiate him out of his generosity.

We enjoyed the last dinner together at Amin's sister's house who lived next door with her husband and their little boy. During the evening, her husband kindly offered to translate our little message to the local into Farsi, the local Persian language.

1. *Hello! We are Thibault and Khanh Nguyen. We got married two years ago. We are doing France-Vietnam by bicycle, 16,000 kilometers (10,000 miles), for our honeymoon and in the hope of collecting donations for underprivileged children in Vietnam.*
2. *Can we pitch our tent in your garden tonight? We will leave very early tomorrow.*
3. *Do you have water to fill our water bottles? Thank you very much!*

The result was perfect because her husband had extremely elegant handwriting. It was also much easier and more natural for us to show that paper to the people we met rather than a glaring cell phone screen.

After three nights at Amin, Asshieh, and Khalil's, it was time to leave. Staying the entire three months with them would've been nice, but we would've gained at least four or five kilos (8 or 11 pounds) more!

Early the next morning, we left Astara and Amin and headed towards Talesh. The north of Iran surprised us with its humid microclimate. Rice fields followed one another along the road. The clichéd image of an Iran comprised of a single barren desert with mountains couldn't be further from the truth! The humidity made our progression difficult. Khanh Nguyen with her hijab and cardigan was sweating profusely. We pulled our breaks and a family, sitting on a large tablecloth next to their car, invited us to share their meal.

Iranians have mastered the art of the "picnic". They always travel with large tablecloths and tea with an infinity of things to enjoy. Reza, Sara, and their young son were no exception to that rule. They even had folding chairs! They were traveling to the city of Mashhad in the North-East of the country. It was so far away. It would take them two or three days to get there. We sat among them. Reza offered us fried eggs that he had just cooked, then dates, tea, fruits and baklavas. I showed them our little presentation paper written in Farsi. Reza and Sara were impressed by our crazy journey. Their son, sporting a cute bowl haircut, suited the *Non-La* hat we placed on his head! We had to resign ourselves to leave for our destination of the day sooner than we would've liked to continue on our way to Talesh.

The road continued to meander through the rice fields. The traffic was dense. It was the weekend, and Tehran's inhabitants had left the capital en mass to enjoy the milder climate and Caspian Sea. Fortunately, the hard shoulder was wide enough to separate us from all the cars. We finally arrived in Talesh and then made our way towards Teymour's home.

Teymour, who we'd contacted via the *Warmshowers* network, was the director of a private school. They taught English there. He had many complimentary comments from other cyclists he had hosted in recent years on his profile. Some of the people he had hosted were even long-distance travel celebrities. I was amused to find the names of several who had inspired us to make our trip: *"Pedal Promise"* for example, a couple who pedaled from Switzerland to Australia two years before. Teymour was, therefore, a mandatory stopover for travelers passing through northern Iran.

Teymour was waiting for us in front of his house. He spoke superb English, which put us at ease immediately. He opened the door of his garage and then took us up to his apartment. Inside, Roshanak, his wife, and Nima, their son, were waiting for us. Without surprise, they also spoke very good English. Roshanak had a smile tinged with sadness. Nima amazed us with his *joie de vivre* and humor. Nima was fourteen years old. Teymour installed us in Nima's room, where he had a large mattress and a blanket.

The five of us spent two memorable days together. Teymour, Roshanak, Nima, and their family embodied Iranian hospitality. We were

First kilometers in Iran, Astara region

With Roshanak, Teymour and their cousins

*The Iranian great sense of hospitality,
Talesh, Iran*

invited for each meal by a member of their family: Roshanak's brother, Teymour's brother, then Teymour's parents. Each time, we were made to sit on gigantic carpets. The dishes were paraded in front of us, each one tastier than the last. They always insisted on serving us first and then served us again and again. The kilos were continuing to accumulate for Khanh Nguyen and me!

At Roshanak's brother, Ali's, we enjoyed *Kotlet*, beef meatballs mixed with onions and potatoes. They were eaten with *Noon*, an Iranian bread, and large pickles. It was a real delight to share this dish in such good company and in that setting. It was a rare privilege for us. Teymour and Roshanak's family were highly educated: each member was a doctor in something. We talked about history, philosophy and Iran. Even France and Vietnam! It was a delight intellectually. Khanh Nguyen intrigued our guests, and she was the first Vietnamese woman they had ever met. They asked a lot of questions about her. The discussions followed one another until our fatigue reared its ugly head. Iranians usually have a late dinner (after nine o'clock) and go to bed very late (after midnight). It's difficult for a cyclist who often needs to leave early the next morning to make the most of the daylight.

As the trust built between us, the beautiful Roshanak with her sad smile revealed the tragedy that had befallen her. She had been the victim of a serious road accident in southern Iran. A bus she'd been traveling on had crashed onto its side. Roshanak's right arm had been completely crushed. Multiple operations had followed to restore her flesh and mobility. We now understood why none of our meals could have been had at their home and why we were invited every time by their family members. Roshanak was on a long journey to restore the mobility in her arm. The self-sacrifice of Teymour, Nima, and their whole family was humbling.

Lessons in Farsi also punctuated those two days at Teymour's. Nima taught phrases to Khanh Nguyen like: "My name is Khanh Nguyen", "What is your name?", "I am from Vietnam", "This is my husband". I also visited the Teymour's English school. It was Boy's Day – where the boys and girls were separated. The twenty or so teenagers asked me a lot of questions about myself, about the trip, about what I thought of Iran and its cuisine. I also asked them questions, one of which was about their dreams: "What is your dream?". I got several answers: to become rich, to have a nice car, to move to the United States, to move to Europe, to be happy. Those answers reflected a certain reality in Iran and the hope of its youth for a better life.

The next morning, we left our three guests with a heavy heart but still filled to the brim with gratitude. We hugged each other, which isn't common in Iran, especially between a man and a woman. Teymour told us that we would be his brother and sister in his heart from now on. I hugged Roshanak.

We were back on the road. We were falling in love with Iran and Iranians. We never expected that in just a few days, the trip would almost end, as much as our lives might've.

It was Muharram, one of the most important religious events for the Shiites. Hussein was the grandson of the Prophet Mohammed. Hussein was the one who revolted against the oppression of the Caliphate of Umayyad in the 7th century. He and his family were captured, and Hussein was beheaded. Gandhi and even Mandela referred to Hussein during their own struggles against oppression. Muharram was the time for all Iranians to celebrate Imam Hussein's memory and cultivate his values.

It was raining as it had every day in the region. We put our rain gear (jacket, pants, shoe protectors) on. Most Iranians were draped in black, testimony of their deep mourning for Hussein. All that black along with a dark sky created a very dull world. We pedaled as best we could through the darkness and the flood of rain. Along the road, there were many stalls distributing meals to all passers-by in honor of Imam Hussein. An entire neighborhood took turns cooking thousands of meals and offering tea to everyone. Some Iranians greeted us warmly and then led us to these stands to drink hot tea and have lunch. Needless to say, in Iran, our budget for food hardly mattered. We were permanently invited to drink and eat by someone every day!

The rain continued to pour. It formed like a continuous screen between us and our line of sight. Our clothes after long hours under the thick liquid, began to take water. At the end of the afternoon, we tried to look for a dry place to spend the night. We were refused several times by a man and his wife and then by a small mosque. The local imam told us that we could try our luck at the Emamzadeh Hashem. It was a holy place that included a mosque and a place where believers could spend the night.

After about ten kilometers (6.2 miles), the Emamzadeh rose straight ahead of us. It was perched on top of a hill. Everything was so black. It was like the battle scene of the Lord of the Rings in Helm's Deep! The climb was steep. Passers-by were staring at us, wondering why we were there. I asked the guard at the entrance if we could put up our tent. He beckoned us to continue a little further. A group of children ran towards us and escorted us to the entrance of a large building where there was an old man with a lot of keys. We had to convince him.

We were at the end of our tether for that day. We were soaked and tired. If he refused to welcome us, we had no plan B. It was already dark, and it was still raining hard. A young girl approached us. She was draped in black, and her face was filled with great softness. A few strands of her curly hair escaped from her hijab. She brought us tea, cakes, took care of Khanh Nguyen. A little angel had fallen from the sky draped in black. Her name was Nazanin. She had come from the great city of Qazvin to Emamzadeh to pray in honor of Imam Hussein. Nazanin brought us comfort at a time when we needed it most.

The old man with his keychain asked us where we came from and made sure that we would stay only one night. He asked us if we were married. We showed him our wedding rings and even our marriage certificate! He made us understand that this was a place of prayer. He joined his hands together and bent over as if to mime the prayer. I didn't know if, at that moment he asked me if I was a Muslim. I just nodded which suited him well enough. We set our tent up in a small alcove of the building. Other Iranians

Night at the mosque, Emamzadeh Achem, Iran

had thrown their own tents all over the ground outside.

Khanh Nguyen first went to the women's bathroom to shower, and then it was my turn to go to the men's. Nazanin was always near us. She made sure that the group of children didn't disturb us too much, served us more tea, and brought us other fruits. We chatted with her using Google Translate: she was living in Qazvin and studying in Tehran. She told us that she was so happy to meet us. We then visited the mosque: one side was reserved for men, the other for women. Khanh Nguyen went to her side, draped with a chador. Inside the mosque, there were thousands of mirrors and silver reflections. We had to kiss a silver-colored grid. The songs of the muezzin resonated in every corner of the Emamzadeh.

It was time for Nazanin to return to Qazvin. We took her contact info; she took ours. Qazvin was our next destination. We promised to contact her when we got there. The hundreds of believers then gradually left the place. Only those, like us, who would spend the night there would remain. We fell asleep to the sound of the muezzin's interminable laments.

Chapter 13

Kalashnikov for me, Sexual Harassment for her

Too many variables in one place makes for uncertain circumstances. In Iran, the end of September marks the annual celebration in memory of Imam Hussein, a respected figure in the Shiite Islamic world. For several weeks the cities and countryside were draped in black in his honor. Northern Iran felt familiar to Khanh Nguyen's homeland with its rain and rice fields, despite the sharp cultural contrasts!

We had just spent the night in our tent at the Emamzadeh Hashem mosque. It was located along a huge highway in the direction of Qazvin (our destination of the day). Endless rain fell from the heavens to the endless wails of the muezzin glorifying the Imam's presence in them. I opened my eyes to the sound of his laments then kissed Khanh Nguyen on the forehead to gently wake her up. The Iranian families who had been sleeping in their tents around ours had already left, padding away like Persian cats.

Khanh Nguyen put on her hijab. It hadn't taken long for the habit to form. We started to dismantle our tent, swigging *Sangak* and chewing some dates for our breakfast. I finished setting up our luggage on Tank as Khanh Nguyen did the same on Monster. It was time to get back on the road. There was only one route to reach Qazvin, which required passing an imposing mountain range. We then had to ride the highway along its shoulder. This would have been mad to do if were it happening in France, but it was casually ignored in Iran. We even passed a parked police car whose driver waved to us warmly through his window.

The Peugeot 405s and Zamyads overtook us along the huge highway at breakneck speeds. After about twenty kilometers (12.5 miles), it grew dangerous. Our bikes arrived in front of an imposing tunnel where the shoulder we had been cycling on suddenly stopped. Cars roared out so ferociously that for the first time, we felt like we shouldn't dare going forward! I turned to Khanh Nguyen, exclaiming: "We're going to hitchhike. We can't continue". Eyes still fixed on the tunnel, she nodded in silent agreement. We left our bikes along the safety railing and waved to the Zamyad, who passed by to stop. The Zamyad were blue pick-up trucks that seemed to be transporting everything and everywhere in Iran.

A few minutes later, a Zamyad stopped. A man reached over and swung open the passenger door from the inside. Short, shaggy-haired, and in a plaid shirt with puffy black pants, he said he was called Ismail and came from Kurdistan. I told him we had to go to Qazvin and threw a "Salavati?" his way. In Farsi, it was a statement that meant we would pray to Allah (strongly) in return for the help we were asking of him. Ismail looked at us warily under his brow, laughing and replied, "Salavati, Salavati.". We put our bicycles in the back with cardboard boxes and vegetables and settled down beside Ismail at the front. Ismail couldn't take us to Qazvin one hundred and thirty kilometers (80 miles) away but only forty kilometers (25 miles) further. He had to leave the highway at that point. "No problem, we'll ask other cars there," I translated on my phone for him to see. We told each other a little about our lives: that his daughter and his wife were waiting for him at home, that he thought we were crazy to cycle like that in Iran.

After about thirty minutes, it was already time to say goodbye. He left us next to a huge dam. We got Tank and Monster down with all our luggage. We took a selfie for the three of us to remember the encounter and left each other with multiple "Khodavez".

We were now above the clouds. The mountain peaks glowing from behind as they were lit by the dying sun. I took pictures of Khanh Nguyen. We had about fifty meters (150 feet) to go to until we'd reach the main road. There was a car with travelers taking a well-deserved break near an unusual-looking building. I thought we might as well wait there for our next Zamyad. We walked, pushing our bikes towards the goal.

As we neared, a man waved and called to catch my attention from the building. I took the building in and realized it was laced with barbed wire, and he was standing in a watchtower within it. It was a military barracks! The car with its amicable passengers had left. The soldier was twenty meters (50 feet) away at the most, and we were the only ones left in his line of sight. I had my camera around my neck. He told me with his hand gestures to take a picture of him. I started to lift it to my eye then stopped. I uneasily remembered that taking pictures of military buildings was strictly forbidden. To be caught taking that picture was a ticket to prison, and Iranian prisons aren't rated well on TripAdvisor... a single star at best! I gave him a curt "no" with my head and bared my most polite if tense smile.

Looking perturbed, he started to raise his Kalashnikov.

My mind thought back to the events of Tarantino's classic *Pulp Fiction*. Two gunmen men drive away from a homicide in a car, arguing about cheeseburgers. One turns to a hostage in the back seat to ask their opinion and accidentally fires a bullet into their head as the car hits a bump in the road. My life could be taken with a simple unintentional pull of that trigger. My heart throbbed so powerfully my whole body beat..

I suddenly thought back to my grandfather. As a child, I'd sit with him on a green bench under the shade of a tree in the countryside as he told me stories. He once told me about his encounter with Furnace Peak on Reunion Island. As a volcanologist, he'd got close to the active volcanos to take some measurements with his team.

Unexpectedly, Furnace Peak had started to wake up, the ground shaking violently beneath him. He told me then: "No need to be a hero. You just run away and try to save your life". They left everything they had behind, running for their lives as fast as they could, as the volcano started

Tank & Monster, well installed at the back of the Zamyad

Two minutes before our encounter with the soldier

to vomit lava.

My mind whirled back to the present. The soldier was still pointing at me with his Kalashnikov. I needed to escape from here with Khanh Nguyen. And as fast as we could. No need to be a hero. Just like Bon Papa had said.

Little by little, I backed out of his line of sight. I managed to make Khanh Nguyen realize that she had to move along too. Abruptly I heard the unmistakable sound of a bullet mechanically moved from its clip into the chamber of a weapon. Time stood still. After what felt like forever, I managed to edge out of its full line of sight. My face now drained of blood, I tried to tell her, "This guy pointed at me with his gun, his Kalashnikov. We have to get out of here and quickly".

We turned to the road, desperate for a car to hitch, as two men started to near us on foot. An old man with a younger man. The younger one had broad shoulders covered with a sweater with the hood pulled up. I explained to them that we were looking for a car to go to Qazvin. The young man gazed at Khanh Nguyen like an object, wordlessly staring into her eyes with a cruel smile as he licked his lips. I made sure Khanh Nguyen stayed behind me. A Zamyad came into our field of vision bringing with it the opportunity of escape! I hurriedly ran towards the driver: "Qazvin!" I yelled after him as he drove past.

Behind me, I heard Khanh Nguyen shouting the Persian words that we had learned a few days earlier. "Im osha Maneh! Im ohsa Maneh": "It's my husband! It's my husband!" I came running back. The guy had made sexual advances. I got in his way, burning with rage. From the corner of my eye, I saw the soldier from his watchtower observing the scene. I signaled for Khanh Nguyen to move away and continue towards the highway ramp. Khanh Nguyen hurried away with Monster. Once she was far enough away, I got on Tank and kept staring at the pervert before pedaling as fast as I could to reach Khanh Nguyen.

Cars were being driven at breakneck speed on the bend to get to the highway. By some miracle, I managed to attract the attention of a Zamyad, which stopped. I shouted "Qazvin" once again, and this time the driver nodded his head. I cried in relief, "Salavati?", but he wanted fifteen dollars. We were in no position to refuse. We threw our bikes on the back of the Zamyad and sat in the open air. The driver shifted into first gear, and the car started the long bend back towards the highway. We watched as the military barracks and men grew ever smaller against the mountains.

The Zamyad entered the highway. It drove so fast the wind made us dizzy. The Elburz mountain range unfolded all around as enveloping us as the Zamyad curved and sped around. We still had seventy kilometers (43 miles) to go. On my phone, I contacted Nazanin, our guardian angel, who we'd met at the mosque from the day before. She lived in Qazvin. She answered and told us she was waiting for us with a prepared lunch.

The Zamyad violently exited the highway. Dust and stones splashed all around us. It wasn't a good sign. We moved further and further away from the highway to Qazvin. What if the driver and his passenger had helped us only to later rob us, rape Khanh Nguyen, or even worse? We felt like fish in a barrel. Should we jump out of the vehicle? Where could we go? Abandon the bikes and all our equipment? We finally reached an asphalt road, and the Zamyad turned left to join it. I look at my GPS. I understood that the driver had just taken a kind of hidden path to exit the highway to avoid the toll booth. I felt stupid for overreacting.

After ten kilometers (6.2 miles), we arrived in the suburbs of Qazvin. I got out of the vehicle, and the driver helped me get everything off the back of the truck. I handed him the fifteen US dollars in rial. He thanked me, nodding and clambered back into his Zamyad. We cycled into the center of Qazvin under the midday sun to meet Nazanin.

Nazanin was waiting for us on the street, oblivious to what had happened to us. She was accompanied by another girl and two boys who parted from the choice of black made by the majority in their style. Nazanin was in a long azure blue cardigan. Only a few hours had passed since Khanh Nguyen, and I had begun our morning with a kiss at the mosque.

Nazanin couldn't welcome us into her home, but she knew a small hotel in the center. She got into the car of her friends that we followed to the hotel. It would do for the next couple of nights. We took a quick shower, put on the only clean clothes we had left, and joined our little azure blue angel and her friends outside.

They took us to a restaurant that offered kebabs - meat cooked on the spit - and rice with saffron or tamarind pulp. We made small talk until I couldn't help but blurt out the contents of that morning. One of Nazanin's friends spoke very good English and translated for us. I saw a bit of fright on everyone's face as I went through the stories. Some of them told us that they were sorry for what had happened, that we had to be careful with some people in Iran. Just getting it off our chest put the dark events of the morning at a distance. For me, easing feelings in abstract, is achieved by solidifying them in words. It's the philosopher Cioran who perfectly identified this process:

"Without the idea of suicide, I would have killed myself since forever."

Chapter 14

In the land of Taarof

Mileage Meter: 6,547 to 6,945km (4,068 to 4,315 miles)

(Qazvin –Qom)

For the whole of the next day, we simply walked with the beautiful youth of Qazvin with Nazanin as our guide. We strolled in the old city, around the gigantic, cool Bazaar. We regained a taste for the simple things, the carefree. I completely forgot the dark events of the day before. After dinner, we said goodbye to Nazanin. Without her having known it, she had been our buoy, our cork, preventing us from sinking, from drifting towards sad expanses.

We took to the road again the next morning, heading south. The climate was so different: temperatures plunged during the night only to rise high during the day. To start before six in the morning was, therefore, to pedal through the cool deserted alleys. We easily left Qazvin to head towards Buin Zahra, about fifty kilometers (31 miles). The landscapes increasingly became deserted. The road, a big straight line in the middle of nothing. Large noisy trucks drove next to us regularly.

I took the opportunity to watch Khanh Nguyen. She impressed me with her ease on Monster while wearing the hijab and a long cardigan. She was such a heroine. She had managed to respond to the gigantic physical challenge while keeping her calm, class, and grace. I felt incredibly lucky to have stumbled upon such a rare pearl.

In Buin Zahra, we were welcomed by Madhi and his family. Madhi was also part of the Warmshowers network. He proudly told us that he had never refused a single request. He was an English teacher, and even though he was often busy, he always had room to welcome travelers like us. Buin Zahra was an oasis in the middle of that desert and had lots of fruits and pistachios on offer. A man even offered us a full bag when we crossed the downtown that afternoon. Madhi had us installed in his basement in his little brother's room. He joined us for dinner with his wife, where his mother had prepared delicious dishes. We went from one subject to another before Mahdi told us that he wanted to give us a gift. He was practicing Persian calligraphy and wanted to write us a poem. He dipped the thick pen in ink and drew elegant characters onto the paper. The poem, in Farsi, said:

"Alone, in the back of my room, you don't know how much I suffered."

I corrected: "Alone, in the back of our tent, you don't know how much we suffered"! It made Madhi and Khanh Nguyen laugh, but like a prophecy that had already come true, this poem made me think back to the events we encountered a few days ago. I remembered the Kalashnikov, the barbed wire, the hood of the harasser... I chased those thoughts away by concentrating on my present and smiling politely at Mahdi. The three of us took a picture with the beautiful poem held softly by Mahdi with his fine fingers.

The next morning, Madhi gave us an appointment at his English school. There we met a group of about twenty teenage girls who were all enthusiastic about meeting us. Some of them spoke impeccable English, and we enjoyed answering their questions in detail. Chuckles often accompanied our answers. Those moments were precious and replenished our souls before we hit the road again. The small group already had to go to class. We took a group photo before leaving them and Madhi to continue south.

The Iranian desert, Saveh, Iran

In Iran, there is an Iranian equivalent of the Red Cross called the Red Crescent. Only men can join the ranks of the Red Crescent, which intervenes during road accidents or natural disasters such as an earthquake. Red Crescent emergency centers are scattered all over the country and near the main roads to make the organization easily accessible.

The blogs we had consulted before coming to Iran had advised us to knock on the door of such a center to inquire about the chance of spending a night there. We spotted one on the difficult road to Saveh and decided to try our luck. The road climbed without the slightest trace of shade. Magnificent red and yellow-tinted mountains with herds of goats moving here and there lay in front, and I took superb photos of Khanh Nguyen on Monster in those surroundings.

The kilometers passed by, and the Red Crescent post inevitably got closer. We arrived there at lunchtime. A man in his twenties welcomed us. His name was Mahmoud. I showed him our small explanatory paper in Farsi, and he immediately beckoned us inside. He set us up in a large room with carpets and invited us to share lunch with his colleagues. There were three of them, and each one was dressed in a red and white uniform. The atmosphere was relaxed until a grim-looking wrinkly policeman and his podgy youthful deputy arrived. The policeman introduced himself and his sidekick: "I'm Ali, and he's Mr. Picnic". Mr. Picnic held his enormous belly and chuckled at the joke made at his expense with the rest of us. Ali asked us a few questions about our trip but without going into detail, then left us with Mr. Picnic as he went on his way. Our friends then took us from the Red Crescent, who took us to a room where we both took a big nap. At six o'clock, Mahmoud came in, asking us if we were going to sleep there all night. I had presumed we were going to, but he looked towards us apologetically:

"We can't accommodate you here."

Immediately my mind drifted back to the police officers, Ali and Mr. Picnic. It seemed like they had put pressure on them to kick us out. I was annoyed, but they had welcomed us that afternoon, offered us the meal, so it felt rude to insist we stay. I told them, however, what situation they had imposed on us. The next town, Saveh, was too far away to cycle to before it grew dark. It was about fifty kilometers (31 miles). Between the Red Crescent and Saveh was the desert. We would have no choice but to improvise and camp in the wild. Mahmoud apologized again and gave us some bottles of water in compensation.

With that, we were back on the road. We didn't have much time left to find a place to sleep. The large trucks continued to pass by. We drove a few kilometers before finding a track that went off to the right. The track faded at the bottom of a valley in the landscape with nothing around except sand and small dry shrubs. I looked on *Google Maps*: it led nowhere. It was a good sign for us because it meant that no one was likely to travel it but us. We waited until there were no more trucks passing by to get onto the sandy track. Once on the track, we pedaled as fast as we could so that nobody could see us. A few minutes later, I spotted a good place to camp: there were some small, stunted shrubs but just enough to hide us. We settled down, laying the bikes on the ground to hide them and sat down next to each other.

    It was a magical moment woven of blue, orange, and red light simultaneously as the sun disappeared behind the mountains. Its journey ended in a silence that stood in sharp contrast to the chaos of the road. A freshness seemed to come after as the ground cooled without its glare. With nobody around, it was time to set up the tent! It was a full moon tonight, which was a gift with a catch. It allowed us to set everything up without using our headlamps, but it made us infinitely more visible for anyone who wanted to find us!

    Khanh Nguyen changed in the tent while I stayed outside to keep watch. I joined her after she finished. We slipped into our comforters before hugging each other. Our eyelids had softly batt closed when suddenly a strong, imposing light projected against our tent wall:

"Shit! We've been spotted!"

"What are we going to do?" Khanh Nguyen answered.

"I'm getting dressed, and I'll go look. Get dressed too and put on your hijab."

I slowly opened the zip of the tent, ready to see at least one car or motorcycle on the sand track... but there was nothing. Nothing at all. Had we both hallucinated? I waited a few minutes to make sure it was nothing, and I came back into the tent. We went back to sleep. Both of us were unable to resist the fatigue. About ten minutes later: the same light projected against our tent! I zipped open the entrance with an alarmed flourish and could see in the distance a bend located higher up where a motorcycle was buzzing along. It was well over a kilometer (a mile) away, but the light of the front headlight of the motorcycle had pierced the desert air to reach us. The bend was so far away that someone could hardly see us from that road even with good eyes. We both felt relieved.

The next morning, well before daybreak, I woke up then woke up my teammate. By now, we were used to our morning routine after a night's camping and had squeezed, rolled, unhooked, and packed all our things before sunrise.

The first moments of the day were fabulously poetic: the sun still hid behind the mountain's highest peak, while the moon waited to see it take its place in the sky. We moved like shadows among the great sand desert, between the sky and earth, between the air and sand, between life and death.

Our small sandy path finally led to the main road to Saveh. The trucks resumed their ceaseless dance. We hadn't had breakfast yet, and a car stopped to offer us a watermelon! The driver passed it to me through the window before speeding off again so fast that I didn't even have time to thank him! We complemented our most recent gift with the pistachios we'd

Improvised night under the tent, Saveh, Iran

Leaving at dawn, Saveh, Iran

received the day before in Buin Zahra.

We continued for a few kilometers (miles) before another car stopped in front of us and firmly signaled for us to stop. The man in the passenger seat handed us green grapes! They were delicious and so sweet. I thanked our generous donors as best I could.

We finally arrived in Saveh after a long descent under the thick sun. On the advice of Mahmoud of the Red Crescent the day before, we stopped by to say hello to the team of the Saveh region. It was a big hospital. I was taken up to the second floor where the director, Mr. Mohammed, was. I told him that I had met Mahmoud. He asked us for our passports and told me that we could only stay there for a few hours and that, similarly, they weren't allowed to receive us for the night. It was a good compromise for us to take a nap and take a needed shower on the first floor instead.

Back from lunch, Mr. Mohammed asked us what our route was. I answered that we wanted to arrive the next day in Qom, one of the most religious cities in Iran. He immediately showed me another center of the Red Crescent on the map:

"You can sleep there tonight before arriving in Qom tomorrow. My team has been briefed and is waiting for you."

It was a gift from heaven. I shook Mr. Mohammed's hand while he gave me a good-natured pat on the shoulder. Khanh Nguyen made him confirm we wouldn't be dislodged like last night. We didn't want to repeat the same experience. Mr. Mohammed assured us that there was nothing to fear. We took to the road feeling light. Knowing where we could spend the night was always a big relief.

Before leaving Saveh, we had to have lunch. We stopped in front of a small restaurant that was offering hookahs. There were only men. Some had the kind of grizzled face you might see on a mobster. I installed Khanh Nguyen at the end of the table, protecting her from their keen eyes. A pot-bellied manager approached me. He spoke English and boisterously asked me what we wanted. I asked to see the menu, and he offered me a visit to the kitchen to choose. It would be spit-roasted chicken with rice.

"How much?" I asked him

"Don't worry... we'll see later! My name is Ahmed, by the way. What's your name?"

"My name is Thibault; she is Khanh Nguyen."

I found it weird not to know the price. I felt like he was going to rip us off:

"You should really try that too! It's really good. I'll bring it to you. You want some drinks too? What are you having?" Said Ahmed.

"Just tea, thank you Ahmed."

A few minutes later, we found ourselves with lots of food and tea. I felt bad not knowing how much it was going to cost. I could already imagine Khanh Nguyen blaming me: that I should have refused, that I should have asked the price... With our twelve US dollars a day, we weren't in a position to overdo it. Ahmed settled down next to us with his hookah. He asked more about us and our trip. He had a restaurant but a lot of other business in import-export markets. He had even been to Vietnam! We discussed it all just before the bill arrived. When I asked Ahmed how much I owed him, he just said no; he wanted us to eat for free. Could he be doing *Taarof?*

Taarof is an Iranian custom, a back-and-forth game that can last a long time between two people. The first begs the other to accept an offering and, the other does everything to refuse. For example, a cab driver would pretend to want to offer the ride to his client, and his client would have to refuse. The driver would insist several times and play the *Taarof* again before the client would insist on paying once more. It was a form of politeness, a ritual between a host and their guest. Since our arrival in Iran, it had baffled us, but by now, we understood. When engaging in a *Taarof*, it's common practice to refuse three times before finally accepting the offering of a host. That way, one can be sure that they really want to make the offering.

Knowing this, I started the *Taarof* parade with Ahmed. I insisted on paying for the meal, he refused. I asked him how much we owed him, he refused. I took out some bills, and with a stern look, he showed I should immediately put them away. With that, I concluded that he really wanted to treat us. I felt so stupid for having judged him by his appearance, to have thought that he wanted to rip us off! We even exchanged phone numbers.

Khanh Nguyen then warmly thanked Ahmed, and I did the same.

The wheels of Tank and Monster took back to the road where the asphalt was practically melting as the sun blazed with all its might. The road leading to the next Red Crescent station was dangerous: it comprised two lanes with no roadside and ran along a ditch. Trucks on both sides crossed at full speed. A small village gave us the opportunity to take a break in the shade. A man on his motorcycle came to see us, offered us pomegranates[1] and soon proposed that we should sleep at his place. I accepted the pomegranates with great gratitude but made him understand that we already had a place to sleep that night.

We continued before we were stopped again. This time, a man on his motorcycle had six corn cobs in his arms, which he held out to me. I asked him for his name: Reza. Reza had seen us in the distance and had time to pass by his cornfield, picked six fresh corn cobs, then caught up to us to offer them! I was so touched by this gift and Reza's frank smile. I signaled that I didn't have room for them all, however. Two or three cobs were more than enough! I shook his hand while Khanh Nguyen immortalized the moment with my camera. We were given so many fruits and vegetables that day we thought we could open a business!

We arrived at the Red Crescent post. I rang the bell. A man in his thirties opened the gates for us. He had a thick mustache like Freddie Mercury. Freddie Mercury was of Iranian origin: he was even called Farrokh Bulsara! The man beckoned for us to go inside. The Director, Mr. Mohammed, had warned him of our arrival. Our host was Mr. Moradi. He spoke perfect English and even a little bit of French. He introduced us to his two acolytes with whom he took care of this station. Mr. Moradi installed us in a small room with two iron beds. The team of three was already at the stove preparing dinner for us. We took the opportunity to share all our offerings of the day with our guests. Mr. Moradi proposed to roast our corn cobs. This was one of the things that Khanh Nguyen really

---

[1] Local fruit

loved: perfect!

Dinner was a moment that I will remember for a long time to come. The food prepared by our three guests was delicious, the atmosphere

Reza and his corn cobs, Saveh, Iran

excellent. Mr. Moradi and his two companions laughed easily with such purity it became contagious. The jokes and situations followed one another so well that we all laughed without really knowing why. Mr. Moradi loved music, culture, and philosophy. We talked for a long time about Nietzsche, Spinoza, and even Derrida, which he loved to read! What an incredible gift from destiny to come across someone like him in the middle of Iran. I love philosophy and can discuss it for hours. Our discussions went on late into the night... Khanh Nguyen was already in bed when I finally joined her. I began to contemplate our day. It had been punctuated with so many beautiful encounters and so many presents. Iran had such a great culture. I fell asleep comforted by the generosity we'd seen mankind capable of that day, far from the military man with his Kalashnikov and the morbid hooded stalker!

Chapter 15

From Qom to Abyaneh: Iran in all its diversity

Mileage Meter: 6,945 to 7,212km (4,315 to 4,481 miles)

(Qom-Abyaneh)

It was seven in the morning, and the sun was already beating down outside. The trucks were making so much noise, their wheels screeching across the asphalt with a deafening noise. Every irregularity on the road sounded like a thunderclap, an explosion that made the whole truck large animals loaded onto them vibrate.

The Red Crescent post, where we spent the night, was like a bunker. A sweet parenthesis before having to go back to the front. Inside, the explosion of noise from the trucks and its vibrating shockwaves were felt but muffled, as if our heads were underwater. Once we opened the thick door again to take out Tank and Monster, we rediscovered this aural warzone!

We extended our goodbyes with Mr. Moradi and his two acolytes as long as we could, and then we resolved to leave. The road to Qom was through a desert. We protected ourselves as much as possible from the ugly sun with cream, scarves, and long sleeves. The road was undulating, passing over the dunes. On the side was an abandoned caravanserai[1]. We took the opportunity to explore it and enjoyed all the shade that its thick stones preserved.

Qom took shape as we approached with its multiple minarets and mosques. It is the most religious city Iran has, along with Mashaad. Millions of believers from the Shia world come here on pilgrimage every year. We didn't know what to expect, whether our bikes would stand out, or even if Khanh Nguyen was too colorfully dressed. The tone was quickly set. All women, without exception wore at least a black chador. Some were even in a burqa with their entire face masked. We snuck through the thick traffic that had formed near a market. The chadors and mullahs sporting their turbans pacing one after one another into the mix.

Mojtaba, who was in the Warmshowers network, could welcome us in Qom for one night but only under some peculiar conditions. . His wife didn't like that he wanted to accommodate cyclists. She thought it would end up in him leaving her for the roads one day. So, cyclists weren't welcome in their home. Mojtaba offered instead for us to spend the night in downtown Qom at his office. We met him in front of his office door. Mojtaba wore large glasses and had a shaved head. He had bright and sparkling eyes. He took us down to the basement to take the elevator to his office. After several months on the roads, our conditions for somewhere to sleep were easy to satisfy. A clean, quiet, and safe place was enough for us.

After a cup of black tea, Mojtaba told us that he had some work to finish for his Doctorate in Architecture. He suggested that we take a stroll by ourselves in Qom but would join us later on for ice cream. Khanh Nguyen readjusted her hijab, and we went out into the streets of Qom. We headed towards the shrine of Fatimah Masoumeh, daughter of the seventh Shiite Imam and known for her great piety. The streets were churning in a sea of black fabric as residents went about their business.

At the entrance to the shrine, men filed to the left and women to the right. The guards took one look at my camera before forbidding me to enter

---

[1] An old roadside inn where travelers could rest and recover from the day's journey

with it. I chose not to visit the sanctuary rather than leave it at the entrance. After five minutes, I saw Khanh Nguyen come back out. She hadn't been able to enter because her hijab hadn't conformed to the regulations. She had to wear a chador. Clearly unwanted, we decided to continue our walk.

Never before had we set foot in a society so culturally inaccessible. No one expressed any aggression or disdain towards us, but we still felt like outsiders. Practices familiar to us were discarded in their daily grind of events. It was a radical experience of alienation. We made a turn at the old Bazar then found Mojtaba for a *Faloodeh* (a kind of ice cream with vermicelli, lemon, and rose water). We shared our experience of Qom with Mojtaba as our *Faloodeh* melted. Mojtaba wanted to go home to his wife and children. He drove us to the office and promised us that he would come back early the next morning to open the doors for us.

With the weeps throbbing from the shrine of Fatimah Masoumeh in the background, I fell asleep next to the printer; and Khanh Nguyen next to the coffee machine.

It was six in the morning and time to return to our world: the world of roads, pavement, and asphalt. We left Qom and Mojtaba and headed on towards Kashan. The road passed by while the sun gave us no mercy. At eleven, we settled down under a bridge to enjoy some shade and take a nap. The landscapes became quite lunar, inhospitable for almost all forms of life. After a night of wild camping in a pomegranate orchard, we discovered Kashan early the next morning.

Kashan was a cultural parenthesis for us. The city was much less rigorous than Qom, and we felt more comfortable there. We found a small hotel that would do the trick. For three days we explored Kashan and its labyrinth of alleys that wound around the old Bazar. There were also big houses like the *Tabatabaeis* House or the *Borujerdi* House. These were

Qom and all its black chadors, Iran

the former homes of rich carpet merchants. Their elaborate architecture, murals, and stained-glass windows projecting wonderful colors into the lavish rooms inside rivaled each other. The highlight of the show was the splendid *Fin Garden* with its ponds, fountains, streams, and trees. It epitomized refinement and elegance. We spent a whole morning there. We were so absorbed by the place.

After three days in Kashan, our bodies and minds were soothed. Our task for the next two days was going to be hard. The goal was to reach the small village of Abyaneh, which was lost in the mountains. Abyaneh is known for the red color of its old houses and the colorful clothes of its women.

We had two options:
- Either take route 587, which climbed for tens of kilometers (miles) and then take a path made of pebbles and dust. We would have to go by a pass at more than 2,800 meters (9,200 feet) of altitude to then go down to Abyaneh. It was a physical challenge, but it promised great scenery.
- Take the road 7 then the 665, which crossed a kind of desert to then pass in front of the nuclear installations of Natanz. Iran enriched uranium here. We were almost certain to be controlled by the military, who would check our passports and inspect our photos. The political climate was very tense at that moment between Iran and the West. However, the road had the advantage of going around the mountain, and the final climb would be toward Abyaneh.

Khanh Nguyen didn't really feel up to climbing a whole day in the sun. We chose the second option: the nuclear option.

We left Kashan in the early morning. After a few kilometers (miles) outside the old city, the desert begins, the real one. Not a single drop of shade or rain. Our water reserves were limited but fortunately, we could count on the Peugeots 405s and Zamyads for assistance in case of an emergency. The environment was so hostile, so rough, so dry. The wind swept the sand from

Lunar landscapes, Qom region, Iran

left to right on the road as the sun melted the asphalt. We weren't very far from the nuclear installations of Natanz. What was expecting us? We still had in mind the traumatic experience with the soldier and creep from a few days ago, but avoiding the route wasn't a luxury we could choose.

At the top of a sandy hill, a white Peugeot 405 pulled up in front of me. An Iranian with a rather dark face, a full beard, and of average size moved towards me with water. I filled my bottle with it and thanked him. He spoke to me with signs, and I began to understand that he was doing everything he could to advise us not to go further. I told him on my phone that there was normally no risk, that other travelers passed by quite regularly without being worried. He looked me straight in the eyes and then mimed with his hands an arrest with handcuffs. My pulse quickened, and I tried to ask him for details, but communication was difficult. He then took out his wallet and showed me his identity card: he was a military man! Now he was dressed in civilian clothes, and I understood that he probably knew more than we did us. He got back in his car, threw me a last glance as if to beg me not to go any further, then he went back on his way to Natanz.

I remained as if stunned by what had just happened... I shared the warnings with Khanh Nguyen. The decision was really difficult to make, but we decided it was better to turn back than risk the Iranian jails. Perhaps they had been instructed for a few days to arrest all foreigners who would pass too close to military or nuclear installations. Recently they had arrested a French researcher and two Australian tourists. We both decided to turn back through the desert. Psychologically it was tough to have to go back under those conditions. Even Monster and Tank seemed to complain about the situation.

After ten endless kilometers (6.2 miles) fighting against the wind and the sand, I signaled to Khanh Nguyen that we would stop in the shade of a row of trees. A grey 405 came out of nowhere. Two men dressed in civilian clothes got out of it. They didn't even say hello to us and asked to see our passports. I answered them in English:

"Can we at least know who you are?"

The Iranian desert, Natanz, Iran

"We are.... the enemy." The younger of the two answered.

I presumed something had been lost in translation. Even today, I'm still not sure what he meant by "enemy". Both men seemed to be part of the secret police. They inspected all of our documents then took pictures. I kept a sufficient distance to avoid any unpleasant surprises. Khanh Nguyen was sitting in the back. After several long minutes of taking pictures of everything, they finally got back in their car and muttered a short goodbye.

The 405 departed, we found ourselves once again both in the middle of the blowing wind, sand, and silence. A deep feeling of unease and insecurity invaded our minds. I started to understand the presence of a dictatorship and its secret police. A sword of Damocles permanently over your head telling you: "Beware, I can fall at any moment and even if you have nothing to blame yourself for. So, in any case, behave yourself". The threat was much stronger and more coercive in abstract than in the actual action. The anticipation of being bludgeoned is much stronger than the bludgeoning itself.

Khanh Nguyen came to hug me, and I hugged her as hard as I could. We left without really knowing where we were going. The idea was to go back to *plan A* and take road 587 to reach the village of Abyaneh. To do this, we first had to pedal along the highway, following the hard shoulder. After the tollgate, which we bypassed, we took route 587. The sun's presence was always so violent over our heads. I saw that Khanh Nguyen had physically cracked. She had stopped advancing. She had sunstroke! Two small benches in the shade appeared in front of a large religious center. We put our bicycles down, Khanh Nguyen lay down then fell asleep almost immediately. A few minutes passed by before I tried to find some alternative routes on the map. Where would we sleep tonight? Where would we stop? Would Khanh Nguyen be able to climb the difficult road ahead after this for several kilometers (miles)?

Khanh Nguyen woke up, saying she felt much better. She gulped down a lot of our remaining water while I handed her what food we had left. I couldn't see myself forcing her to go back on the road at the risk of her health, so I proposed to hitchhike the rest of our route and see where it would take us. I still had the bad memory of the hitchhike to Qazvin that ended in Kalashnikov and sexual harassment.

After just a few minutes, a blue Zamyad stopped. It was a family: two parents and their child. They could take us about ten kilometers before our paths separated. It suited us, and we were carried further along the road. When we had to get out, they kindly offered us tea and dates and then went on their way. We got back on our bikes and took a photo of ourselves at the intersection towards Ghohrud and the village of Abyaneh

Five minutes passed before another Zamyad arrived. He was a man, alone, in his fifties. His name was Faruk. I showed him our little paper written in Farsi and asked him if he could take us. Luckily, he was also going to Abyaneh! He lived in a small village a few kilometers away. Faruk made us get in the back of the vehicle with Tank and Monster. We mountain-gazed from the car for an hour. Some summits were so high you could see the snow-tipped caps. I was relieved to have made that choice instead of pushing Khanh Nguyen to continue by bike. The slopes were so steep that we probably wouldn't have gotten very far..

Faruk stopped to take a break. I took the opportunity to go into a convenience store and offered him a drink and vanilla ice cream. He smiled with all his teeth and thanked me. We were on our way again. From the village of Ghohrud, we suddenly left the asphalt road to take a track that got lost in the mountains. We crossed a river then continued to climb again and again. Arriving at an intersection, Faruk braked then cut the engine of his Zamyad. It was time for us to get out. Faruk took the left road towards his village. For us, it would be on the right towards Abyaneh. We still had about thirty kilometers (19 miles) to go. We threw dozens of "Thank you"'s his way which were pronounced the same way as in French ("Merci"). Faruk wished us good luck, restarted his Zamyad, and soon disappeared behind the relief.

Once again, we found ourselves alone in the middle of the great outdoors. Only a small path tracing the mountains. It was already five o'clock, and we would have to find a place to sleep for that night.

What immediately shocked me was the total absence of sound that reigned. All I could hear were the mechanical whirs and clicks of my bike and my jerky breath as we continued to climb. The dirt road finally reached a high point and then went back down. We took the opportunity to disappear from the small path and look for a good place to pitch our tent. After a few minutes of searching, I found a place without too many stones and roots: we would sleep there! We set up the tent and prepared our dinner: lentil soup with vegetables, scrambled eggs, and *lavash*[1].

Sitting down to enjoy our evening meal, we contemplated the mountains and their colors that faded as the sun went down. It was already so cold at 2,000 meters (6,560 feet) above sea level. We put on our coats, put all our gear away under the canopy of our tent and allowed ourselves to be absorbed by the eternal spectacle of the sky. It was Lucretius who said in De Rerum Natura:

"Tired that we are of the spectacle of the sky, we do not dare any more to raise our eyes towards these temples of light."

We found it hard to leave the beauty of the stars. However, fatigue finally caught up with us, and we went to bed in thick sheets woven of silence.

The early morning dawned. The night had been perfect; calm and restorative. I woke up before Khanh Nguyen and took the opportunity to admire the sunrise. I moved far enough away from our tent to notice its smallness in front of the mountains surrounding us. Khanh Nguyen woke up too. We prepared coffee and finished installing our bags on Tank and Monster. We hadn't showered since Kashan. It would have to wait until we found a

---

[1] Iranian bread with air bubbles

stream. I hoped in my heart that it would be soon because we were running out of water.

We found the sand track that led us to the village of Abyaneh. The dried yellowing grass at the edges of the small path dominated the play of colors. After a few kilometers, we entered a gorge with mountains on each side, limiting our route. A herd of goats was located higher up, braying as a shepherd played with his voice to lead them. As I looked up, the large dog craned its neck down before starting to bark at us. The whole gorge echoed with those barks so fiercely it was as though we were inside its mouth. Other dogs arrived. There were five or six of them coming down towards us from both sides. They started barking too.

I summoned Khanh Nguyen to stand in the middle of Tank and Monster with me. They would stand in the way of the big dogs. At the same time, I shouted with my whole body in the direction of the shepherd for him to order his hairy henchmen to retreat. The alpha male of the group got closer as the other five surrounded us. I looked him straight in the eyes and pretended to pick up a stone from the ground. He backed away a little. Khanh Nguyen shouted with all her strength, and I continued to shout towards the shepherd. After two long seconds, his voice finally rebounded off the stones. The big dogs stopped dead in their tracks with looks of disappointment, unable to continue their game. Then the six of them went back up towards the shepherd, leaving a cloud of dust behind them.

We came to our senses and continued to climb towards the summit of the pass at 2,800 meters (9,186 feet) high. Our breath became shorter, and our heartbeats jerkier. On the way, we met a tiny grey donkey and its black-haired mother. They seemed surprised to see us. Tank and Monster looked a little bit like donkeys, too, with all their cargo! After a long descent, we met another donkey, this time of adult size. It moved in total freedom in the valley. Khanh Nguyen offered it one of our last cookies. The donkey, let's call it Eeyore, instantly bound himself with great affection for her and Monster. Eeyore started to follow us for several kilometers (miles). We formed a beautiful team of three! Eeyore crossed the road from right to left, always following us like a faithful follower. We were getting closer to Abyaneh, and I didn't really feel like going back to the village with Eeyore. There was no better way to attract attention. So we tried to make it understand that it had to let us go. But in vain... I tried to cut it off, to make big gestures... nothing helped! It always managed to go around me, sneak among the stones, and find Khanh Nguyen. Eeyore must have considered me as an embarrassingly inadequate rival who was getting in its way. Its liveliness impressed me as it jumped over any and every ditch and rock in its misled quest.

At a bend in the road, I managed to block it. I shouted to Khanh Nguyen to keep moving away while I blocked Eeyore. I threw a couple of stones next to Eeyore, hoping to scare him. Eeyore didn't bat an eye. Khanh Nguyen was now very far away. I pushed Eeyore away one last time and went to escape by pushing my pedals with all my strength, but Eeyore chased after me! It held the distance between us until he ran out of breath and stopped dead. I rejoined Khanh Nguyen and told her the scene that had just taken place. I cried with laughter, and so did she. We quickly got back on the road for fear that Eeyore might reappear. A small river appeared, which widened the further we pedaled. Trees finally appeared, then walls and houses. Abyaneh was finally uncovering itself before our very eyes. Its houses were made of red dried mud brick. The history of Abyaneh was a thousand years old, and I quickly understood that it would be nothing without that small river which had formed in the mountains we had just crossed and was flowing gracefully through the village.

What impressed us immediately were the women with their colorful outfits. They contrasted with the black of all the women from the conservative city of Qom. They were mostly old women who chatted with each other here and there, at the foot of a large staircase or next to the flowing river. Abyaneh was a touristy place, but recent geopolitical events had dried up their visitors. We visited the village almost alone, pushing our bikes through the narrow streets and taking a break for some pictures. It was good to discover Abyaneh together for a few hours. We also took the opportunity to have lunch, refuel and do our laundry with the river water. We took a cold-water shower using the river as it flowed past. I made sure

Meeting with Eeyore, Abyaneh, Iran

to hide Khanh Nguyen well so that no man could see her. I had lain down to take a nap when I heard Khanh Nguyen screaming. A tiny little mouse had just escaped from one of her saddlebags! It had probably snuck into it during our last night in the mountains. Fortunately, it hadn't relieved itself inside it.

We were thinking of spending the night in Abyaneh, but the few hotels were too expensive. At the end of the afternoon, we decided to turn back to sleep again in the tent. We found a place at an elevation far enough away from any glances allowing us to spend an undisturbed night together.

Chapter 16

Leyla and Mustafa

Mileage Meter: 7,212 to 7,430km (4,481 to 4,616 miles)

(Abyaneh-Isfahan)

The next morning, time rewound itself. We went back the way we had come the day before and even found Eeyore! However, his owner hadn't appreciated its love escapade as he was firmly attached to a lanyard!

The long descent we had made the day before became a long ascent. But, at the place where the sheepdogs had surrounded us, we turned left and took a new path south towards Meymeh. The path was littered with stones that were hard to negotiate. Khanh Nguyen had difficulty as her tires slipped and almost fell several times. Khanh Nguyen finally fell to the ground with her bike, hurting her shin. Tears she'd been holding back now flowed hot and fast. I went back to her as fast as I could.

"What am I doing here? What am I doing here?" she shouted with all her might.

She had tremors all over her body. I hugged her, placing her head in the hollow of my neck. As her tears soaked my shirt, I tried to talk to her, to tell her that we were almost done with the path. Her breathing, jerky and irregular eased. I kissed her wet cheeks. With steel in her eyes, she told me

Leyla and Mustafa, Isfahan, Iran

we could continue.

I let Khanh Nguyen pedal in front before following her to make sure everything was okay. We got out of the mountains, finding the path to Meymeh. There, we spent the night in the family home of Sina, another member of the *Warmshowers* network. He wasn't there but had asked for assistance from his old uncle, who opened the doors for us. We spent a strange evening together in their big, otherwise empty house. I checked the news of the day on my phone: France had just joined the United States and Saudi Arabia. A few days ago, a Saudi pipeline had been targeted by missile launches. The United States immediately accused the Iranians. France had remained neutral, waiting for the UN report. On that day, our president, Emmanuel Macron, was standing behind Trump and pointing to the Iranians for being responsible for the attack. I gave my phone to Khanh Nguyen saying sullenly:

"Well, given the situation, we will now be good little tourists and stop taking lost paths. I don't want to be arrested for spying by the Guardians of the Revolution..."

"And then you never know if you are near a military zone or not... Imagine if we camp a few kilometers away from a military base without knowing it... "

"We play good little tourists, and we don't camp anymore. We go to Isfahan, then Shiraz, and we see how the situation evolves!"

"Ok... "

The recent arrests scared us. Especially the two Australian tourists. When France remained neutral and played its role as an intermediary on the nuclear issue, I considered the political risk for us to be negligible. But from that day, it was no longer the case. The police check that we had undergone near Natanz also contributed to our paranoia that played in the background. It was now a question of keeping our risk-taking to a minimum before leaving Iran.

The wind returned the next morning as we went down to Isfahan. We swallowed up the hundred kilometers (62 miles) that separated us from the big city in a few hours. Thick traffic became denser the closer we got to the city center.

We were fortunate to be welcomed by Maha and his whole family. Maha was another supporter of the *Warmshowers* network. He had cycled from Isfahan to Tehran by bike in a single day, was a follower of meditation, and an expert in everything related to coffee. Maha welcomed us to his family, who lived in a large apartment in the outskirts of Isfahan. His girlfriend Fatima was waiting for us in Maha's room. She was studying for her upcoming exams. We bonded immediately with them both: they were a modern, relaxed pair. It was like we spoke the same language; we suddenly felt that we could express ourselves freely.

As a specialist of the art, Maha prepared some coffee for us! We hadn't had any since Georgia. Beverage consumers in Azerbaijan and Iran usually opt for tea. People like Maha seemed to be trying to convert the population one by one to take up the global craze. Maha made us smell his coffee beans before he ground them, then made us taste the result. A true delight! Good coffee always evokes the start of Khanh Nguyen and I's relationship for me. Vietnam is one of the world's largest coffee exporters, along with Brazil. The foundation of our relationship was practically around a *caphê sua da*[1] which we'd met over on our first date. The contrast of circumstance made my mind realize the passage of time. I felt far from the man I had been, who had shared those first simple pleasures with Khanh Nguyen in one of the many small alleys in Saigon.

I watched Maha and Fatima adjusting, tuning into each other. I thought back on my journey with Khanh Nguyen. We had been glued together for five months straight. My express return trip from Georgia to France for my grandmother's funeral, Maman Zouzou, was the only exception. Absence is sometimes the reminder that enables you to reappreciate your partner. Nights under the stars in a tent can be romantic. Sometimes, however, flatulence can steal the show with an urgent: "Where is the TP?", "Ha, you'll be careful not to go to the right side of the tent. Go to the left if you have

---

[1] Vietnamese coffee with condensed milk and ice cubes

to go to the toilet. Okay?"

As Khanh Nguyen talked with Fatima and Maha, I devoured her with my eyes. We were living our dream together, and we had accepted all the consequences. Many couples never do the work to understand themselves and each other better throughout their relationships. One day those couples wake up facing that reality. I think back to the maxim of La Rochefoucauld in his *Maxims*:

"There are people who would never have been in love if they had never heard of love."

I would never have been in love if I hadn't met Khanh Nguyen.

Maha saw me daydreaming and asked me:
"What are your Persian names, Thibault and Khanh Nguyen?"
I hesitated for a few seconds before blurting out:
"Leyla and Mustafa!"
The four of us start laughing heartily. Nobody expected Mustafa to pop out! With that, we were baptized: Leyla and Mustafa could now celebrate their Persian life!

~

Isfahan was a modern city with a relaxed youth. It was good to walk along Chahar Bagh Boulevard and see groups of young people. Girls and boys walked and laughed together. As we walked, three girls on skateboards passed us. It cannot be said enough: Iran is such a varied country. Between the conservative Qom and the carefree Isfahan, there was an infinite number of cultural worlds. The Great Bazar and the Jameh Mosque were both small masterpieces of architecture that represented the best Isfahan could produce. The shapes and blue of the Jameh Mosque were unforgettable. With Maha, we gazed at them, appreciating all their details.

In the evening, Leyla, Maha, and Mustafa strolled on bridges gracefully spanning the Zayandeh River. As the evening arrived, the inhabitants gathered there to share a dinner, sing, or simply observe the spectacle of water below. Then we had to run to catch the last bus, where the women sat in the back, and the men sat in the front. There was a grey area in the center, a buffer zone, where women and men could sit side by side. We arrived late at Maha's house. We collapsed onto a pile of thick Persian carpets that formed a comfortable layer between us and the ground.

In Isfahan, we took care of Tank and Monster. We had cycled more than 7,000 kilometers (4,350 miles on them by that stage. We had them both inspected in a specialized store and changed their chain. They came out of the store as good as new, ready to face even greater challenges.

We also needed to renew our Iranian visas, which would expire in a few days. We didn't know, but it would be an interesting experience! We could extend our tourist visa for 30 days, which was more than enough for us to reach Shiraz. Before going to the immigration department at the police station, we had our passport photos taken. Leyla had to wear a hijab and hide even the slightest bit of her hair that slipped out. With Maha, we laughed a lot when we saw Leyla like that: she looked like an Indonesian or Malaysian girl, certainly not a Vietnamese woman! Then Mustafa's turn came for an even more Iranian-looking photo. When the photos finished printing, we discovered a real little Iranian couple ready for a big wedding: Leyla and Mustafa, princess and prince of Isfahan!

We then went back to the police station. At the reception desk, an officer checked what we had, then asked us to put our phones in a plastic box. We would get them back at the exit. Mustafa took the door on the left, Leyla the one on the right. We then found ourselves among a dense crowd, mostly Iraqis and Afghans. There were dozens of numbered counters where everyone elbowed their way through to stand at one. I remained as if dazed, not knowing where to go. A man told me that we had to get a file first then go to counter seven, which we did. We got a first stamp and were then directed to counter eleven. We waited at the door. A man was inside getting yelled at by a police officer. He was shouting, yelling, begging, even crying a little. I saw on the man's passport that he was an Iraqi. It was soon the turn of Leyla and Mustafa. We were afraid of suffering the same fate. The little Iraqi man was dismissed and the police officer, closely shaved, called us with a scowl. I prepared myself for a similar rebuke but as if by magic, his face changed completely. His stormy face gave way to a calm and serene sea:

"Hello! Where do you come from? Ha, France and Vietnam. Wonderful! You're married: congratulations! What do you want? You want to extend your visa and go to Shiraz. Very good. Here's your stamp. Thank you and good luck in Iran."

We came out after only a minute and were happy to have had such a good time. We went up and down the floors among the compact crowd of Iraqis and Afghans. The administration still had some beautiful days ahead of it. I really felt like I was reliving the scene from Asterix in the *Twelve Tasks* where it was necessary to obtain the A-38 pass in the "house that drives you crazy". Without too much difficulty, we got one last stamp. The last officer asked us to come back after lunch.

A few hours later, we returned to the police building. We queued up to get our visa extension. I took the opportunity to take a closer look at a poster I saw on the wall. It was divided into two. On the left, a candy flew as though flung in the air without a wrapping. On the right, a candy was wrapped with nice paper. Flies were devouring the candy on the left; the one on the right was intact, and the flies had left it alone. At the bottom of the poster was a woman with her hair loose and her skin showing, opposite her was a woman perfectly dressed in a long hijab. The message couldn't have been clearer or more explicit: "Woman, if you want to avoid the sexual harassment symbolized by the flies, cover yourself properly. Wear it like a nice candy, and you will keep your dignity and intimacy". That poster made my blood run cold and even today, I still think about iter. It showed a tone-deaf and destructive culture of violence against women. I thought back to the harassment Khanh Nguyen had been subjected to on the road to Qazvin, perhaps only because she was a woman and wearing a hijab

Between modernity and religious rigorism, Isfahan, Iran

too casually. With gender relations in Iran one wonders if some men are innately more perverted than others, and the women need to be protected, or that by putting women's bodies on a pedestal by covering them, men develop devastating sexual impulses as soon as they catch a glimpse of a tiny piece of skin?

It was our turn. I took my eyes off the poster with disgust and put them on the more pleasurable sight of freshly stamped ink on our visas instead. With those bits of ink, we had secured another thirty days in Iran! We spent one last evening with Maha and his family. Fatima, Maha's girlfriend, really wanted to welcome us to Shiraz. Maha would meet us there.

From Isfahan to Shiraz, there were five hundred kilometers (310 miles). Between the two was the great province of Fars and Persepolis within it. Early in the morning, we prepared Tank and Monster, embraced our dear Maha, the only one who was up at that same ungodly hour, and we disappeared into the unique coolness of the starting day.

Chapter 17

The province of Fars and the Qashqai

Mileage Meter: 7,430 to 7,790km (4,616 to 4,840 miles)

(Isfahan-Aspas)

The province of Fars had some beautiful encounters in store for us. We pedaled gaily. After several days of rest, getting back on the road was always a source of satisfaction and tangible joy for me. Everything was in motion again. The mountains followed one another, and so did the desert landscapes. Here and there were irrigated lands that supplied the region and the country with vegetables and fruit. After two days on the road, we arrived in the small town of Abadeh. At the entrance was a long military barracks. I signaled to Leyla to drive straight ahead, as fast as she could and to not look at the barracks. I heard a man calling out to us from his watchtower. I pretended not to hear him and drove straight ahead.

In Abadeh, we had an appointment with Mehdi and his family who welcomed members of the *Warmshowers* community from time-to-time. Mehdi studied sports at university and spoke very hesitant English. So, we used *Google Translate* to communicate, and it worked well. Mehdi introduced us to his family: he lived with his parents and his sister. Bono, his mother, Honi, his sister were the two pillars of the house. Bono was a sports teacher and coached a volleyball team. She was a strong and motherly woman who managed her universe with proficiency. Bono was a great cook and had prepared a succulent *Abgoosht*. It was a tasty mix of chickpeas, tomatoes, potatoes, onions, and sheep that was eaten with Sangak, our favorite bread in Iran! The evening went well with the whole family. Everyone laughed when I said that my name was now Mustafa and that my wife was called Leyla. "No terrorist Mustafa, no terrorist," exclaimed Bono and Honi and everyone laughed again!

The whole family also wanted us to discover their region. The next day we left in two cars to visit what was supposed to be - according to the Iranians- the oldest tree in the world. It was in the neighboring province of Yazd, a gigantic awe-inspiring cypress with 4,500 springs. It was said to have been planted by the prophet of Zoroastrianism, Zarathustra.

Mehdi and his family then led us through a desert, one that you might dream of: its dunes stretched as far as the eye could see and were completely arid. The car skated on the sandy tracks as the sun began its crazy race to sink behind the dunes. I set my eyes on the gas meter, which had long since reached the limit of the red zone. A few minutes later, it finally gave up. We found ourselves in the middle of the desert without petrol. Fortunately, we managed to contact the second car, which came to our rescue. With the help of a hose, we transferred the precious gasoline from one car to the other. With that, we set off again and soon reached a nomadic camp where a huge fire was crackling in the center. Musicians played all around. We listened to them playing for a while. Bono then suggested walking straight among the dunes and stars. They felt so clear and close. Everyone stood at the top of a dune then rolled playfully down. Each descent was accompanied by the cries and laughter of the whole group. It was my turn. I frantically fell into the sand and rolled. I landed at the bottom with a big twirl as pure laughter sounded from Leyla and the whole family up above.

The sky contained so many stars that there scarcely seemed enough room for them. I contemplated them, dreaming, my hand in Leyla's hand. Tomorrow we would be back on the road. The mountains were waiting for us readily!

On the way to Abadeh, Iran

The day before departure, we looked at a map in Mehdi's room. To reach Shiraz, Mehdi advised us to take a secondary road, rather than following the main road. It presented more relief but had the merit of discovering the beautiful landscapes of the province of Fars. It would lead us to the millennium Persepolis before reaching Shiraz. A two to three days wait would be necessary before we could finally see Persepolis.

As usual, we packed up early in the morning so that we could beat the midday sun. We quickly left the main road and its dilapidated trucks to join a quiet road that went up towards the town of Eqlid. A strong gust of wind picked up before the ascent. We had to protect ourselves behind a row of cypress trees to avoid being pushed off our bikes. Trees lined the roads, especially walnut trees, big and proud to grow the walnuts characteristic to Eqlid.

On my GPS, I targeted the Rasool Allah Promenade for our lunch. A famous fountain flowed peacefully there. Iranians liked to have lunch or camp there for the night. Shortly before noon, we crossed the main street when a police car came up to us. There were two policemen inside: the older one in the driver's seat while the younger one was clutched a walkie-talkie. Let's call them Starsky and Hutch. The older one, Starsky, rolled down his window. I smiled at him and unfolded our little introductory paper in Farsi. He asked me where we were going. I told him "Shiraz," our direction for the next few days. He greeted us and then rolled up his window.

We continued to cross the city to reach the Rasool Allah Promenade. There was a small hill to climb to reach the top of its hill. As soon as we reached the top, the same police car appeared again. Starsky and Hutch had obviously followed us. They didn't seem to tolerate our presence in Eqlid for too long. Hutch asked us if we were going to spend the night there. I answered that we might camp. He and Starsky made a face that seemed to say, "Ok but at your own risk". Starsky left us his phone number before leaving. We expected that they would come back to see us again later.

We left *Monster* and *Tank* so we could sit on a bench and enjoy our lunch: leftover Abgoosht of Bono from the day before, *Sangak* bread, tomatoes,

Fars province, Iran

Lost in the middle of the desert, Yazd province, Iran

cucumber, and fresh cheese with nuts. As soon as we settled down, two men came towards us. They were both dressed in blue polo shirts. Both could speak English: they were brothers, and their names were Mahmood and Ali. After a brief introduction from me, they proposed that we join them for lunch with their two parents. The four of them had settled down in the gardens of Rasool Allah Promenade and had seen us passing by on our bikes. I played a bit of *Taarof* with them: they insisted and soon won. We found their parents sitting on a large tablecloth on which rested the same intimate dishes, bread, rice, fruits, and tea. Their father didn't speak English but significantly enhanced the meeting. Whenever he laughed, his gigantic mustache would wave. Their mother, also dressed in blue, was more discreet but she had a gentle, maternal look. We exchanged with them the stories of our past and future journey. I could read in their eyes that they judged the adventure we were on to be impossible to complete. Ali was doing his military service while Mahmood was an electromechanical engineer. I shared the beautiful discoveries we have made in Kashan, Abyaneh, and Isfahan with them. They approved, but for them, the most beautiful city was clearly Shiraz!

It was then time for them to go. Ali asked us if we were planning to sleep there that night. I tried to make him understand that we were going to set up our tent outside. Ali and Mahmood started to laugh:

"Sleep in the tent here? But it will be cold tonight! Come to our place, friends."

"It's really nice of you. But is it safe with the police? They've been following us since noon, and we don't want to cause you any problems."

"No, don't worry. Come on! This is our address. See you later, friends."

The four of them got back into their white Peugeot 405 - a decidedly ubiquitous presence in Iran - and drove away. We rested in the shade. Khanh Nguyen took the opportunity to nap. The goal now was to reach their house without the police spotting us. Sleeping at someone's home as a tourist isn't always tolerated in Iran, and I didn't want us to be a source of problems for our benefactors.

We left the Rasool Allah Promenade. At the entrance of the Promenade, I suddenly recognized familiar faces. Yes! It was Bono and Mehdi. What a happy coincidence! They had come for the afternoon to visit the Promenade and seeing them again was a real moment of joy. We explained that we would spend the night in Eqlid at a family's house, and we thanked them again for having welcomed us in their house in Abadeh. The big and strong Bono smiled at us once again and wished us good luck for the rest of the trip.

Now it was a matter of arriving at Ali and Mahmood's house without being spotted by Starsky and Hutch. Rather than taking the main street, we meandered through the alleys of Eqlid, which added distance to our journey but hid us perfectly from their eyes. A little old lady dressed in black saw us coming into her little street with an aghast look. She certainly wasn't used to people who looked like us! We then took several smaller streets to arrive at a block lined with splendid walnut trees. I called out for Ali, who immediately came out and opened the door. He didn't seem to be worried about the police as we rushed into the courtyard of his house. No one had seen us come in... which assured us of a quiet evening and night, theoretically.

The family had a beautiful home with several fruit and walnut trees. Ali helped us unpack our bags and accompanied us inside. His mother was already busy preparing a meal. His father was happy to host us and kindly waved for us to make ourselves comfortable on the thick carpet in the living room. We were offered tea and cookies. Mahmood asked questions about our relationship:

"How were you able to meet each other? Vietnam and France... it's so far away."

I told our story, realizing through Mahmood's subsequent questioning how much of a curiosity we really were to them. The people we had met were usually living sedentary lifestyles. We were nomads without limits or borders. Globalization had gifted us the opportunity to travel. It had enabled me to live in Vietnam and subsequently meet the woman who would become my wife. I had infinite respect for them, staying almost all their lives in the same place. To begin a family and develop their own community without dreaming of fleeing elsewhere were valid and legitimate goals. However, I don't know if I would be able to do that.

The door of the main room then opened. Two of their cousins came in. They wanted to show us Eqlid! We all got into the Peugeot 405 to discover the peaceful little town. The voices of the muezzins of all the surrounding mosques rose as the sun disappeared deep into the horizon, behind the mountains. Then the two brothers and two cousins led us to a pastry shop on the main street. The main street was synonymous with Starsky and Hutch for us. We got off the 405 like two fugitives and rushed into the pastry shop. "Choose what you want, folks!" There were hundreds of different cakes. Leyla pointed out to some of them at random and I tried to pick some others based on how good they looked. Suddenly we had a big box in our hands, which of course we couldn't pay for, Mahmood and Ali insisted.

Back at their home, we all settled down around the meal. Their mother had spent so much time cooking us the best she could that I did my best to compliment her. I insisted that Mahmood translated all my praises. His mother swept them off with a polite wave of her hand and a delicious smile. The dishes were varied, succulent, and the plate of Eqlid walnuts was first to be devoured. The atmosphere was relaxed between our nomadic couple and that sedentary family. After an hour or two, Leyla started to yawn. It was time to go to bed. Ali insisted that we stay one more day. I declined as politely as I could: we had to reach the great Shiraz on time.

Our nights in Iran were among the best I have spent in my life, especially in the countryside. The air was fresh, silence reigned, and the plush Persian carpets we lay on soothed and resuscitated our aching bodies as we slept. It must also be said that I could sleep even more peacefully thanks to the absolute confidence I had in our great hosts and their divine way of hosting us like royalty.

The next morning, the cool night had slipped away just as we had to leave for Persepolis. Ali, Mahmood, and their parents accompanied us to the iron gate. "Thank you, thank you," Leyla addressed them. We took pictures in front of the gate and the walnut trees, kissed them with our eyes, and spun the pedals of Tank and Monster forward.

The journey resumed. Not a single tree was there to protect us from the sun. The road stretched like a strange silvery cobra, snaking through the sand and the mountains. We were two little parasites pedaling on its back. Not a cloud floated above us. The road should have led us to the small village of Aspas. A long tunnel, very dangerous and polluted according to Ali, was in front of us. In the beginning, we wanted to do it by bike, but a car stopped next to me. The driver made a funny face and seemed to mimic suffocation due to pollution. Dissuaded, I proposed to approach the tunnel and then to hitch-hike. It took us about a minute to find a driver who stopped with his green Zamyad. He threw us in the back among tomatoes and watermelons. The tunnel wasn't that dangerous: it was well lit and not that polluted. I was still happy to do it by car! Once we got out, I hit the driver's rear window, and he stopped dead. We got off with the bikes and took a selfie that he sent to his wife. He wished us good luck and left in his little Zamyad.

There were few cars on this secondary road to Persepolis and even fewer bicycles. I must specify here that we hadn't met any long-distance cyclists like us for almost a month. The locals were even more surprised to see us riding on this small road through the desert. I even saw one man at the steering wheel of his car tap a long index finger on his little head while looking at us as he crossed by us as if to tell us that we were fools. The landscapes became quite sublime. Being the travelers we were, we let ourselves be gradually swept away by the atmosphere and elements.

On our right, I spotted a large flock of sheep accompanied by shepherds moving away towards the mountains. A little further on, there were white cloth tents whose ends float deliciously in the wind. It was the Qashqai! The Qashqai aren't a Nissan car model... but great people who live in Iran. Most of them live in the Fars province of Iran. In previous centuries, they were mainly nomads and had pastoralism as their main resource. They are known and recognized for their high-quality wool and carpets. The Qashqai nomads were a bit like us in regularly changing where they set up their tent to sleep! Many of them had settled down since the 1970s and now lived off the agriculture in small villages.

We arrived a little before lunchtime in the tiny village of Aspas. There was a small store that sold a little bit of everything, including hot coffee. I bought what we needed for that night and the following morning and returned outside where Leyla had waited, sitting on a fragile plastic chair. I handed her a coffee and started blowing on mine when a man greeted us warmly. His name was Reza. I introduced us, and he offered us lunch at his parents' house, just three hundred meters (1,000 feet) away. Reza had a face that I liked, and he told us, "My mother makes the best *Ghormeh Sabzi* in Iran!" That was all it took to convince us... It went against everything our parents taught us since childhood: "Never accept sweets from a stranger at the school exit", "Never accept to follow someone you don't know". Yet I had absolute confidence in Reza and his mother's *Ghormeh Sabzi*. Reza called his parents for permission to invite us and then signaled for us to follow him.

We followed Reza to his home. I was immediately impressed by a splendid pink, red and yellow hedge of flowers that led through to a small courtyard inside. Reza belonged to the Qashqai people: his parents were nomads, but they had settled down a few decades ago. We were moving our bikes forward when suddenly Zahra, Reza's mother, came to the front porch. She was dressed differently from many Iranian women we had met. She wore several items of clothing: a celestial blue dress, covered with a dark grey patterned garment, and finally, a black veil hemmed with golden colors to top it off. Zahra welcomed us with all the customary warmth Iranian people should show in this situation. I tried to keep a good composition despite a morning spent on the road. Zahra seemed especially impressed by Leyla: a woman who traveled by bike and with such Asian features. There was something magnetic between the two of them.

Reza then introduced us to his younger brother, Ali, and his father, Karim. Were you to do a simple *Google image* search and type in "Qashqai man," Karim would have popped up. He had sun-kissed features, dark skin, and an impressive thick mustache. We were to sit in their large living room where the sun's rays pierced through the small spaces between tiles. I told Reza that we would like to leave after lunch, as our journey ahead was still incredibly long. We settled comfortably around a meal prepared by Zahra. It was great! Her fabled *Ghormeh Sabzi* was a fabulous burst of flavors and nuances. The *Ghormeh Sabzi* is a lamb stew with herbs and chickpeas with an ingredient that makes all the difference: pomegranate. I enjoyed it as we discovered more about each other. Reza worked in Isfahan as an electrical engineer. He visited his parents regularly. As we talked, I forgot the fatigue and the hassles of the road. I was just joyful to be there. To feel present. Zahra and Karim forced us to refill our drinks several times. After the meal, we both had food comas.

Reza installed mattresses and pillows for us in a room adjoining the living room. We were out as soon as our heads had hit the pillow. I woke up about thirty minutes later, and everything was numb while Leyla was still sleeping. I didn't see us rushing back to the road that night when we were already so settled. I got up and crept towards Reza with a light in my hand, bouncing a dim glow across the room as I went:

"Reza, do you think we could stay here tonight? The afternoon is already well advanced, and I don't really know where we can sleep on the road..."

"Of course, Mustafa, stay as long as you want. We're really happy and touched that you both want to stay with us."

"Thank you, Reza... Thank you so much..."

I let Princess Leyla wake up by herself. Once her two little eyes were wide open, I told her the good news and observed with satisfaction the calm stretch onto her waking face. Zahra then entered the room: she wanted to share something special with Leyla. Zahra was busy looking for something in a large wardrobe: a Qashqai wedding dress!

She took out a pile of clothes from the cupboard. I got out to give them some privacy, surveying the flowers in the courtyard as I waited. A few minutes later, a real Qashqai princess appeared, my princess. Leyla was splendid in her those traditional clothes: silver, gold, and black weaved and spun in a glorious surge around her body. On her head, Leyla wore a transparent veil on which rested a pink turban, a *Dastmal*. The result was unique. She was so beautiful, so majestic. Comparatively, I was like a poor hobo in my clothes beside her. An Aladdin to that Jasmine. We snapped photo after photo in the courtyard. Then, I photographed Leyla with Zahra, then Reza. The pictures were unique: a Vietnamese woman wearing a Qashqai wedding dress in the province of Fars in Iran. I thanked Zahra for opening the doors to these special moments.

In the afternoon, Reza took us to a neighbor's house with a large garden where Qashqai weddings were regularly organized. It was my turn to wear the traditional outfit of those beautiful nomads: a long garment with golden colors and red tips with some butterfly-shaped patterns. My waist was circled with an amber-red fabric, and I wore funny headgear that could be folded on both sides. I looked a lot worse than Princess Leyla, but I could still be mistaken for a Qashqai. We rejoiced in the beautiful little house of Zahra and Karim.

Dinner was served: a *Kotlet*[1], waiting impatiently for us. We enjoyed these precious and timeless moments together. I thanked Zahra, Karim, Reza, and Ali again. Princess Leyla glided back to her apartments and me, Mustafa the hobo, dutifully followed her.

⁓

The early morning rose and enveloped us with its lively freshness as we prepared Tank and Monster for the day ahead. There were one hundred and twenty kilometers (75 miles) to cover, and we had to leave without delay. Karim had already left the house with his car. I asked Reza to say goodbye to him for us. Then came the time for some difficult farewells with Zahra,

---

[1] Meatballs mixed with potato and onions

Leyla and Mustafa with the Qashqai, Fars, Iran

Reza, and Ali. I thanked them for their graces. For having welcomed us as the friends that we eventually became by force of circumstance. We would stay connected; it was mandatory.

The road resumed among the Qashqai Mountains. About thirty minutes after leaving Aspas, a car passed by us: it was Karim! He stopped his engine and came to wish us good luck.

After only five kilometers (3 miles), we passed by a small school. A small group of children saw us coming from afar and waved to tell us to come closer. There was still another hundred kilometers (62 miles) to go for today, but I made the decision, quite irrationally, to visit them. The schoolchildren, ranging in age from five to fourteen, seemed to have never felt such excitement. They were shouting, running around us so much we felt dizzy. Their teacher, who wore a very dense black beard, alerted by the din, came to meet us and invited us to have tea inside. There were at least two hundred kids in the courtyard: the little girls wore a veil and a pink or black uniform, but the little boys didn't seem to have a particular dress code. The crowd of small individuals formed a circle all around us. They wanted to touch everything: the bikes, the Non-La hats, the saddlebags, our faces. I took the opportunity to get off Tank and took pictures of this joyful and dense little crowd clustered around Leyla.

Soon I remembered that we still had a hundred kilometers (62 miles) to go. We quickly drank the tea offered by the teacher while the schoolchildren inspected Tank and Monster from every angle. I explained to the teacher that we, unfortunately, had to go to Persepolis and got up to go, but the students followed us, begging us to sign an autograph! Others demanded we visit them at their home, pulling our hands. Two little girls even started arguing about who would be the family that would welcome us and one of them even started crying. I stopped the argument by explaining to them that we had to go on and that visiting them was completely impossible. Their teacher shook his head, laughing behind them, his hands on his face. All the students started shouting "Khodâfez , Khodâfez!" waving at us while we were still in their field of vision until we disappeared into the distance.

The road became more difficult as a small pass appeared in front of us: the asphalt rose steeply with some incline gradients around twenty percent. No shade could support us. We sweated a lot, even catching up with a big truck that was similarly struggling to cross the pass. At the top of the pass, a car handed us drinks and cookies; inside was the teacher we'd met at the school! Taking the refreshments, I exclaimed, "Thank you, thank you! Khodâfez! "After the pass, we took advantage of a road that wound its way down among the rock carved by eons gone by. A village appeared in the distance, at the very bottom. I suggested to Leyla that we should stop at the *Emamzadeh Esmaieel*, a place of worship, for lunch. I also wanted to spend the night there, if possible. Between this village and Persepolis, there wasn't really a place where we could stop otherwise.

The village seemed to be under construction, and the main street was smashed up. I entered the *Emamzadeh*: no one was there apart from an old woman resting in a corner and two or three lost children hanging around. The atmosphere was weird. We decided to rest for a few moments in the shade and have lunch. It was already two o'clock, and we still had sixty-six kilometers (40 miles) to go before Persepolis. We had to get back on the road and quickly. " Do not ride at night" was an important rule for our safety that we had told ourselves. Fatigue set in as the kilometers (miles) went by. Suddenly a guy came into our field of vision on a motorcycle without a helmet and started to follow us for several kilometers (miles).

There was absolutely nobody in the valley, just him and the two of us. For me, he didn't seem to be particularly threatening. Perhaps he had been bored to death and then tried to distract himself by tailing us. Leyla, on the other hand, felt uneasy: "He's waiting for the right moment to attack us or rob us. I don't feel good about that guy at all." The guy then passed in front of us, and I took the opportunity to stop. Leyla did the same, grabbing her pepper spray and putting our little kitchen knife in her pocket. The guy had gone far ahead but then stopped too. He seemed to be waiting for us. I was starting to get a little scared too. The guy then restarted his motorcycle and disappeared.

Leyla and the schoolgirls, Fars, Iran

The following kilometers (miles) were subsequently cycled in fear of an imminent attack. We were as attentive as possible to every detail, to every shape that might emerge from the stunted and dry bushes along the road. But nothing, absolutely nothing. Fatigue started to play its own score, elevating a fear that we had let play complacently. We would never see that strange guy on his motorcycle again, however. We had forty kilometers (25 miles) to ride, and it would be dark within two hours.

The landscapes didn't disappoint us. The ridges of the mountains looked like a stretched-out dinosaur spine. I admired them, but knowing that the clock was ticking against us, it was difficult to enjoy them fully. Muscular fatigue had slowed us down, and each little hill was a cause of suffering enhanced by the stress of the danger brought by night. I tried to find a place where we could camp, but no opportunity presented itself. I also remembered that we had forbidden ourselves to camp before Shiraz to limit the risks of being stopped by some overzealous Revolutionary Guards.

The night gradually fell on us. Leyla was on the verge of breaking. I tried to negate that by using words of encouragement as we cycled. We put on our reflective jackets and turned on our front and backlights. There were no streetlights. We were two little cyclists in the dark of the night. On the map, I spotted a small hotel seventeen kilometers (11 miles) away; so, we had a good hour left to pedal in the dark. We pedaled with a little trepidation without knowing what was going to fall on us or when the headlights of a car would flood us with their blinding light. Then out of nowhere came an angel, our knight in shining armor. A man waved to us from his grey Peugeot 405. He showed me a business card that happened to be the small hotel where we wanted to spend the night! He lived next to that hotel. He called the manager who told us that there was a room waiting for us! We were saved! Our benefactor then proceeded to escort us for fifteen kilometers (9 miles)! He made sure to drive behind us to give us sufficient light to see and oblige the cars that passed by us to have enough space between them and us. We immediately pedaled more serenely in the dark of the night. The grey Peugeot 405 protected us, sheltering us from danger

Last kilometers before Persepolis, Iran

until we arrived at the hotel.

By that time, I had no more energy left. I thanked our angel of the day: Hassan and his grey Peugeot 405. Without him, I really didn't know what would have happened to us. The hotel manager led us to our room. It would be twenty US dollars for that night. I accepted his price, which seemed reasonable enough to me. After a short dinner and a shower, we collapsed onto the bed.

We had experienced all our emotions through all those landscapes. Time had dilated so much that I had the feeling that morning had been a week ago: Karim, the schoolchildren, the pass, the *Emamzadeh*, the weird guy on his motorcycle, the dinosaurs, Hassan. The following day, Persepolis was waiting for us.

Chapter 18

Persepolis and Shiraz: finishing Iran in style

Mileage Meter: 7,790 to 8,012km (4,840 to 4,978 miles)

(Persepolis – Shiraz)

In *In Search of Lost Time*, Proust described the narrator's experience who idealizes the church of Balbec. Swann gives him the most beautiful description of it, even describing it as: "almost Persian". From then on, the narrator idealizes the church of Balbec as one of the most beautiful buildings in the world. When he discovers it, the narrator is completely disappointed by the church and its surroundings: the reality doesn't correspond to his expectations, doesn't match his desires, and the grandiose image he had of it.

As not to spoil the surprise like the narrator of Proust's *In Search of Lost Time* with the church in Balbec, I didn't inquire about Persepolis before setting foot there. All I knew is that the place was over 2,500 years old. That was all I knew. If you want to know too much, if you want to learn about everything, if you want to optimize your trip at all costs by seeing what is most beautiful, if you want to avoid being disappointed, you are inevitably disappointed. Our adventure taught me that the most beautiful things are received by accident, by chance, at the bend of a path or an alley. A bit like the truth, the more we want to find it, to define it, to fix it, the more it escapes us, and the more elusive it is. Knowing how to enjoy beautiful things at their true value is more a disposition than an exact science. One must love to get lost in unknown places, to sometimes have the delicious impression of being in the right place at the right time.

Before arriving at Persepolis, we drove past the impressive Naqsh-e Rostam: it is a necropolis whose first vestiges date back more than three thousand years ago and where the Achaemenid kings Darius and Xerxes rest. We dared not leave Tank and Monster all harnessed on the parking lot as we visited. So, we just took pictures from far away. We also took a quick photo to celebrate the eight thousand kilometers (almost 5,000 miles) traveled. It meant that we were already halfway through the journey!

There was a long straight line that led to Persepolis for several kilometers (miles). The road was lined on both sides with endless rows of trees and wide-open spaces for tourist buses. The large spaces were completely empty: not a single bus. We deposited our bikes in a small hotel where we would spend the night; also empty. It must be said that the geopolitical tensions between Iran, the United States, and Saudi Arabia must have stopped a lot of tourists from coming. After having left our saddlebags and Tank and Monster in our room, we advanced towards the eternal city of Persepolis.

Our ticket came to just 2 US dollars. We discovered the ancient capital of the Achaemenid kingdom by ourselves. It was an astonishing superposition of styles and techniques patiently applied for centuries until Alexander the Great sacked and burned it to the ground in 331 BC. It was a wonder for me to see its bas-reliefs so well preserved, which brought before our eyes all the diversity of the peoples of the Achaemenid kingdom. The site was monumental in its size. It was elevated and overlooked the surrounding area. With Leyla, we enjoyed traveling among the ruins of Persepolis, getting lost through the millennia. We had left my small village in the Vendée, now here largely by the strength of our calves. It made me dizzy to consider it. As the hours passed, we gradually climbed up a hill to the point that overlooked the city below. We then had an ideal point of view to enjoy a slow and unforgettable sunset over the ruins. I was sitting next to Leyla, hugging her. We were both quiet observers of that still and silent spectacle.

8,000 kilometers (5,000 miles)... halfway there, Persepolis, Iran

The road that led us to Shiraz the next day wasn't the most pleasant. It was very busy with, you guessed it, Peugeot 405s and Zamyads. But unfortunately, it was the only route. We passed, once again, by a military barracks.

A soldier called us from his tower. I ignored him. He shouted louder and louder until I finally gave in and threw him a "hello" with a wave of my right hand without even looking his way. After a final climb came our reward: the long descent to Shiraz and Fatima's house. Fatima was Maha's girlfriend who welcomed us in Isfahan, if you remember. She was waiting for us impatiently at her house. We would stay together for one joyful week before our flight to Delhi in India.

Fatima opened the gate that opened onto a wide courtyard where we would let Monster and Tank rest. I was so happy to find a familiar face! But Fatima and Leyla were like two reunited sisters. Fatima lived in an apartment with her mother and brother, who worked for the Iranian army. She settled us in a room before suggesting that we find Maha who had come to visit her from Isfahan and who was leaving in a few hours.

After a few subway stops, we found our good old friend Maha, sitting benignly in the corner of a small coffee shop! Seeing Maha again was like finding an old brother, an old friend. With Leyla, we told him about all our adventures from Isfahan to Shiraz. Maha gave us some news about him and his family. The minutes passed quickly before Maha had to catch his bus back to Isfahan. I took him in my arms one last time, Leyla too. 'Goodbye Maha, we will see each other one day, old brother!'

The week in Shiraz was a mix of meals with Fatima and her family, naps, wandering around Shiraz, small restaurants, naps, and yet more naps. Shiraz was known throughout Iran for its slow pace of life and the laziness of its inhabitants. We got caught up with delight in its cottony torpor and caught up on years of missed sleep in just a few days.

We also had to find boxes to carry Tank and Monster in the luggage bay of the plane. Fatima helped us by calling several stores. One of them offered us two boxes: perfect! We would get them in the morning, as well as enough bubble wrap and tape. It was necessary to methodically disassemble Tank and Monster in order to make them fit in their cardboard box. It was also necessary to take care to wrap them well with bubble wrap to avoid any breakage during transport. It took hours and hours. Fatima assisted us both with Tank and Monster. It looked like playing the video game Tetris: we had to make the wheels fit in the box without damaging the derailleur or the bike's chain. It was endless. After a long battle, everything finally fit. We then had the challenge of protecting the cardboard boxes by multiplying layers of tape on the edges and ends to deal with. But soon enough, Monster and Tank were mummified and packed: ready to travel!

From Shiraz, I remember the pink mosque the most. You had to go there early in the morning before the crowds to see the rays of the eastern sun passing through its stained-glass windows. The vivid blue, red, green, and yellow colors then spread throughout the room in a prodigious infinity of combinations and shades. I watched Leyla cross the rays, scattering the light. We posed here and there. It was so unique. Unfortunately, visitors quickly accumulated, and it became impossible to enjoy the place in peace. The pink mosque was suddenly black with the clothes of the new arrivals. It was time for us to leave.

The days came and went with Fatima and her family. Time slipped away by. Then it was time to pack our bags. Our plane was at four in the morning. The blare of our alarm clock rudely woke us. Our two cabs were already waiting for us downstairs. We hugged Fatima, thanked all the Persian gods for sending her our way. Would we see each other again? Only they knew. We hoped Fatima and Maha would come and visit us in Vietnam one day so we could return their kindness and hospitality. We loaded the big boxes containing Tank and Monster onto the roof of the cab. Once the engine started, we were propelled over the deserted roads of Shiraz. Shiraz airport represented a final test before leaving Iran. Every employee was trying to make money off our backs: the luggage carriers, those in charge of wrapping the luggage, everyone! We had to refuse several times, struggle, or negotiate. Leyla even got her little pepper spray confiscated during the luggage check. We should have put it in the luggage bay, but we forgot. A little knot formed in my belly: what if the immigration officers refused to let us go? What if the local police were looking for us because we had camped near a military

The famous Pink Mosque, Shiraz, Iran

base? Paranoia set in for me. I switched to the men's side: thankfully, the immigration officer stamped my visa without batting an eye. I waited for Leyla on a bench. Five minutes went by. She still wasn't there. What if the officer had refused to let her go? The wait was interminable, but Leyla finally appeared at the end of the terminal with nothing to report. The steward called for the passengers to board the plane. We sat down, side by side. As long as the plane was on the ground, I couldn't relax. I felt like I was in a bad version of Ben Affleck's film Argo, where the hero of the film tried to escape six members of the American administration trapped in Tehran during the hostage crisis in 1979. All the passengers were on board, waiting for the plane to take off. Emotions mingled, crossed, and crossed again. I kissed Khanh Nguyen, who could finally take off her hijab. As we took off: Leyla became Khanh Nguyen once more, and I said goodbye to my alter ego too. Euphoria consumed us both as we acknowledged each other again.

If you're waiting for our mid-journey summary at this point, we had now covered 8,000 kilometers (5,000 miles) and collected $8,585 for *Poussières de Vie* and for all the children, the association helps. We were halfway. Psychologically, it was important for us. It meant that each additional pedal stroke brought us closer to Vietnam and that the second half of the journey would decrease as we went forward, that we were closer to the finish than to the start.

Iran had marked us for life, to our bones. We'd had our fair share of dangers, fears, and anxieties. But it was nothing, absolutely nothing, compared to the good encounters we'd had, to the landscapes we crossed. We had gone beyond our fears, beyond ourselves, to have the opportunity to meet the greatest humanity had to offer. People who welcome without reserve, people who don't calculate, people who trust, who love. To our dearest Iranian friends, if you are reading this, you made us better. You push us every day to become even better. Thank you for that gift.

India was waiting for us and a very special guest would be joining us in those coming weeks...

Chapter 19

Northern India: teleportation to a new civilization

Mileage Meter: 8,012 to 8,354km (4,978 to 5,190 miles)

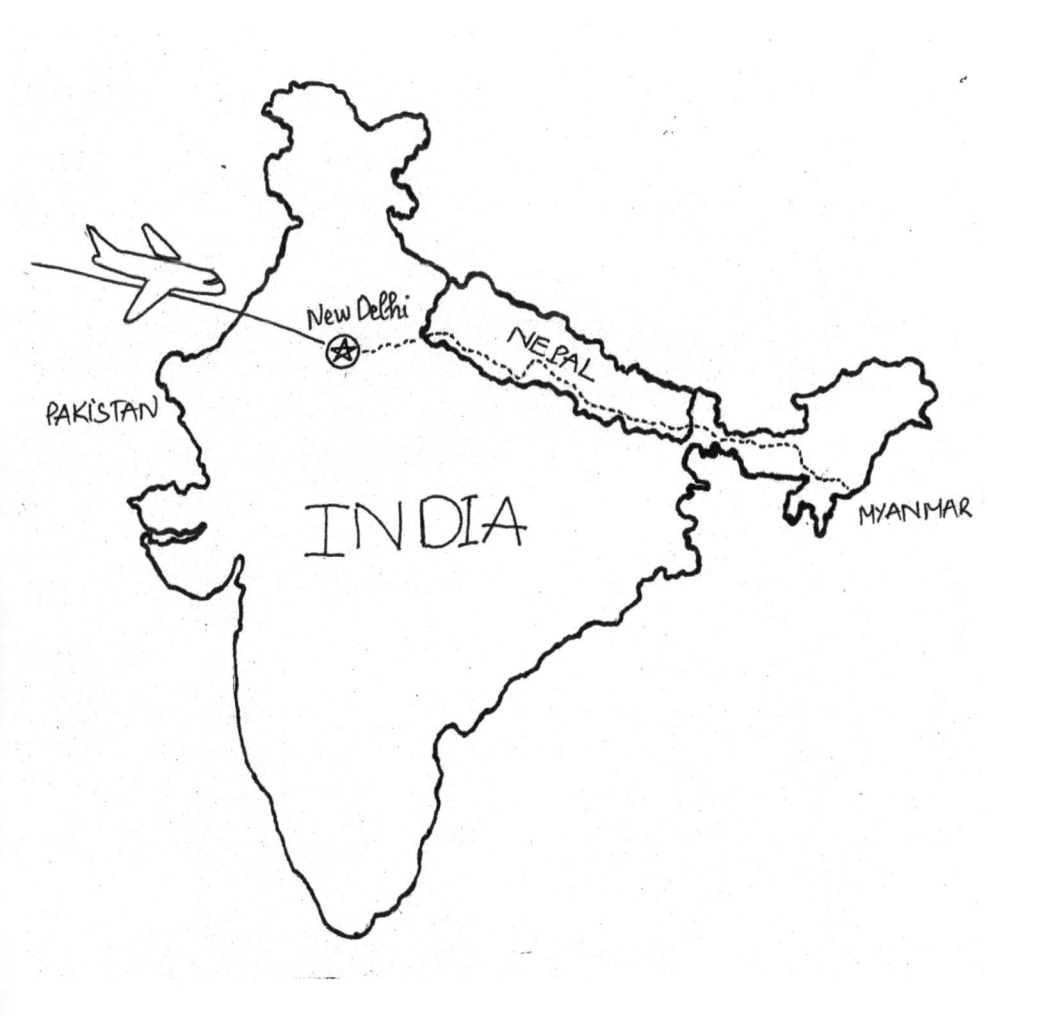

Before I flew to India, I thought that teleportation was a reality only science fiction could produce, but I was soon proved wrong.

In less than twenty-four hours, we were thrown from one civilization into another: from Iran to India. In between Pakistan, which we had decided to avoid for practical and security reasons. We, who were used to moving slowly from one country to another were suddenly thrown into a gigantic country in which we had to relearn everything. It was brutal.

Honestly, we had considered completely avoiding India. It was a country that to cross by bike seemed insurmountable. Especially in densely populated regions. We had also heard many stories from travelers: scams, robberies, violence, and rapes. However, the fact that we were avoiding China for visa reasons made India inevitable for us. It would have undermined the Non-La project to take a plane even further east to Myanmar or Thailand instead. Fortunately, we had a decompression chamber. One of my old friends from business school, Paul-Arnaud, had arrived a few weeks before in Delhi for work. He had contacted me while we were in Iran, offering us a place to stay in his apartment in Delhi.

There was also the prospect of my younger brother, Amaury, who would join us for a few days in Delhi! I'd made my first big bicycle trip in Europe six years ago with Amaury from Vendée to Slovenia and then Italy. He would cycle with us for six weeks to Nepal. The previous journey I'd made with him was something that had given me the confidence to embark on this even greater adventure. It was a weight off my mind to have him with us to cross India. With just Khanh Nguyen and I, it would be harder to stop anyone who meant to cause us harm. Amaury would arrive in two days.

The arrival at Delhi airport went without a hitch. We picked up Tank and Monster, which seemed to be still in one piece. Their boxes, in any case, didn't have any tears or holes, which was a good sign. We then found a cab that could take us to Paul-Arnaud's house – I will call him "PA" to simplify! We were quite amazed by the dense and chaotic traffic. Passers-by looked miserable battling through a thick cloud of pollution, which permeated everything and made things look dull. "We are going to have to pedal through this?" exclaimed Khanh Nguyen.

PA was on a mission in Kolkata and would be back in three days. His apartment was in a beautiful residential area of New Delhi, and we rested there for a while. We left the apartment to do some shopping, get a sim card, and get our vaccinations. On the menu: Hepatitis A, B and Japanese Encephalitis for Khanh Nguyen; Typhoid and Japanese Encephalitis for me. For dessert: enough anti-malaria pills for almost two months. The vaccines tired us a little more and prolonged our lethargic state between waking and sleeping. I also took this opportunity to fix up Tank and Monster. It took me several hours to reassemble, clean, polish, and lubricate them while fighting against the humidity and mosquitoes. They hadn't suffered any mechanical breakdowns during their transport in the bay or their transfer to Doha airport. We had been lucky.

A new sun rose behind the thick polluted clouds of Delhi. Amaury would land in a few hours; PA that afternoon. I went to pick up Amaury at Delhi airport and let Khanh Nguyen rest again in the apartment. Once at Indira-Gandhi airport, I waited patiently in front of the exit doors. Around me was India in all its glorious diversity: faces, outfits, and attitudes so varied between individuals. There were also many Sikhs on my right who were wearing their famous turban: the *Dastar*. They came in all colors: red, mauve, green, and yellow. I finally saw Amaury and his Greek shepherd's beard appearing! It was quite unreal to find him a world away there in Delhi after so many months on the world's roads. He looked good! I shared some anecdotes and highlights of the last few months with him in the cab: Iran, Georgia, the Hungarian mosquitoes. We were back at the apartment. Khanh Nguyen opened the door and shouted, "Amaury! Welcome to India. It is so great that you can do part of the trip with us".

We needed to find a bike for Amaury quickly. Delhi has no shortage of bike stores. We spotted one on Google Maps that seemed to be suitable. The store had a lot of small warehouses all over the street and offered several second-hand bikes. One of them seemed to please Amaury: it was a Giant, still in good condition and with a good enough casket. All it needed was a change of tires and a stronger rack installed. After a short negotiation, the store offered us the bike for US$ 300. For six weeks on the road, it was a reasonable price. Besides, we knew that it would be possible to resell it once we were in Pokhara or Kathmandu in Nepal.

It was then the turn of PA to arrive in Delhi. Our reunion after several years was all the stronger in ways we hadn't even expected. For those few days, we traversed Delhi with PA as our guide. Diwali was soon celebrated, and Delhi was full of all kinds of purchases: food, spices, clothing, jewelry, and decorations. Diwali represented one of the most important festivals for Hindus: it was the victory of light over darkness. The old market was saturated with people, carriers, smells, and sweat. There wasn't a single square centimeter available around us. What impressed me was the calm and respect with which people passed each other and snuck among the crowd despite the heat and the thousands of souls that formed an artist's palette worth of colors.

"Let's go to the spice market!" proposed PA. The old market of Delhi housed a whole block of buildings entirely dedicated to spices for their trade. As soon as we approached the main entrance, our nostrils itched. An explosive cocktail of pepper, turmeric, cinnamon, cumin, cardamom, saffron, and mustard. I snuck among the shirtless carriers with their big bags on their shoulders. The air became completely unbreathable. Our whole group started to cough and splutter without interruption. My eyes stung. My throat itched. We had to get out of there! A small staircase on the left allowed us to escape to the roof of a nearby building. There, the air was breathable once again, and the view of a waltz of spices, men, and sacred cows was breathtaking. As I contemplated that curious spectacle, I wondered how we would be able to pedal through Uttar Pradesh and its millions and millions of beating hearts.

Delhi and its millions of souls, India

Among those millions of beating hearts, I saw men and women completely emaciated. Their clothes were in tatters. They wandered along the gutters without purpose, without life. If they had died, no one would lift a finger to help. They were the "untouchables". Under Ancient Rome, there had been their equivalent: the *Homo Sacer*. They were people who were excluded from the rest of society. They could be killed with impunity by anyone. I understood with horror what the *Homo Sacer* still breathed in modern Delhi. The idea of people being beyond assistance as a human being was impossible for me to comprehend. As a result, I found it hard to feel fully emotionally invested in India, despite the fascinating aspects of its incredible civilization. .

After a long week of resting and preparing in Delhi at our dear PA's, it was time for us to start our next 8,000 kilometers (5,000 miles). Having made that great leap from Iran to India had given us the impression that we were getting closer to Vietnam. But that wasn't really the case.

Our immediate goal was to reach Nepal in three or four days from Delhi or travel 350km (217 miles) heading East. We chose to play the "security and lung protection" card rather than cross all of Delhi by bike, undergoing its thick cloud of pollution in the process. We decided to rent the services of a van that would transport us over twenty-five kilometers (16 miles) to reach the outskirts of sprawling Delhi. The van would pick us up at five in the morning. Of the three of us, I woke up first. In the silence of those early hours, I woke up Khanh Nguyen, then went to the next room to wake up Amaury. We let PA swim in his dreams as we set our hands on all our adventurous equipment. Not a sound stirred, except for the occasional dog bark.

A van's headlights flooded the alley in a brilliant white. The driver helped us with the saddlebags and the bikes. I sat at his side at the front. I wanted to make sure he brought us where we needed to go. Amaury and Khanh Nguyen sat in the back with the bikes in the open air. The driver turned the ignition on, the van jerkily started, and we set off. We experienced a deserted Dehli. Kilometers (miles) passed quickly. For the first time on the trip, the traffic was on the left side of the road. It would be necessary to get used to that. At the slightest irregularity in the road, Khanh Nguyen and Amaury had to endure shocks and vibrations due to the meager suspension in the back. Cars and trucks started to pile up around us as the night's darkness ended. Watching chaos forming through the window, I was relieved that I didn't have to pedal through it; we were riding on gigantic multi-lane roads and endless ramped highways!

Arriving in the city of Ghaziabad, the driver parked on the left and signaled that we had arrived. I rushed to the back to see the state of my troops: Khanh Nguyen and Amaury were still in one piece. We took the opportunity to take everything down and get on our bikes. The pollution scratched my lungs after just a few first pedal strokes. The clouds that enveloped us made everything around us milky, dull, and inconsistent. The few Indians who paid attention to us were relatively surprised to see three travelers leaving Delhi by bike in those conditions.

After only twenty minutes, my front tire punctured for the first time. We had to find a place a little bit away while I inspected it, gradually removing a small metal spike, then installing a new inner tube. Within five minutes, we were back on the road. I pedaled for the next three hundred meters (1,000 feet) with difficulty. My front tire was still weakening. It deflated again. Our start in India was proving far from ideal. We tried to find the cause of those two punctures. We found nothing, even while passing our fingers all over the strip of the tire. Maybe the spare tube had already been punctured? I installed a new one, and the three of us set off again.

I pedaled, trying to make up for lost time, before groaning as my front tire deflated yet again! We were cursed! Khanh Nguyen became impatient with our flagrant lack of efficiency and offered to inspect the tire by herself. Within thirty seconds, she had put her finger on a tiny piece of metal that poked out of the inside of the tire. Our thick male fingers had been unable to find it. That piece of metal came from the very structure of my tire, which had weakened over time. I grabbed my pliers and gently pulled it out. Now we were on our last tube, and we couldn't afford to lose it. Once the tire was installed, I got back on Tank. A minute passed, then two, without incident, and I was finally able to sigh with relief.

The road out of Delhi wasn't very interesting but had the merit of having a large shoulder that isolated us from the traffic. A motorcyclist without a helmet sidled near, observing us without crossing our gaze, before riding right next to us and asking us in English with a strong Indian accent:

"Where are you from? Where are you going? What's your name?"

We answered, and he asked one final question:

" Can we take a selfie together?"

Looking at each other we all stopped. We took dozens of photos with him, and he left, phone in hand, already sharing them on social media. The first few times it happened with people it was an endearing game. But after ten, twenty, or even thirty times in a single day, it started to drive me mad! Even when I turned them down, they insisted. By the end of that day, I was doing everything I could to avoid them. At the insistence of one man, I got aggressive and said that we had to move forward. We had already lost far too much time that today.

At least in the state of Uttar Pradesh, we didn't have time to get bored! There was always something going on by the side of the road. From a bridge, I could see a wedding taking place a little further down. It was a Sikh wedding. The groom proudly rode a beautiful horse. He was surrounded by an imposing orchestra, which was playing as loudly as they could to drown out the traffic. The colors of that great procession impressed me with their variety and vivacity. The men wore their *Dastar*, the women their traditional dress. We saw the procession moving away from the main road and towards a small path curling into the countryside. With them gone, we were left curious about what the countryside had to offer us!

As soon as the opportunity arose, we left the main road to take a small

Amaury, our new team member, just outside Delhi, India

Sikh women returning from the fields, Uttar Pradesh, India

country road. What immediately stood out was the great diversity from one village to the next. We passed a Hindu village, then a Muslim village, before passing through a Christian village complete with a church before we ended up in a village where Sikhism dominated. The Sikhs impressed us with their imposing beards and turbans. We even posed with two elderly Sikhs with white beards resting in the shade on their motorcycles. We met a whole group of women who wore an imposing bag on the top of their heads.

The small path that we took soon turned into another, which led us through some rice fields and a tiny wooden bridge crossing a small river. Amaury was in charge of helping Khanh Nguyen cross while I took a picture of the scene. A little further ahead, two men were watching us. Once we had crossed, one came towards us:

"Hello! Why are you passing by here? You are the first foreigners I've seen crossing this bridge! Come and have tea and cookies at my home!"

He was a Sikh called James. He didn't sport a turban but he did have a mustache. He had the belly of a man who had eaten and drank more than he should have but didn't regret his greed. We followed him until we reached his home. A man with a large white turban was sitting, preoccupied with drinking his cup of tea with milk. He was James' father. He was resting in the shade under a huge tree and invited us to sit with him. They were all speaking a high level of English, and it was a real pleasure not to have the language barrier we'd had sometimes in Iran or Azerbaijan. We could talk together about various subjects and could more easily understand each other. James's mother brought us a small tray with coffees, milk, and a lot of cookies. The break was welcome. I took the time to tell our story and asked some questions to better understand the Sikhs and their culture.

James' father explained that Sikhism was a relatively recent religion. Less than five hundred years old. Everything had started with its founder, Guru Nanak. Through his education and experience, he had taught a new religion that had a single god. Unlike the prevailing polytheistic religion of the country, Hinduism, with its thousands of gods, Sikhism was monotheistic. Guru Nanak had particularly deplored the caste system in India: religion should be a force to bring people together, not separate

Happy to return to the rice fields, Uttar Pradesh, India

Tea with milk with James and his family, Uttar Pradesh, India

and divide them into classes. Sikhs could also marry, in theory, whoever they chose. James smiled when his father mentioned this possibility. I also smiled, exchanging a knowing glance with Khanh Nguyen, and finished my cup of tea.

We quickly understood that Sikhism, with its monotheism and egalitarianism, was often not received well by some Hindus. James's father complained about the policies of Narendra Modi, the Indian Prime Minister. His head and ribbon waved more and more violently as his voice rose. Narendra Modi had recently implemented pro-Hindu guidelines that were directed against the Muslim community in particular. National unity in India was fragile, and any imbalance rightly worried James and his family. I savored those moments when, through the voice of those who embody the effects of religion or policy, I'd appreciate them for the first time.

I swallowed one last cookie before letting James and his family know that we had to continue our journey. The three of us thanked them and exchanged *Instagram* accounts. James thanked and praised his god for allowing our paths to cross.

We took to the road again in the direction of Nepal. It was about noon, and the sun was beating with all its strength. Shortly after leaving James' house, we crossed a small village. There was a gathering of some kind in front of a building where a large white and purple tent stood. "Is it a wedding, you think?" said Amaury. A man in the crowd came and grabbed my arm, wanting us to go inside. We hadn't had lunch yet, so we decided to give it a try! We left our three bicycles between the motorbikes of the guests along a wall. It was not a wedding, but a party, organized by the newly elected mayor. Lunch was offered to all passers-by: rice, beef, eggs, fish, and chapatis. You should have seen all the guests' completely astonished look when they saw two French men and a Vietnamese woman arrive on the scene! Some of them urged us to serve ourselves and sit down. A small but dense circle of people gathered around us. All eyes were on us. The newly elected mayor arrived with a beautiful white shirt and a big smile. I hastened to stand up, congratulating him and thanking him for welcoming us. Khanh Nguyen and Amaury joined us to take part in an official photo.

With a full belly, we had to leave again to pedal the remaining one hundred and twenty more kilometers (75 miles). A large group composed mainly of children eagerly accompanied us from the tent to our bikes. Some of them started to run beside us as we went, then pensively came to a stop as they realized that we weren't going to slow down. We gave them one last wave before disappearing among the rice fields.

Kilometers (miles) passed by on a set of completely flat roads. After inevitably taking a good ten selfies insistently requested by several bikers without helmets, we had to find a place to spend the night. On *Google Maps*, I spotted a school for Christian children: I proposed to our group that we ask to spend the night there. We had nothing to lose, and I saw that Khanh Nguyen was getting tired. Thirty minutes passed, and we arrived in front of the school gate. A man who was busy watering the plants turned and saw us. With a smile, he came to welcome us. He was also the school janitor. I asked to see the Father in charge of the school: he let me go in. The janitor showed me a small house surrounded by an elegant little garden with a beautiful lawn adorned with flowers.

I knocked on the door which a man opened: it was Father Andrew, the school principal. I introduced our party to him in English with a lively voice and asked him if we could spend the night there. His answer was an immediate yes! I hastened to announce the good news to Khanh Nguyen and Amaury. Rather than sleeping outside in the tent, Father Andrew proposed to provide us with a room in his own house! He also invited us to shower and announced that dinner that night would be served at seven o'clock after mass. What an incredible welcome! The three of us couldn't believe it, and we couldn't contain the smiles that spread over our faces full of dust and sweat.

Other fathers arrived, including Father Peter. He was short, with only a few white hairs left on his balding head. He wore small glasses with round lenses. He also spoke English, which made discussions livelier. Their school had several thousand students, all in uniform. The next morning several fathers were traveling to Kolkata by train for a large gathering. Father Peter blessed the Lord for our good fortune.

We settled down in our small room for the evening and then enjoyed a good shower which consisted of a large bucket of cold water. I felt as if I had been regenerated: the cold water relieved me of all the dust, all the aches and pains, sweat, and fatigue that had accumulated that day. I put on my pants and shirt to be more presentable for mass. Father Andrew and Father Peter were both wearing their beautiful white *Alb* and were heading to a small room where the faithful were waiting. Amaury and Khanh Nguyen were also ready, and we entered the room with great circumstance. The evening worshippers looked at us with wide eyes: they hadn't expected us at all! We settled down discreetly at the back of the room. The small procession began. I looked with complicity at Amaury, and we both held ourselves back from laughing. A young woman read passages from the Bible with an English accent that was impossible for us to understand. A few songs here and there were interspersed between the readings. Some parents disciplined their children when they got too distracted. Father Andrew finally called the faithful to come and eat the body of Christ in the form of a wafer.

Once the short mass was over, our meal was served. We settled down with all the fathers around a round table in the middle of which the dishes could be rotated. For that evening, it was fish and vegetable curry with chapatis and rice. Father Peter asked us about the continuation of our journey and fussed when I told him that we were going to cross Nepal:

"It goes high up there! Nepal is only mountains. I don't know how you do it..."

"We are starting to have good legs, *Father* Peter! Don't worry too much about us."

"God bless you, my children."

After dinner, we apologized to the fathers and asked their permission to go to bed. The day, once again, had been endless, and the three of us could barely keep our eyes open.

The night wasn't going to be restful. Mosquitoes were very present, and we didn't have a mosquito net. Our only weapon of defense: a huge iron fan that blew stronger than a wind announcing a storm. At least the mosquitoes wouldn't dare come near! I put on my sweater and socks and snuggled against Khanh Nguyen under the comforter.

The next morning, the result was irrevocable: a sore throat for Amaury and I. Khanh Nguyen had survived without too much damage. Most of the fathers had gone before dawn. Only Father Peter was left, who had breakfast with us: chapatis, masala sauce, and tea with milk. The four of us enjoyed that final meal. The good Father Peter promised to pray for us and our safety throughout the adventure. In return, I asked God to bless him and protect his entire community.

***

The road through Uttar Pradesh resumed. The kilometers (miles) went by along with their daily selfies. We also found ourselves in gigantic traffic jams, where it sometimes took us more than an hour to escape. That was the case in the city of Moradabad. It was impossible for us to make our way among the tuk-tuks, sacred cows, motorcycles, and all the children returning from school. Nothing moved. I took the opportunity to take pictures; Amaury to talk with a local Muslim. There was always a kind of euphoria in belonging to that joyful mess. Thanks to our bikes, we finally managed to escape and cross the bridge over the Ramganga River. From the top of the bridge, hundreds of buffaloes immersed themselves in the river water, some rolling in the mud. It was a delight to see.

What else can I say about those four days from Delhi to Nepal, except that I was pleasantly surprised that most of the Indians we met had a lot of respect for us. After having scoured the blogs before arriving in India, I had expected daily harassment and having to keep a watchful eye on Khanh Nguyen, but I was proved wrong. Uttar Pradesh, on the other hand, with its population density, its noise, its pollution, its constant demands, depleted all our energy, and we had to draw on our reserves. It was impossible on the road to have a minute to ourselves. Trucks and cars honked their horns, reminding everyone of their presence as they crept through traffic at a snail's pace. In the evening, my eardrums beat with the echoes of the noise they'd taken that day. The small hotels that we found for the night became our refuge. We didn't leave them except to buy what would be our dinner.

After more than three days on the road and more than 350 kilometers (217 miles), we were finally at the border to Nepal, our thirteenth country! We would come back into North-East India, as far as we'd planned, before entering our fourteenth, Myanmar.

Chapter 20

Nepal: between the Himalayas, the tigers and Buddha

Mileage Meter: 8,354 to 9,594 km (5,190 to 5,961 miles)

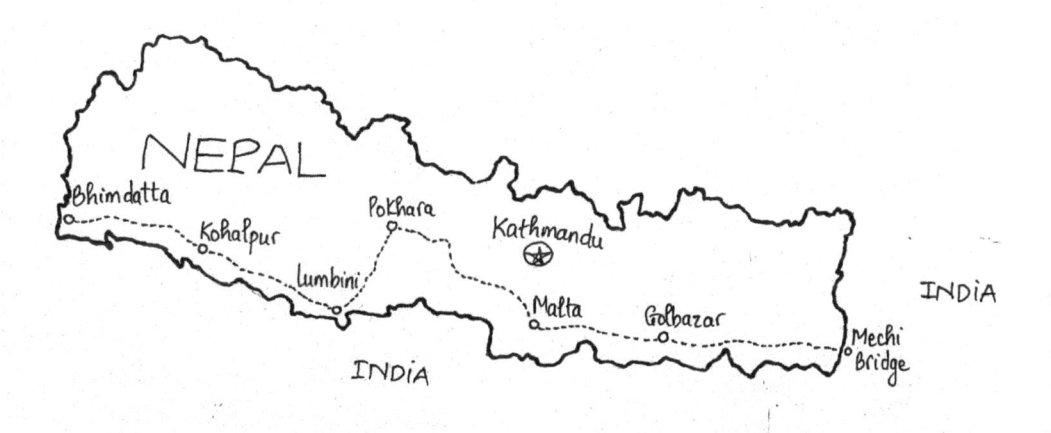

It was possible to get a visa at the Nepalese border for fifty US dollars. As we approached the border post, the atmosphere quietened down, and our headaches slowly subsided. A small army of bicycles replaced the splutter and blare of the cars' engines and horns.

We crossed a bridge over the tumultuous Sharda River, which drew all its water from the rocks of the Himalayas. At the end of the bridge, a cheerful traffic jam formed. The Indian border guards had closed the barriers to let those who wished to travel to India circulate. I looked all around me to see the bikes, some of which were trying to get between Khanh Nguyen and Amaury. Before our impatience got the better of us, the flow of cars, motorcycles, and bicycles had dried up. Only a skinny man on an iron bike blocked our path. The barrier lowered on his side as ours raised up again. We desperately took the opportunity to swallow the few centimeters of asphalt between us, trying to avoid his feet.

We passed under the barrier. The road finally widened. We welcomed the return of our personal space! Our exit stamps from India were obtained in a tiny wooden hut that looked nothing like an immigration post. A little lady welcomed us into a very small room cooled by the shade. She quickly stamped our passports, scribbled on a piece of paper, then told us we could continue to Nepal.

A short minute went by without any corresponding Nepalese border post. Had we passed it? Where was it? A man ran up behind us and gestured to where the border post for foreigners was. It was almost impossible to see him from the road that extended towards Nepal. Three officers drank milk tea from little cups inside. They offered us a broad smile as we passed the doorway. Two of them got up to take care of our passports while the third tried to offer us various services: 'Perhaps an organized tour? Hotel? Transportation?' His face betrayed a cold love of money, however, so I answered without enthusiasm. Seeing that there wouldn't be much to get out of us, he handed me a flyer, slumping out of the room for a cigarette. The two officers had just finished with our passports: we handed them our beautiful brand-new dollars, which triggered the heavy noise of the stamp falling on the blank pages of our passports. To Nepal we went!

Our first few kilometers of pedaling in a new country always made us anticipate the possible discoveries it had in store. Our senses, full of the smells and tastes of the previous country, soon abandoned them in order to become impregnated with those we were entering. The contrast with India was striking. Everything was cleaner and more peaceful. The women we met impressed us by their height and the colors they wore. On the road, there were a few trucks, and bicycles reigned supreme. I took pleasure in passing them. Sometimes they were schoolchildren, sometimes a couple with the woman sitting on the luggage rack, sometimes a wise old man. For the first time on the trip, the bicycle seemed to be the most used means of transportation in the country we were crossing!

The Nepalese also seemed much shyer than their Indian counterparts. They rarely waved at us and certainly never came to speak to us. That wasn't really a problem for us, however. We'd had an overdose of encounters and selfies in India! We fully enjoyed our newfound breathing room. Our first culinary discovery was the *Dal Bhat*. It was presented to us in the form of a round tray on which we had white rice, lentils, curry, and vegetables. I was very happy to discover those new flavors. I hadn't expected that I would find them almost daily for that whole month in Nepal, however! Since I didn't know at that stage, however, I took full advantage of the opportunity to eat and taste as much as I could

---

We chose to begin by taking the *road number 1* because it went through the *Terai*; the least mountainous part of Southern Nepal. There were many nature reserves. It is the breadbasket of Nepal; rice, vegetables, and fruits are grown there.

What impressed us was that the road passed through nature reserves where elephants, deer, crocodiles, thousands of birds, and even tigers roamed wild. Many signs alerted drivers to the presence of the tigers. It didn't reassure us much. Often, we were pedaling on *road number 1* without a single soul for company. I was afraid to see a hungry tiger leap out from the undergrown to hunt our small group! I saw Khanh Nguyen and Amaury watching out for the slightest movement that came from the dense forests. I kept behind them and turned my head regularly to make sure that nothing popped up unexpectedly too. Many monkeys here and there clung to the surrounding branches or otherwise tried to approach us searching for food or entertainment.

The road meandered through national parks and "buffer" zones, so we didn't always know if we were still pedaling through a park or not. The night was approaching, so we decided to camp near a river. There was a village nearby which suggested wild animals didn't venture into the area. Whether it was a foolish assumption or not, we set up our tents. One for the married couple, the other for the bachelor! Before the sun went down, we swam in the fresh water of the river. I bathed first in the company of my brother, and then it was Khanh Nguyen's turn. Despite the humidity, there were few mosquitoes, so we relaxed outside and took the time to cook our dinner: pasta with *masala* sauce and vegetables from the market. Once the meal was finished, we made sure to pack everything well and hide any remaining food or cake in a nearby tree branch. We wanted to avoid attracting monkeys or, worse, predators!

Before we went to our tents, I looked at Amaury and softly said:
"I'm so glad you joined us Amaury."
"Of course! I wanted to accompany you, even just for a little while. It was important to me."
"It's kind of amazing how one thing leads to another, isn't it? Just a few years after our first 4000km trip through Europe, you and I have now shared an even greater adventure?"
Later, I took Khanh Nguyen's hand in mine, relaxed and fell asleep.

At dawn, I opened the zip of our tent and observed the few birds and cows that had come to drink in the river. The humidity level was so high that the whole wall of our tent was soaked; Amaury's too. We would have to take a break at lunchtime to dry our tents in the sun. The food I hid from the monkeys the night before was still there. We packed up our luggage and took *road number* 1 again.

We started our day with the Bardiya National Park, which also had its share of tigers, elephants, and crocodiles. From the top of a large bridge over the great Babai River, we took a short break to admire the view.
"Truly magnificent! Look at the color of the water," said Khanh Nguyen in wonder.
"We should have camped here last night! The scenery is perfect!" replied Amaury.

Crossing of natural reserves with tigers and crocodiles, Nepal

"You bet it is! Look here! And there!" I teased, pointing at a couple of huge crocodiles drying themselves in the sun.

They weren't the only ones. Many squatted on both banks of the Babai River with their permanent crocodile smiles. One waddled close to our small group, letting us admire its magnificent elongated jaw. Its skin glowed in the sun. It was fortunately at a good distance and located below us. I thought back to the night before and how we could have had crocodiles as housemates. I took this vision as a warning, and knew we would have to be much more careful next time. A Nepalese soldier came up to us, politely moving us along. It was forbidden to park too long, even with a bicycle.

The road resumed through the jungle and small villages. Each house was well kept, with a small garden and flowers. Animals were littered outside: cows, chickens, dogs, and cats. Today was a special day: it was the beginning of the Diwali festival. We had seen the preparation of this festival while we were pedaling through India. Now it was time for the celebrations to start. As we went along, we came across several groups, mainly composed of teenagers and young adults, all dressed in fine costumes, going from house to house.

At each, they started to dance and play songs. The musicians stood in the center as the Nepalese youth danced in a circle around them. Their twirling multi-colored clothes produced a beautiful effect. Very regularly, we were invited to join the circle and participated in the party. Comparatively, in our traveling gear, we looked drab. The songs and dances were rhythmic, filling us with joy and imbuing us with life. Suddenly the group stopped. Everyone started to dance without restriction. Khanh Nguyen, Amaury, and I looked at each other and quickly gave it our all! We only knew three or four dance steps between us, though! Dancing among the Nepalese youth was such an experience. Giving all the energy we had was all that really counted. It didn't matter that our dance steps weren't particularly creative. Nobody was there to judge us. Our sweat almost caused us to slide off our saddles when we got back on our bikes! As the dancing ended, we took multiple pictures with our dance partners. Everyone smiled widely and thanked us for taking part in Diwali with them: "Happy Diwali, my friends!"

I was gratified that we'd finally been able to get a little closer to the Nepalese in that way..

We decided to spend the night in a small guesthouse for three US dollars a night per person. Our hosts greeted us with necklaces of orange flowers and invited us to join in the evening celebrations. The music became progressively techno and psychedelic. Some highly intoxicated youths were letting off steam, wiggling their hips in hysterical and disjointed movements. At that stage, the fatigue from the kilometers (miles) we'd pedaled reared its head, and we ended the evening early to go and sleep.

The first reliefs took shape as we got closer to Lumbini. Amaury, who had a big bike and light equipment, took the climbs easily. Our saddlebags, however, seemed to be trying to pull us back with all their might. We climbed at a steady pace, but Amaury took the lead several times. We would find him again and again, waiting for us patiently to catch up on a stone bench or under a tree.

The humidity was hard for Khanh Nguyen and me to bear. We were used to dry weather, especially in Iran. Every climb came with inevitable and omnipresent sweat. It quickly spread up and around our bodies, soaking our entire back and face. We saw it drop and fall into the earth we were cycling through. It became difficult to enjoy the places and people with those small streams flowing along our spines, particularly when they reached the estuary formed by our buttocks! We began to dream of the refreshing embrace of a cold shower.

The road continued, however, and Lumbini got closer. Lumbini is a place that is important for Buddhists, which includes Khanh Nguyen's family. When we told her that we would be passing through Nepal, Lumbini quickly became an obligatory stopover. Lumbini was where the Buddha, Siddhartha

Celebrations for Diwali, Nepal

Gautama, was said to have been born in 623 BC.

Thirty years ago, Lumbini was an abandoned and neglected place. Through his vision and strength of conviction, Huyên Diêu, then a young Vietnamese monk, convinced the King of Nepal in 1993 to grant him the right to build a pagoda near the birthplace of Buddha. With very limited resources and little support at first, Huyên Diêu managed to set up the pagoda. Over the years, he managed to get the whole local community on his side and many countries that agreed to build their own pagoda on the Lumbini site, including France. Lumbini became an essential pilgrimage site where Buddhists from all over the world come to discover the birthplace of the great Siddhartha Gautama.

As we headed towards Lumbini, we hoped we'd be able to meet him. Very few visitors had been able to meet him. Huyên Diêu is a discreet, traveling, and elusive man. Many pilgrims coming hoping to meet him could spend days or even weeks in Lumbini without seeing a trace of him. With an indecisive, soft pedal stroke, we were inevitably getting closer to the birthplace of the Buddha. The sun set, letting beautiful pink and orange colors filter and evaporate within the sky. We arrived at the site of Lumbini, which was surrounded by a wide moat. I signaled to the guard that we were expected at the Vietnamese pagoda. He let us enter and showed us the way. The setting sun reflected on the tops of the pagodas and stupas, which were covered with gold leaf. We pedaled in front of the Chinese pagoda, which forked in front of the French pagoda to finally arrive at the imposing Vietnamese pagoda of Huyên Diêu.

The place seemed very peaceful, almost empty. A Nepalese guard opened the imposing iron door and left to alert the master immediately. We installed our bikes near a beautiful garden where flowers and reeds were mixed. I hoped so much that it would be Huyên Diêu who would appear. Footsteps were heard and then a shadow appeared. A young monk introduced himself to us. His features and appearance were not those of an experienced and wise monk. The welcome was rather cold, detached. Khanh Nguyen explained to him in Vietnamese who we were, our journey, and our project. He softly agreed to let us spend one night in a room adjoining the pagoda. Khanh Nguyen thanked him and asked him if the venerable Huyên Diêu was there.

"No, I don't think so," replied the young monk. "He is on a trip."

"Ha, very well, thank you for your welcome," answered Khanh Nguyen in a voice full of disappointment.

The young monk nonchalantly disappeared into his apartments. We were hoping for a slightly warmer welcome. The three of us agreed to leave early the next day when a new character came onto the stage: Lanh. He introduced himself to us with a big smile and offered us tea. He was a young Vietnamese student who offered his services as a volunteer at the pagoda. For several weeks he had been taking care of the decoration in several rooms at the pagoda.

I saw Khanh Nguyen's face light up as she expressed herself in her native language. The last time she'd met one of her countrymen, we'd been in the Czech Republic. Lanh was from Saigon and his good mood comforted me. He got enthusiastic as we shared anecdotes from our trip with him. For dinner, he accompanied us to a small restaurant where many monks of all nationalities went: Thai, Chinese, Burmese... On the evening menu: *momos* which consisted of steamed ravioli with *masala* sauce. After a while, Huyên Diêu came up.

"We are really disappointed that we can't meet him. He's on a trip apparently," began Khanh Nguyen.

"Yes... But he's already back in Nepal! And he might arrive late at night in Lumbini," answered Lanh.

"Oh but that's great! We might be able to meet him then!"

"He will be very happy to meet you, I think, and to discuss you about your trip with you."

A big smile then appeared on our faces. For Amaury, it had not been a significant issue to miss the monk, but for Khanh Nguyen and me, it was a welcome turn of events. The day after would also be my birthday, my thirtieth birthday. After dinner, Amaury went to his room and we to ours.

At the mere thought of our possible meeting with Huyên Diêu, we initially found it difficult to fall asleep. However, fatigue took over, and I fell asleep beside her.

On my thirtieth birthday, everything had a cinematic quality. I left our room, watching the morning sunlight pass through the branches of the tall trees around us. The gong of the pagoda rang several times. Several magnificent Sarus cranes came to land in the small pond in front of the pagoda, their heads covered in beautiful bright red feathers. Then, from the top of the pagoda, a voice started to sing Buddhist prayers. The sound was melodious and resonated with the song of the Sarus cranes. Could it be Huyên Diêu?

Khanh Nguyen then Amaury joined me in the small garden and settled down beside me around a small wooden table. The three of us remained silent while the singing that came from the heights continued as well as the one of the cranes. Lanh then joined us and whispered to us: "This is the venerable Huyên Diêu". The song ended, and footsteps could be heard on the stairs. A few seconds went by before we finally saw Huyên Diêu! He looked simple in appearance but exuded an aura hard to describe. He wore a taupe-colored monk's habit, with a shaved head and small round glasses. Small but deep-set wrinkles furrowed his face here and there.

"Hello, how are you?" Huyên Diêu asked us in perfect French.

"Hello Thây, we are so happy to meet you! And you speak French so well. How is it possible?" I answered.

"I studied in France in my youth: at La Sorbonne. I have wonderful memories of it. What you do, your bicycle trip, is remarkable. You must write a book and inspire the youth."

"Thank you very much, Thây, I'm simply following my dream. What you have achieved here is on a whole other level."

"A lot of people said I was 'crazy' when I first came here. There was

Meeting with Thây Huyên Diêu in Lumbini, Nepal

nothing here: only swamps and mosquitoes. People who believed in my project could be counted on one hand. And then, through hard work and conviction, things gradually evolved into what they are today. It wasn't easy: we had few means initially, and then there was the war from 1996 to 2006."

"This site is remarkable! There are so many foreign pagodas. It's a true success!"

"Thank you, Thibault. You are welcome here. Stay a few days. I will show you around, and I understand that today is your birthday."

"It is! Thank you, Thây, for your welcome. We will stay a little while a course."

Thây Huyên Diêu impressed me with the simplicity of his attitude and words. He put himself at our level and presented his life and work simply, without false modesty. All things considered, his words resonated with our adventure. Few people believed in us, especially in Khanh Nguyen. Some even on social networks said that we were crooks: that our fundraising for street children in Vietnam was actually destined to end up deep in our pockets. And then, through hardship, kilometers, and perseverance, there we were in Lumbini, Nepal, seven months later, talking to Huyên Diêu. Our journey had taken on a real mystical, spiritual dimension by that stage.

The two days we spent with Huyên Diêu and Lanh would engrave themselves in our memories. The young monk who welcomed us so coldly the day before did everything he could to avoid us. He wouldn't speak to us the entire time. We didn't really try to interpret that attitude and simply enjoyed the time we had with our host. Huyên Diêu took us on a tuk-tuk tour of the Lumbini site with all its pagodas, each with its own style. Each visit was always accompanied by our discussions about life, travel, France, Vietnam, religion. I enjoyed talking about these subjects with a man who embodied what he defends and advocates in life. Philosophies are best appreciated when embodied by the believers in their lifestyle and rhetoric. On the evening of my birthday, Huyên Diêu surprised me by preparing a cream cake! We celebrated my thirty springs together in the small garden of the pagoda.

Huyên Diêu instructed us to take our time to observe the Sarus cranes that came to land in the small pond. He had been a key person for the protection of those fabulous birds. He knew them all, even the multiple meanings of their songs, their flights, and their testimonies of love towards their offspring. We tried to get ourselves into his mindset and observed, soon feeling the magnificent spectacle of nature that was slowly unfolding before our eyes. The day before leaving, I felt that unique encounter with Huyên Diêu had created a beautiful space in my body, in my heart, for how best to observe nature. It was one of those encounters that can't help but influence the course of your life, multiplying it into infinite consequences, variations, and colors.

The next morning, it was time to say goodbye to Huyên Diêu, Lanh, the pagoda, and the beautiful Sarus cranes. Huyên Diêu wished us all the best for the rest of our trip. He offered us two of his books that we intended to carry to Saigon, but that wasn't been everything. He offered us two of his books that we intended to carry to Saigon, but that wasn't everything. He gave us an envelope containing a large sum of money for our fundraising. We thanked him with all the sincerity and strength we were capable of. Huyên Diêu joined us for a photo then said:

"Have a safe trip Khanh Nguyen, Thibault, and Amaury. Our paths will hopefully cross again. If you encounter any problems during your remaining days in Nepal, please contact me on my phone."

Amaury got on his bike, Khanh climbed on Monster, I jumped on Tank's back and off we went. We passed the pagoda gate one last time. I took a last look at Huyên Diêu and the cranes. Then we were on the Nepalese roads again with the feeling that our journey and our lives had taken a new course.

The road and all its dust were back. Our goal for the next few days: the city of Pokhara where Amaury would leave us to return by bus to Delhi in India.

The one hundred and fifty kilometers (93 miles) that remained for us to arrive at that tourist city weren't in the best conditions. Potholes, puddles, mud, and trucks were multiplying. We lost a lot of time and energy by making our way through that small chaos. To make matters worse, the road that led to Pokhara climbed higher and higher the further we went. Nevertheless, all our efforts were rewarded by breathtaking views of the rice fields, mountains, and waterfalls that cascaded down.

Our route went North towards the Himalayan ranges. Snowy summits were starting to appear far away on the horizon. Temperatures cooled down as we climbed the Himalayan colossus. I enjoyed those last few days with my little brother. Our trio had worked marvelously well together, and I had a little knot in my stomach as I remembered that he (and his long beard) would soon no longer be with us. As with Fanny in Georgia, Amaury had brought all his energy with him on our road from India to Nepal. The dynamic of three people is different from the dynamic of two; another kind of social balance is formed. I didn't really know which one I preferred.

Our small trio stopped in the town of Tansen, which formed a brave stronghold among the mountains. To get to the center of Tansen, we had to take a street that looked more like a climbing wall than anything else. It seemed to climb up to the heights as fast as possible and would stop the most daring cyclists. But after long months on the road, our muscles seemed to have no real limits. Each one of us gained momentum and changed speed as quickly as possible to reach the smallest gable. You should have seen the inhabitants of Tansen, aghast to see three cyclists loaded like mules in such a small pedestrian street. Khanh Nguyen quickly let us go ahead, putting her feet to the ground. She would end up on foot.

With Amaury, we then engaged in a playful race to see who would arrive at the top first. Two Nepalese women started to encourage and applaud us as we passed in front of their small store. The climb was awesome: my legs were burning, and I felt like Tank would explode under all the pressure and force I was putting on him. Amaury stuck out his tongue in exhaustion but stayed at my level. A bluff? I increased my efforts, and he cracked. I savored

On the way to Pokhara, Nepal

my small and ridiculous victory as I reached the top of Tansen. Amaury arrived just as breathless as I was a few seconds later. Khanh Nguyen was even further away. I left Tank against the wall of a small store and rushed towards her to help her get through the day's final event. The view from the top of the street was breathtaking. So much so that I wondered how I had managed to stay on my bike until the top.

Kilometers (miles) and days went by until we finally reached Pokhara, located at an altitude of 1,400 meters (4,600 feet). It is a city popular with tourists and it made me feel good to find a little "western" touch. Since Delhi, we had been immersed without interruption in the local culture and food. After more than a month, I began to get tired of *masala* sauce and *dalh baht*... To taste a good French crepe with cider and munch an *apple crumble* with a cappuccino felt like a privilege. We even found a Vietnamese restaurant nearby. We found a small hotel with a memorable panorama of the mountain ranges to stay in.

Before Amaury took his bus for a thirty-six-hour ride back to Delhi, we had to find a buyer for his bike. We went around the stores in the city, which all offered us an insufficient price. We ended up settling a price with the small hotel owner who bought it for seventy percent of the price Amaury had paid in Delhi. His bike had held remarkably well during all its kilometers (miles) from Delhi to Pokhara. There had been no technical problems or punctures: a perfect companion, just like him.

After one last evening with Amaury it was time for him to go. In the Clemenceau[1] family, we do not show much emotion, especially in public. I hugged and kissed him hard but did not overdo it; neither did he.

As Amaury walked away, we were once again a duo. We did not know it yet, but we would be right until Laos. We resumed our habits as an old, adventurous couple! Two choices were available before us: to pass quickly

---

[1] My family name

again through India and cross the region of Bihar or to continue full East in Nepal to join West Bengal in India. The region of Bihar is one of the poorest in India and is unfortunately known for its violence. Very quickly, we chose to continue to enjoy the Nepalese calm rather than plunge back into the Indian chaos.

Our route would be: Bharatpur, Hetauda, then the long *road number 1 to* Siliguri, which would mark our return to India. We quickly resumed our little routine together: getting up, preparing breakfast, adjusting the bikes, and putting the saddlebags in place. A few hours after leaving Pokhara, I decided to follow a track by the Seti Gandaki river rather than follow the national road. It would take us at least a day to reach the end of that track where, I hoped, a bridge would allow us to reach the city of Bharatpur. We prepared the necessary stock of food: rice, pasta, eggs, vegetables, fruits, and cakes.

The asphalt road disappeared quickly to give way to a track, sometimes sandy and sometimes stony, along the river. We passed by a few inhabitants who lived in modest wooden houses with tin roofs overlooking the river. Very quickly, Khanh Nguyen had met difficulty. Her tires jumped on the rocks, and I saw that she lost a lot of energy in the process. We multiplied the breaks, and after several hours, I suggested that we should stop for the day, which she accepted gratefully.

I saw a spot a little off-center from the track: a kind of beach with big white and gray pebbles that followed the "S" curve of the Seti Gandaki. The water was a stunning teal blue and flowed slowly. I scanned to make sure that there were no crocodiles. We opened our saddlebags and lay our floor mats on the pebbles. Khanh Nguyen stretched out all the way, closed her eyes, and immediately sank into a deep sleep. It wasn't the first time that it had happened to her, and I understood that she was at the end of her tether and needed rest.

While she slept and regained strength, I started to set up the tent and prepare the meal. The silence was so pure. Only the wind and sound of flowing water. As I cooked, three children came up the river. They were ten years old at most and trying to skim the stones. They were barefoot and wore vague copies of soccer shirts in the colors of FC Barcelona, Paris Saint-Germain, and Arsenal. They took a long time to spot us when finally the tallest of them waved to his two friends that there were two strange beings in the distance. I continued to cook, ignoring them, as they continued to slowly approach us halfway between curiosity and fear. I greeted them, touching my chest with my right hand and saying "Thibault", to which I got no answer. They were intrigued by our stove that ran on gasoline. I took the time to display to them how it worked. Then, to continue to distract them, I showed them our bikes, the water filter, and our tent.

Khanh Nguyen then woke up looking a little lost. Then she smiled at our three new friends.

"How do you feel, my love?"

"Much better, I had no energy at all. But now I'm fine!"

"Can you watch the rice cooking? I'm going to take a bath in the river. Don't worry about the three kids. They're just curious, that's it. And I feel that this place isn't dangerous. Even if they report us to their village, no one will come to visit us during the night."

Once finished and dried, it was Khanh Nguyen's turn to wash herself. I made sure to keep the attention of the three little Nepalese kids while I cooked some vegetables and eggs. After a while I saw Khanh Nguyen sneaking back into the tent to change behind them.

Keeping the attention of our friends, I started a skimming contest. All three of them could play well, especially the tallest with his FC Barcelona jersey. As I picked up my next pebble, a female voice rose from the forest. The three little friends raised their heads, looked at each other, then ran towards the forest without saying goodbye.

It would soon be dark, and it was probably their mother calling them for dinner. I saw them hurrying among the pebbles, scattering them until they disappeared deep into the thick forest.

Crossing the bridge, Nepal

Night next to the Seti Gandaki River, Nepal

We enjoyed our dinner to the sound of the wind and the lapping of the river. A man a little further away seemed to be fishing but he didn't pay any attention to us. At nightfall, we washed the dishes, brushed our teeth, and settled down in our small hotel with ten thousand stars in line with the sky that offered itself to us. Khanh Nguyen placed her head on my chest. I placed my arm around the back of her neck. Very quickly we fell asleep to the sound of the stream, lost along a Nepalese river.

The sun's heat on the wall of our tent told us it was time to wake up. The night was peaceful, and all our equipment and bikes were still there. We had few doubts about it, but it was always comforting to wake up in the middle of nature and see everything was still there.

After having breakfast and loading everything on Tank and Monster, we took the long track, which should have led us, in theory, towards a bridge. The first hours of pedaling were lonely before we came across a village with several tens of houses: a good sign. At the end of the track, there was a monkey bridge, suspended well above the river. It was only possible to cross it on foot or by pushing our bikes. We passed by some Nepalese women all loaded with wares who had come back from a big market on the other side of the monkey bridge. We made the crossing without much difficulty, which left us the time to admire the Seti Gandaki one last time whose sound had rocked us to sleep so well last night. At the end of the bridge, we reached the main road that would allow us to continue our trip.

During the week that remained before we reached Northeast India, we would have few highlights, few encounters. The kilometers followed each other straight eastward day after day without much flavor. All was quiet on the Eastern front. We crossed national parks, saw monkeys, swallowed *momos*, but our conical Non-La hats weren't arousing much interest anymore. We were now firmly in Asia. We spent our last Nepalese nights under the tent well hidden by trees and high grass.

Chapter 21

Northeast India: hugs and food poisoning

Mileage Meter: 9,594 to 10,902km (5,961 to 6,774 miles)

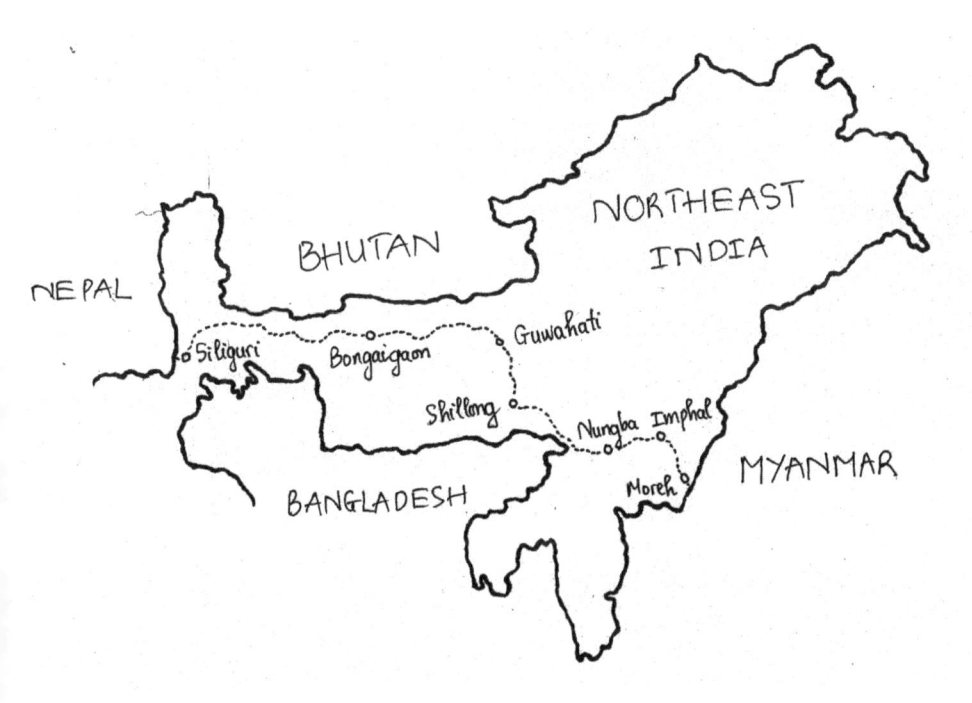

Northeast India and the state of West Bengal were finally in sight. A gigantic bridge allowed us to cross the Mechi River. It was an adventure to find the small immigration post to get our entry stamp. Several soldiers pointed us in the wrong direction so that we entered India without a stamp... A rather permeable border if ever there was one! We had to turn back to finally find a small, isolated immigration post. While the officer took care of our passports, I asked if other cyclists had passed through there recently. A Dutch couple had preceded us by a few days. It was up to us now to try to catch up with them!

Northeast India wasn't at all the "Bollywood" vision one might fantasize about. The "Seven Sisters States" that compromised the country included many peoples who spoke Tibeto-Burmese languages. There were two hundred and twenty different languages in these Sisters States! The cultures, the faces of all these peoples were much closer to the peoples of Southeast Asia than to an Indian from Delhi or Mumbai. It must be said that these various peoples and cultures were attached to India during the British period. During the British colonization and especially after India's independence in 1947, multiple separatist movements developed. There was a lot of violence. The result was a strong Indian military presence and its multiple *checkpoints*. We would experience them during these hundreds of kilometers (miles) to the Burmese border: we would find the military uniforms, the berets, and the Kalashnikovs.

The first of the seven sisters we met on our way was the State of Assam. Rice fields dominated there, reflecting the beauty of the season with their yellow and green reflections. The atmosphere was much calmer and more serene than on our trip from Delhi to Nepal. The people we met greeted us and smiled but didn't harass us for a photo or a selfie. The possibilities of not following the main road were almost infinite: a small path that wound between rivers, a road shaded by hundred-year-old trees, crossing a river on a frail wooden boat... We started to enjoy pedaling in Assam.

Another really welcome thing was that there were many hosts from the *Warmshowers* community along our route in Northeast India. The vast majority of the messages we sent got a positive response. This was how we met Rahul, who welcomed us in the city of Alipurduar. He lived in a beautiful house with his mother, his wife, and his son. Rahul was very inquisitive, and as soon as we arrived, he threw a battery of questions about France, Vietnam, and our journey at us. Alipurduar was an obligatory stop we had to make towards Burma, and as Rahul was the only *Warmshowers* host in the city, he had seen a lot of long-distance cyclists: from Europe, the United States, South America, South Korea... but it was the first time he'd encountered someone from Vietnam.

"Khanh Nguyen, describe your country to me: its food, its climate, its economy, its political regime. I'm curious, you know," Rahul said.

Khanh Nguyen took her time to explain Rahul what her beautiful country was made up of, which only inspired more questions. On the second floor of Rahul's house was a large room where we set up our tent. We had direct access to a small bathroom, which for us was now synonymous with great luxury! After a cold shower, Rahul's wife invited us down for dinner. She had prepared *chapatis*, broccoli, and chickpeas with a delicious curry sauce: what a treat it was! Later that evening, there would be the annual festival of the city of Alipurduar in honor of a Hindu deity. Rahul proposed that we go, which we immediately accepted despite our fatigue. There were several thousand people at this festival where stands of food, clothes, jewelry, and all kinds of attractions were mixed. There was also a large tent for concerts and dances. I liked mingling with the crowd, observing families wandering here and there, to understand what united them that evening.

As we were the only foreigners, the local TV quickly spotted us. A rather unusual interview followed. The Indian accent of the journalist was very harsh, which made it difficult to understand her questions. The "R" and "L" were mixed and confused. I tried to catch a word here and there and ventured to give banal and unremarkable answers with my French accent. I hoped viewers would at least understand something in the interview. The director then offered us two scarves typical of the Assam region with their red and white squares. We posed for the official photo, then after two or three laps among the stands, we decided to go back with Rahul's whole family in the tuk-tuk.

The next morning, after breakfast with Rahul, many thanks, and a group photo, we continued eastward towards the small village of Gossaigaon.

I was not sure what was waiting for us in Gossaigaon, but I was excited to get there. It had all started a few days ago when Hassanul called me on my phone. I contacted him via the *Warmshowers* website, and he called me immediately. Hassanul was a young teacher at a private school in Gossaigaon: *St. Anthony's English Medium High School*. He wanted to welcome us but was currently in Kolkatta, more than seven hundred kilometers (434 miles) away: his mother was seriously ill, and her surgery was coming soon. Hassanul offered us the following:

"Father David, the Director of the school, can welcome you. It would be great if you could present your adventure to all the children. I'm sure it will be a wonderful moment for them and you. Please pray for my mom and family."

The opportunity was too good to pass up. To be able to present the stories of the ten thousand kilometers (6,200 miles) we'd already covered in front of children and teenagers was a dream. We immediately accepted and prepared our presentation as we got closer to Gossaigaon. The school was located near the main road. I was expecting to discover a modest little school, but imposing buildings on several floors soon appeared in front of us and in the middle, a church. It was Sunday, and the school was pretty empty. We got off of Monster and Tank to push them to the front of the church. A very skinny sister welcomed us and guided us to Father David.

Father David introduced himself to us in all simplicity and made sure we didn't need anything. He had dressed in a beautiful white shirt. He offered us tea with milk and cookies while we told him all our stories.

"Tomorrow, about 600 students will come to listen to you. I'm sure your story will be a great inspiration to them!"

"Thank you, father," I replied. "We're biking across the world to experience exactly this kind of moment. And being able to speak in English with everyone is a great help for the discussion."

"Here, English is the language to communicate. Our students each speak the dialect of the community they belong to. With English, they can communicate with each other."

"I can hear some music inside the church. What are you preparing?"

"We are preparing for a big concert next week! There will be songs in English and young people from each community are also preparing songs in their own language. Go and meet them!"

Once our cup of tea was finished, we headed towards the church. About fifty students accompanied by drums, bass, and electric guitar were in full rehearsal. With Khanh Nguyen, we greeted them and settled in as discreetly as we could. The youth group started a Bodo song. The Bodos were an important ethnic group in the state of Assam. Although I didn't understand them, the lyrics of the song were beautiful in both sound and rhythm. The young people who sang them too, by the diversity of their faces and all the energy they displayed. One of the sisters even handed us a small booklet with the songs written in phonetically and we awkwardly tried to accompany them. Everyone looked at us with a curious and benevolent look as the songs followed one another

Time passed so fast that it was already dinner time. It was quick and efficient, still in the company of Father David, who quickly took his leave from us. One of the sisters, Sister Rosalyne, then led us to a beautiful room where everything was made of wood. I spent some time with Khanh Nguyen finishing our presentation: we had to select from thousands of memories, photos, what we wanted to say, and transmitted it to all these little beings. With red eyes full of fatigue, we went to bed, both well protected under a mosquito net. .

The next day, we had breakfast: rice, fish, chapatis, and peanut butter.

Our adventure was always under the sign of permanent adaptation! As the minutes went by, a clamor from the schoolyard gradually came towards our ears. I walked a few meters (feet) to get out of the building and discovered thousands of children in front of me. The beginning of classes would soon ring out, and a multitude of students were running and playing in all directions. They all wore an elegant red and white uniform: pants and blazer for the boys; skirt, shirt, tights, and hair tied up for the girls. It was impressive to see and a little intimidating to think that we would have to captivate all these little people for more than an hour! A voice resounded in the loudspeakers, and suddenly, all the pupils rushed to place themselves in line for their respective classes. Once calm was restored, prayers and songs in honor of the Virgin Mary rang out in the courtyard.

Father David, who today was wearing his most beautiful white Alb, beckoned us to settle in the room. We set up Tank and Monster on the stage, prepared the overhead projector, checked that the microphones worked properly. Then all the students, like the successive red and white waves of a great tide, entered the large room and came and sat on the floor. I caught some glances here and there. Father David introduced us to our small audience, who were admirable for their calm and attention. Hundreds of little hands applauded us, and it was time for us to take to the stage, the stage of *Saint Anthony's School* in Gossaigaon. .

After a small presentation of who we were, I launched into a rather hazardous pun:

"Our destination is Saigon... *We will go to Saigon...* And here we are in Gossaigaon... GO SAIGON!"

I expected it to flounder, but the pun went well with our beautiful audience! The students laughed heartily and repeated: "Haha, Go Saigon, Gossaigaon!" Phew... it had worked. .

We spent a long time introducing them to Monster and Tank, some of the highlights of the trip: the beautiful European forests, the snow in Switzerland, Maria and Vojtech in the Czech Republic, the nights in the tent in Bulgaria, the desert in Iran, Reza and the Qashqai, Persepolis, the Pink Mosque in Shiraz, Delhi, Nepal... I was not quite sure that all those places meant anything to them. Returning to all those moments, all those images, was quite dizzying for me. . My house seemed so far away, and I suddenly felt battle-worn, as if I had already lived too much for one man. I could already sell my business so to speak, and I had already burned up all my quota of the intensity one can experience in life. At that moment, I missed my family. I missed my friends too. What was the point of living this kind of thing so far away from home? What was the meaning of it all in the end?

As Khanh Nguyen told them about Iran, I looked at our small red and white audience. They were captivated. Some reacted to the slightest sentence as if they resonated with everything we said. I told myself then that if we inspired even one of them, one of these children, to one day follow their own dream, then we would have won everything. That was worth something.

Once our presentation was over, arms were raised, and questions soon came flying. We were asked how we managed to get enough water and food, if we had been afraid when we'd slept in the tent, which country we had preferred more than others. After ten or so enthusiastic questions, Father David put an end to the proceedings, proposing to take a picture of us all together. All the students applauded for a long time and came up to join us onstage. The photos were magnificent: a Vietnamese woman, a French man, two bicycles, and two Non-La hats among a red and white forest of beautiful little souls!

Then perhaps one of the most beautiful moments of our entire adventure came. Once the picture was taken, hundreds of students lined up in front of the stage and went up to us one by one to thank us. Some of them shook our hands but many of them clambered all over each other to give us huge hugs.

We gave hundreds of hugs, and it lasted a good ten minutes. Each hug made us grow, gave us strength. Once all the hugs had been received and given, we left the room into the open air. Many students were waiting for us outside and even asked us for autographs: in a notebook or just on their forearm! A little girl caught my attention. She stood radiantly with ribbons in her hair, patiently waiting her turn behind the grown-ups to get an autograph from Khanh Nguyen on her little notebook. It was then her turn, and you should have seen her eyes: full of admiration. Khanh Nguyen knelt down to reach the same height as the girl then embraced her. That was meaningful too.

After our second and last night in Saint Anthony, we resumed our tireless route towards the East. The cities followed one another: Manikpur, Barpetta, Guwahati... Men and women worked in their rice fields as November ended. From the top of our two bicycles, the agricultural display was permanent. We had also just passed the symbolic 10,000 kilometers (6,213 miles) mark. We were at 10,324 US dollars in donations! The mileage meter was starting to get dangerously close to the donation meter... We hoped that the trend would be reversed! I remained confident. I was convinced that the closer we got to Vietnam, the more people would be talking about *Non-La Project*; with even more donations coming in as a result.

Leaving Guwahati, we discovered the second of the seven sisters: Meghalaya, which embraced Bangladesh. Rice fields gave way to mountains and jungle. We often shared the road with convoys of large tanker trucks that made everything around us shake. They crossed rivers and streams on feverish wooden bridges that threatened to collapse under their weight. It was rather easy for us to camp in the forests: there were few people in this region, and spring water was abundant.

After several days of going up and down, we reached the third of the seven sisters I previously mentioned: the State of Manipur. The military was once again the ones to check our passports. It must be said that Manipur had suffered many acts of violence of an independent nature that had been exacerbated at the beginning of the 21st century. Ambushes against convoys of tanker trucks had regularly taken place. Many soldiers in combat uniform

Presentation, autographs and hugs with the students, Gossaigaon, India

patrolled along the roads, but I didn't feel unsafe. Those conflicts concerned the Indian State and those ethnic groups: not two bicycle travelers. However, we avoided riding at night, and I ensured that the place we slept was safe.

One afternoon, as we continued to climb among the mountains and jungle, we decided to take a well-deserved break in a village. A church overlooked the village, and I proposed that we rest under a porch. A small group of children played next door: they threw a ball back and forth and ran in all directions. Our presence didn't affect them any more than that. The sunset that day would be at half-past four. We had one hour to find a place to sleep, so pitching our tent next to the church seemed to be the best option. While we continued to watch the children play, a motorcycle arrived with two men. The passenger in the back carried a Kalashnikov on his shoulder, but I didn't see him as a threat.

The motorcycle driver got off, greeted us, and came and sat down next to us. He was about thirty years old, with a stern look, fine features and a rather slender body. He spoke English well. After explaining to him who we were, he introduced himself:

"Good afternoon, friends. I'm Tangboy, son of the village chief. Here you are on the land of the Kukis."

"Hello Tangboy," I answered him while reaching out to him. "We didn't know the Kukis before we met you. It's easy to remember this name!"

"Where are you going to sleep tonight?"

"Do you think we can sleep in the church? We don't know where to stop for tonight. We have a tent."

"Let me check with my father."

Tangboy spent a few minutes on the phone, then came back to us. He had decided to invite us to his place! "It will be safer for you," he told us without much enthusiasm. It was hard to get a smile out of Tangboy's face. We pushed Tank and Monster to his house, located about 100 meters from the church. All the children followed us, touching our bikes and Non-La hats. The house, entirely made of wood, had a small courtyard where we put our bikes. Many women were busy in the kitchen and showering the children.

Chickens pecked here and there.

"This is your room for tonight. Does it suit you?". It suited us perfectly! We had a large bed and a mosquito net. Tangboy invited us to shower before joining him for dinner. With a plastic pan that we plunged in a big water-filled barrel also made of plastic, we sprinkled our body, then soaped and rinsed ourselves. The small troop of children watched our every move. Our bicycles still intrigued them. The prepared dinner consisted of rice and chicken curry with a few vegetables. Tangboy told us about the recent problems in his village: a big flood had destroyed part of the school. The children were still there, sitting all around us. I offered to show them photos and videos of the trip on my computer. A small crowd gathered between Khanh Nguyen and me and looked at these images from so far away. Tangboy looked too, always without much reaction on his face. He then ordered the children to sing songs for us. The twenty or so little brown heads started singing songs in English and the local dialect. The older ones led the dance while the younger ones tried to follow the rhythm and the words. Each time they finished a song, we applauded them heartily. It became late, and we started to get tired. Tangboy told us that he had to go visit his sister and that he would come back later in the evening.

We prepared to go to bed. With no sign of Tangboy, we started to plunge into a deep sleep. Suddenly vigorous knocking sounded on our bedroom door: "Thibault, Khanh Nguyen! It's Tangboy, wake up!" It took me a few moments to get up and open the door for him. Tangboy sat on a chair near our bed and said:

""Thibault, you are like a brother to me. I would really like to have a memory of you and for you to keep a memory of me."

"What would make you happy, Tangboy?" I answered as I was still between sleep and wake.

"I would love to have your black jeans, the ones you were wearing tonight. I brought you a pair of jeans that belong to me!" The blue jeans that he wanted to give me were very large. He had definitely never worn them. I absolutely didn't want to part with my black jeans... They had accompanied me for more than 10,000 kilometers (6,213 miles) from France... Especially to trade them for jeans that were much too big for me.

"Don't you want another pair of my pants? I have these in gray? I bought them in Iran? Or a T-shirt?"

"Try my jeans on, Thibault. I want you to try them on", asserted Tangboy starting to frown.

The situation started to get a bit weird. Khanh Nguyen was still dozing. I took off my shorts and found myself in my underwear in front of Tangboy before putting on "his" jeans, which were way too big for me. I let out a little laugh as I tried to make Tangboy understand the absurdity of the situation.

"You see, Tangboy, They don't fit. Thank you so much for your gift but these jeans are way too big for me..."

I took the jeans off and found myself back in my underwear.

"I want a memory of you, and you must have a memory of me. It's important. I won't wear your black jeans, don't worry."

"So why do you refuse to take the grey pants that I bought in Iran? They mean a lot to me too. If you're not going to wear them, what's the difference with my black jeans?"

Tangboy scowled. He crossed his arms and didn't say a word. He was as stubborn as a mule! He didn't want to accept any of my arguments: he wanted my black jeans, period. The situation was really absurd. I started to get afraid it might get dangerous. Faced with his long silence, I kept trying to argue. He still didn't answer. It went on for almost an hour before Khanh Nguyen finally got out of bed.

"Why don't you accept his gray pants, Tangboy?" she tried to convince him with her softest voice. "These pants mean a lot to Thibault. It's a nice gift."

"Thibault is like a brother. It would make me so happy to have his black jeans... I don't understand why he refuses."

I thought back to the Kalashnikov I had seen that afternoon and thought that I shouldn't play the game too long with Tangboy. He was starting to get threatening and disturbing me. After a bit of deliberation, I gave in to Tangboy's whims. He would have my black jeans!

"Thank you, thank you. I'm so happy. I leave you my blue jeans, Thibault. Thank you!"

TanTangboy acted like a little boy after a successful tantrum. He snatched my black jeans and disappeared from the room in seconds. I lay back next to Khanh Nguyen, and we told each other that we had just lived a completely absurd and timeless moment. We relived the moment several times in order to rationalize Tangboy's attitude a little bit. It was pretty clear to me: he needed new jeans and wanted to get rid of a pair too big for him. Despite what just happened, it didn't take me long to get back to sleep.

The early morning dawned, and one of the women of the house invited us to have tea with cupcakes. Tangboy arrived nonchalantly with "my" black jeans on. He asked us which road we were going to take. Tangboy then introduced us to his father, the village chief. He was at least ninety with a huge turban perched on his head. I thanked him for welcoming us to his Kuki village. Tangboy and my black jeans then came to say goodbye to us. "Goodbye, my brother, come back and see us one day".

With that, I left my dear black jeans after more than 10,000 kilometers (6,213 miles) from France in a Kuki village in the state of Manipur. I just hoped that Tangboy would meet his future wife while wearing them. What am I going to do with the oversized jeans he gave me? The call of the road became insistent, and we left, still in the direction of Burma.

For lunch, we stopped in one of those little wooden and tin bistros by the roadside. The cooks handled the food and money with their hands and then served us large metal plates. The fish had a strong, unpleasant smell, but I told myself that it was probably the sauce. After a few hours, Khanh Nguyen started to weaken and complain of stomachaches. We were still in the middle of the mountains, and each climb was a real difficulty for her.

After a long break for lunch and medicine for dessert, she was a little better, but soon the pain started again. A night under the tent didn't help either: in the morning, Khanh Nguyen complained about her stomach cramps again. On my map, I spotted a small hospital located about 20 kilometers (12,4 miles) away, still uphill.

Those kilometers (miles) were among the most grueling of the entire trip. Khanh Nguyen's body batteries were flat, and she could barely move forward. Finally, we entered the village of Nungba. At the very top was a small hospital. After more than eight months of traveling, this was the first time we had to enter a hospital. The steep little street to get there was a final test. We didn't really know what we were going to stumble upon. I left Tank at the entrance and entered the hospital. A doctor in a white coat introduced himself to us. He looked like one of those typical uncles you find in Vietnam: an alert and laughing face and a real friendliness that gave a smile to each of his interlocutors. His name was Adim, and he spoke impeccable English. I introduced him to who we were and explained to him the pains of Khanh Nguyen in a few sentences. "It's food poisoning, she needs a lot of rest, and I will prescribe her medication. You can put her in my room. I will sleep in the dormitory with the other staff of the hospital."

Adim welcomed us with the utmost care. I accompanied Khanh Nguyen to her room and took all our luggage upstairs. Each step caused Khanh Nguyen to be in strong pain. Once back down, Adim introduced me to his team: Tana, Lungjin, and Panmei. Tana impressed me with his size and his face: with his long mustache, he looked like one of those proud Mongolian riders who cross the steppes. That beautiful team of doctors treated, vaccinated, and protected all the minorities of the region. They sometimes had to walk long hours in the jungle to reach the most remote villages. The good mood they radiated was rare: jokes and bursts of laughter fused. Tana told me:

"You both impress me! I wouldn't even dare to travel here from my village by bike... So you! You come from France. You're a bit crazy, aren't you?"

"And it's a great Mongolian rider whose ancestors rode horses all the way to Europe who tells me that!" Tana's long mustache wiggled even more beautifully as he laughed heartily.

"Lunch is almost ready! I want you to try some of our tribe's specialties."

I went back to see Khanh Nguyen who was sleeping soundly: I brought her water and some food and then went back down to have lunch with our new family. Tana and Lungjin were great cooks: they had prepared several dishes, including wild pig. It was delicious!

"Brother, here you are at the Rongmei Naga," began Panmei, who wore glasses and had hair curling over his temples. "We have our own traditions and customs and a long history."

"Two days ago, we were welcomed by the Kuki". When I pronounced the word Kuki, I saw that some of their brows furrowed.

"Brother, we're very different from the Kuki: our origins, our culture, and our history distinguish us. Among the Rongmei Naga, every decision in a village is made by an assembly of elders, whereas among the Kuki, the village chief has all the power. One thing that characterizes the Kuki: they are very stubborn!"

"I can confirm it," I answered Panmei in a burst of laughter as I thought back to the story of my black jeans...

"Brother, at home, the sense of family is very broad. Each member of our tribe is a sister or a brother. Here, all problems can be solved with the offering of a pig or a cow. A pig if it's a crime; a cow if it's a felony."

"If I own a lot of pigs and cows, I can afford to do a lot then!"

Panmei, Lungjin, Tana, and Adim exploded with laughter. I really liked our new adoptive family. Once the meal was over, I went to go and spend time with Khanh Nguyen. Her condition was stabilizing, and she was suffering less. I lay down next to her and ran my hand through her hair and over her forehead. Very quickly, she fell back into a deep sleep.

I went back down and met Adim, who was wearing a blouse. He had just helped a woman from the village give birth. The small village of Nungba was beautiful: from the roof of the hospital, we had a clear view of the mountain range, from above the cottony bed of the clouds. You could see the cars or the buses passing in front of the market with little people coming to sell or buy something: a whole theater of trade. The temperatures here were cool and pleasant. The air was pure and good to breathe. I felt good here in our new family, and I thought back to an aphorism of Nietzsche::

"*Always at home.*

One day we reach our goal – and now point with pride to the long travels we undertook to reach it. In fact, we were not even aware of traveling. But we got so far because we fancied at every point that we were at home."

We spent three days with our new family Rongmei Naga while Khanh Nguyen recovered enough strength to continue. They took care of us, pampered us, coddled us. Each meal was an opportunity to talk about our respective cultures, anecdotes, and philosophical reflections on a good life. Once back on her feet, Khanh Nguyen joined our conversation. All our brothers called her "sister". She really looked like a local girl. When we both walked around Nungba, the local old women had to indulge themselves in all the gossip: "Oh, where did she get that foreigner? Are you sure she's from the village? Isn't she more of a Kuki?"...

Time passed, and trust established itself. Everyone began to tell more personal stories. Out of respect to them, I won't reveal them here. But I want to mention so to highlight how special the bond became between all of us in just a few days. This was the beauty we often found throughout our adventures. Each event, even an unfavorable one - a flat tire, food poisoning – always gave us the opportunity to share in our common humanity with others. Our journey was alchemical: it could transform lead into gold. The opportunities to discover, to grow, to love were inexhaustible.

After three days, Khanh Nguyen was more or less able to leave. We still had about one hundred and twenty kilometers (74 miles) before

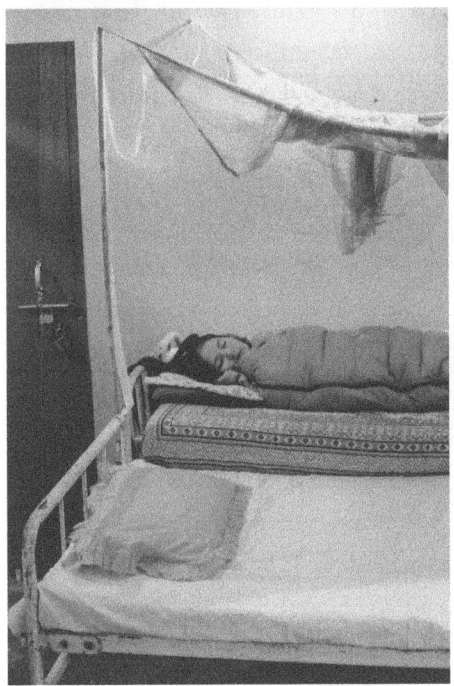

Before, during and after food poisoning.
With Panmei on the third picture, Manipur, India

reaching Imphal, the last big city before Burma. We still had two or three passes to cross to reach Imphal. For our adoptive father, Adim, there was no way we were leaving by bike: "Khanh Nguyen's stomach is still fragile. It's likely to relapse if you go back on the road quickly. Take the bus to Imphal". Adim was right. We would take the bus.

On the morning of departure, we left our hospital in Nungba, our house, our family. It was still the early morning when we got off the bus with our bikes. A sea of clouds was under our feet, there in the valley: what an epiphany! The bus to Imphal cost us about fifteen US dollars each. Tank and Monster would be placed on the roof. The driver, a small inexperienced young man, mistreated our two mounts. I told him to be careful. He even installed Tank on the derailleur side, which was the worst thing to do. I yelled at him to stop before installing the bikes by myself with cords so that they didn't move.

All our friends were there to say goodbye: dad Adim and our Rongmei Naga brothers: Panmei, Lungjin, and Tana. We thanked all of them one by one, then destiny for having enabled that magnificent meeting. Tana, the beautiful Mongolian rider, even offered us a typical Rongmei Naga necklace with its yellow, black, and white colors.

On the bus, we were accompanied by five other people: three men and two women. The road was riddled with holes, and the curves followed one another. After only a few minutes, one of the passengers started to vomit. Every time the bus ran over a pothole, I prayed for Tank and Monster. The young driver had poor visibility and risked it all every time the bus rounded the road curves. Hours, turns, and military checkpoints followed one another. About thirty kilometers (18 miles) from Imphal, the small bus stopped: everyone had to get off. The driver explained to us that today he would stop there and that it was non-negotiable. I looked at the other passengers, who seemed to resign themselves. I, however, couldn't let that go: the contract had been to drive us to Imphal. Khanh Nguyen was still weak, and she would have to pedal for thirty kilometers! I pushed the driver to drive us further. He refused, so I refused to pay. He either had to reimburse us for everything or drive us to Imphal. His boss, with a head full of scars, arrived. Rather than making things worse, I calmly explained our situation to him. He still refused to drive us to Imphal and so made us pay one ticket instead of two.

The goal now was for Khanh Nguyen to be able to pedal to Imphal. Fortunately, the road became flat again for about thirty kilometers (18 miles). We left the mountains to join a large valley where the capital of Manipur was located. In less than two hours, we were able to reach Imphal without any further stomachaches.

In Imphal, we built up strength for what was to come. We also took the opportunity to change Monster's bike chain, which was beginning to weaken. The last time we had changed it was in Iran, in Isfahan. Tank's chain, I hoped, would hold until Vietnam.

We made another vital purchase: new black jeans that I found in a local market! Due to the lack of space in my bags, I left the XXL size jeans that Tangboy, the son of the Kuki village chief, had given me. Since the latter had my phone number, I asked Khanh Nguyen to take a picture of me while I was wearing Tangboy's *gift*. I looked like a pound shop Charlie Chaplin with my XXL size jeans! Now, if Tangboy ever asked me: "Thibault, are you wearing my gift?" I could promptly present pictures of me in his jeans to him. That way, I would avoid any diplomatic issues, which would surely lead to a devastating war with the Kukis tribe!

After a few days in Imphal, Khanh Nguyen felt capable of leaving. We needed to cycle a little more than one hundred kilometers (62 miles) through the mountains to reach the border with Burma, which was located at the level of the city of Moreh. Rather than spending the night in a shabby hotel in Moreh, we chose to spend one last night in India under the tent in the mountains. In the morning, we met a group of soldiers who magically appeared among the bushes and tall grass.

Northeast India had been a real gem for us. Before heading down towards Moreh and the border with Burma, I thought one last time about the hundreds of school children from Gossaigaon and their hugs, about Tangboy and my black jeans, about Nungba, our family Rongmei Naga, and our first visit to the hospital, which I hoped would be the last. However, the greatest of all dangers still remained omnipresent: a road accident; perhaps a careless semi-trailer driver. I touched the necklace the Rongmei Naga had given me for protection around my neck. After more than eight months on the roads, we were finally going to return to Southeast Asia. Vietnam seemed so close on the map, but there were still 5,000 kilometers (3,100 miles) to go to Saigon. It was the same distance from Vendée, France to Bulgaria had been!

Chapter 22

Myanmar: Cat and Mouse with the local police

Mileage Meter: 10,902 to 12,237km (6,774 to 7,603 miles)

The passage between India and Myanmar was through the city of Moreh known for its trafficking and the black market. We didn't linger there. There were no problems at the border: the immigration officers didn't even bother to scan all our luggage. Arriving in the small town of Tamuh, we exchanged our currency for local currencies, purchased a Sim card, had the first meal, discovering the national flavors in the process. Myanmar is a country that has always fascinated me by its culture and its people. It was a country apart from the others we experienced for many reasons.

Many Burmese people apply thanaka powder, obtained from the bark of a tree, to their face. It's off-white or even yellowish. Men and women put it on their faces for its cosmetic virtues, protection against the sun, and simply for aesthetics. Many Burmese citizens apply the powder in patterns and curves of their choice in an expression of their individuality. Some that we saw had drawn adorable little circles on their cheeks, others long grooves with the help of a Banyan leaf, and all were the personification of elegance. Culturally it is necessary to pay attention to the clothes they wear and that they are always clean. I hoped that we wouldn't look too uncivilized with our dusty bodies and clothes drenched in sweat.

Myanmar is also a country where Buddhist practices are central to their way of life. Prayer and festivals punctuate the days of the Burmese. Each village had several pagodas and stupas. The monks - both male and female - were omnipresent. Every morning we could see them walking in long lines along the roads in search of offerings. It had taken a lot of money to build all those pagodas: we regularly came across stands along the roads, located near the construction of a pagoda where women asked for offerings from passers-by. They didn't fail to greet us every time we passed in front of them!

More than cultural specificities, what would be the biggest challenge for us were the tourism rules. The Burmese were prohibited from welcoming foreigners into their homes. It was, therefore, illegal to ask a pagoda or a church to accommodate us for the night. We could only sleep in hotels that had a license to receive tourists. I looked at our Myanmar map and quickly realized that sometimes two hotels that had such a license were located more than one hundred and fifty kilometers (93 miles) away from each other. To complicate things even further: camping was strictly forbidden! There had been copious anecdotes from travelers on blogs about their encounters with the local police: a night at the station, a confiscated tent or even a jail stay for some! Khanh Nguyen had reflected when we researched it all: "It will take us a lot of energy is to find a place to sleep every night!" But I hadn't realized quite how right she would end up being.

Our first Burmese days were a flavor of first times: the landscapes, the locals living all around us, the trees, their shadows, and the animals. Even the wind seemed to whisper new sounds into our ears. We pedaled effortlessly on beautiful roads entirely absent of cars or trucks. Most of the children we met said "hello" or "bye-bye" to greet us. We experienced great generosity. I was offered fruit or tea several times. On one occasion, a young Burmese boy silently came and had lunch next to us. Before finishing his meal, he asked us where we came from. When he was ready to leave on his motorcycle, he announced to us: "I invite you for lunch! Enjoy our country!" He then left at full speed on his motorbike without either Khanh Nguyen or me having the time to thank him or catch up. Cycling in Burma during the day was thus done in a good mood and in a state of total relaxation.

As we pedaled southbound, a silhouette appeared on the horizon on the other side of the small road. It was a bike! We had the sun blinding our sight, and it was difficult to distinguish if it was a local or a long-distance traveler. We stopped to wait for the meeting which soon arrived. It was a long-distance traveler, and of a certain age! He had two saddlebags at the back of his bike but without the two saddlebags at the front, like on Tank and Monster. The man stopped at our level and started the conversation:

"Hello friends, where are you going? My name is Frank, and your names are?"

"Hello, Frank! My name is Thibault, and this is Khanh Nguyen! I'm French, and she's Vietnamese. We are married, and it's kinda our honeymoon," I answered, still short of breath.

"I come from the Netherlands. I landed in Hanoi, Vietnam, and I'm going to Delhi, India. And what about you?"

"We left France, and we are planning to arrive in Saigon, also in Vietnam!"

"Ha, it's beautiful! You are going to see Myanmar it's great. It climbs up steeply sometimes..."

"What about where to sleep? Do you have any advice? It sounds complicated..."

"I travel without a tent, so I have to find a hotel every night. Once, I had to take a cab because the night was falling and I couldn't arrive by myself... Otherwise, do it like a couple I met about a week ago: you wait until nightfall and pitch your tent behind the bushes out of sight! You'll have to pack up early in the morning," replied Frank with an air of challenge in his eyes.

"Let's try it then! For what awaits you, it will be easier to find accommodation in North-East India. You can always count on the hospitality of the locals as well as the welcome of the churches."

"And, if it's not too indiscreet, how old are you?" asked Khanh Nguyen politely.

"I'm... seventy years old!"

"Respect!" I replied with admiration.

Frank still had a long way to go that day. He had time for a quick picture, then away he went. I hoped that when we reached our seventies, we would have half of his spirit: still exploring new parts of the world by bike. Regularly throughout our journey, we came across people afraid of the unknown, of failure, persuading themselves that they were condemned to a life in bondage, without bounce, and without panache. Several times during the trip, I had heard: "I would love to do something like you... but I'm too old." or "Ah, if I were still young...". The people who uttered such sentences weren't even close to seventy but sometimes fifty or forty years old! What had happened to cause such restraint? By the diversity of its postures, ambitions, and renunciations, the human soul takes more than a lifetime to understand in its most subtle mechanics. What worthier investigation could you undertake? What better way to find answers than risking it all? For me, the best time to start is before you have to ask yourself the question, but the second-best time would be that day.

The afternoon was beginning to stretch to its end, and we needed to find a place to sleep. Northwest Myanmar is home to a large Christian community. Near the city of Khampat, I decided to try my luck with a Baptist church. I felt that the police would surely try to evict us, but I counted on beginner's luck. A nice lady was overseeing the decoration of the church with garlands – it would be Christmas soon. She indicated a small wooden house where the pastor lived. When we arrived at the house, his wife opened the door and called her husband who was somewhere in the neighborhood.

Two minutes went by, and out he came: around fifty years old with a beautifully trimmed mustache. All smiles, I asked him if we could spend the night, but he seemed embarrassed at the question and told me that he had to check with his superiors: "There are no hotels for foreigners in the city, so I should be able to welcome you," he said more confidently. After a brief call in Burmese, he turned to us: "It's okay! You can sleep here tonight. The only instruction is that you shouldn't go out after dark". We thanked him for his hospitality. We could shower outside and sleep in the small office where volunteers worked during the day. But I never really felt comfortable. I always had the unpleasant feeling that the police would come out of

First Burmese kilometers, Tamuh, Myanmar

nowhere at a late hour. I had trouble falling asleep that night.

The next morning, I opened my blue eyes wide, sighing in relief at processing that the police hadn't come knocking! I thanked the pastor and his family several times for having welcomed us in such good conditions. Our discovery of Myanmar continued. Our first climbs arrived as well as our inevitable perspiration. That day and its eighty kilometers (50 miles) passed by steadily. A few hours before nightfall, the same question arose: where would we be able to sleep? On *Google Maps*, I spotted a pagoda, isolated from the main road. If nobody from the village saw us, it could be attempted.

We had to turn right onto a dirt road to reach the pagoda. The street was deserted: we were going! I arrived first in a large courtyard in front of a gigantic pagoda which was two hundred meters long. There were only two young Buddhist monks there with shaved heads, wearing beautiful orange robes. They didn't speak English so I prepared a short translation on my phone for them, illustrating who we were and if we could spend the night. The taller of the two answered a big "Yes" and got us to hide our bikes behind the stairs. I understood immediately that it was to avoid attracting the attention of one of the potential snitches in the village. He then beckoned us upstairs, where a much older and corpulent monk sat on a small wooden chair. He had a deep and authoritative voice tinged with benevolence. We were certain he was the head monk of that pagoda. I tried to make a little conversation via my phone, which amused him. He offered Khanh Nguyen a cookie packet and told us that we could leave him. The youngest of the monks then led us inside the gigantic pagoda. The wood that it was composed of was immense but decorated in a pleasingly straightforward way. The short monk installed us behind two large screens: where two floor mats and pillows were positioned. For the shower: we'd have to go outside. Khanh Nguyen, fearing that she'd be exposed, decided to fill a large bucket with water and washed in the bathroom, out of sight.

We rested behind the screens for an hour while the sun set. "Would the police arrive that night?" I thought. I hoped they wouldn't.

The sun set. The open sky, not quite blue anymore, suddenly filled with beautiful tangerine orange. The two young monks then gathered in front of the Buddha; the old monk stood in front of them, also in front of the Buddha. Khanh Nguyen beckoned for me to sit behind them to join in with their prayers. Inside the huge room, there were only the three monks and us. That moment was among the most mystical of our whole adventure. The three monks chanted melodiously in a loop of phrases projected throughout the pagoda and echoed reason as if by magic. I closed my eyes and let myself be carried away by the heady melody. The songs lasted a few minutes or a few hours. I almost lost track of time. Everyone then bowed three times. Finally, the youngest of the monks stood next to the gong and struck it five times in different places. Each of his percussion had a different tone that fit as if it were in harmony with the others. It required great mastery to express so much with so little. Once the last note was played, the five notes slowly dissipated, giving way to a deep silence.

My eyes were still closed as I heard the three monks get up and leave the room. I opened my eyes at the same time Khanh Nguyen did: we looked at each other without saying anything, convinced that we had experienced something out of time. We spent a few hours alone in the pagoda until the two young monks came back and went to bed in the corner of the room. I dozed off serenely, without fear. I felt confident the police wouldn't be coming that night: Buddha had welcomed us into his home.

Around four in the morning, we heard a noise in the pagoda. The monks were there, as well as some of the faithful. It was the morning prayer. We participated right away, despite our sleepiness. Once the prayer was over, the old monk then told us to go to the dining room. A table had been set up just for us. There were about ten vegetarian dishes accompanied by rice. Each dish was tasty and deliciously prepared: eggplant, sweet potato, bindweed. The old monk was having lunch at another table next to ours.

We enjoyed the variety and flavors of the dishes in silence.

Sleeping in Myanmar seemed to be less of an obstacle course than I had imagined. We respectfully greeted our three hosts for an evening that would stay with us forever.

We continued to follow the main road, which led us to the majestic Bagan. Buffaloes and goats grazed here and there; tamarind and jackfruit trees spread all around. After about ninety kilometers (56 miles), we started to gain the confidence to find a place to spend the night.

We used the same technique: I spotted a remote pagoda on the map, and headed towards it as discreetly as possible. The pagoda was even more splendid than the one from yesterday and with an imposing stupa that shone gold. People from the village were walking around the pagoda. The same scenario we'd experienced before followed: a young monk welcomed us and made us go upstairs to his master. The master was young this time but still accepted our request for the night. However, he took a picture of our two passports which he sent on his cell phone to one of his contacts. I thanked him from the bottom of my heart for welcoming us. Two small monks prepared our room on the second floor: they swept, brought mattresses, quilts, and two blankets. A shower was also available on the second floor. We were truly blessed. After a life-saving shower was taken, we went back down to visit the surroundings.

A group of women, all with thanaka on their faces, prepared flowers to decorate the different corners of the pagoda. As we walked around the imposing stupa, a man in longyi greeted us and offered to take a picture of us with all these beautiful women and their countless flower bouquets. The proposal was so rare that I immediately accepted it. A bit taller than me, the man smiled at me with his teeth full of red stains, characteristic of betel. After some photos were taken together, Khanh Nguyen went back up to our room. I took one last picture, and then it was my turn to go back up.

But very quickly, I realized that I was being followed. There were three men in longyi accompanied by the one who was pretending to be our friend. In a fraction of a nanosecond, I immediately understood that

Night at the pagoda, Myanmar

The Burmese countryside, Myanmar

it was the police. I feigned nonchalance as I strode back to our room. Khanh Nguyen was sat down and watched me enter. I told her, "It's the police". She regained composure before seeing the men in longyi arrive in our room. I sat next to her on the carpet as the men in longyi came inside. All five of them got down and sat in front of us without saying a word. A strange minute followed where we looked at them in the whites of their eyes without really knowing what to do. None of them spoke English. The youngest one, who had slicked back his hair, started mimicking a passport. I handed him our papers.

The five police officers meticulously inspected every page of our passports, going through as though secret entries were suddenly going to be revealed to them. The wait was starting to get interminable when a young woman entered the room. She spoke hesitant but comprehensible English:

"You can't stay here tonight. It's too dangerous..."

"Do you mean that the pagoda is a dangerous place?" I asked her, playing the fool.

"No..."

"You mean we are dangerous then?"

"No, I don't mean..."

"I don't quite understand then why it's dangerous..."

"It's that according to the laws of our country, you can't stay here. This is for your safety. You have to sleep in a hotel for foreigners."

"It's already dark, and the next hotel for foreigners is in Gangaw... more than fifty kilometers (31 miles) away. We can't get there tonight by bike... Riding at night is too dangerous."

"These policemen tell me that they have planned a small van to take you to Gangaw. It should arrive in twenty minutes."

"Very well then... " I agreed spitefully.

The young monk in charge of the pagoda then entered. He chatted with the police for a few moments. By his voice and gestures, I understood that he was trying to convince them to leave us there for that night. The young rooster with his slicked-back hair seemed determined not to give in, however. After a few rounds of negotiations, the young monk left the room.

It was all over for us. I got up, so did Khanh Nguyen. We began to pack up while darkness reigned outside.

A few moments passed before the small van they'd arranged made its entrance in the pagoda's courtyard. The five policemen helped us with our luggage and got everything into the van. The night was going to be cool, so we put on our coats. On a second-floor balcony, the young monk stood, spectator to our hasty departure. I said goodbye with my hand and tried, as much as I could, to apologize with my look and my attitude for all the disturbance caused by our fault. He gave a small, benevolent smile.

The slick-haired young policeman and one of his acolytes sat in the back with us. He was just doing his job, but I couldn't help but not want to be cordial. The driver of the van started the engine. We sped into the dark Burmese night towards Gangaw and its fifty kilometers (31 miles). The fresh wind rushed in at the back of the vehicle as we went. Khanh Nguyen huddled up close to me, trying to take the least uncomfortable position possible. The slick-haired policeman made several calls. He showed me his phone where a hotel in the town of Gangaw was displayed: the *Gangaw hotel*. Assuming that he would get a commission on our night that night, I indicated another hotel where I wanted to sleep to him instead: the *Gangaw Aung Si Hein Motel* to which he pouted and scowled. He turned off his phone and didn't speak to me for the rest of the journey.

After more than an hour trying to conserve what little energy we had left, we arrived at the *Gangaw Aung Si Hein Motel*. The policemen accompanied us to the reception. The night there was fifteen US dollars and non-negotiable. I accepted immediately and gave our passports in. With two policemen, I went to get Tank, Monster, and all our luggage. I tied our two mounts under the stairs and joined Khanh Nguyen in the elevator with all our luggage. I said a short goodbye to the two policemen who helped me with the luggage, ignoring the slick-haired one.

We pushed open the bedroom door and slumped down on our double bed. At least there, we could hug each other and regain our intimacy as a couple. It had been an emotional roller coaster of a day. I didn't have a spark of energy left in me. The little game with the police had pumped me up with a phenomenal amount of energy, and our day's experience had discouraged me from having any temptation to do it again over the following few days. Our small convoy had at least allowed us to advance fifty kilometers (31 miles), though. We were only two hundred kilometers (124 miles) away from the Kingdom of Bagan and its thousands of pagodas, where a small surprise was awaiting us.

Sleep and night could finally play their part at the *Gangaw Aung Si Hein Motel*.

Gangaw woke up slowly, and so did we. We went downstairs to have breakfast in a shop next to the hotel. While we drank our tea with milk, paranoia invaded us little by little. We now had the impression we were permanently being observed by police officers or informers. "And don't you think he's a cop with his newspaper? And him with his glasses and his coffee?" Khanh Nguyen laughed.

Our little daily routine was back on track: Tank and Monster tire pressure checks, luggage installation, sunscreen, water bottle filling, and off we went. The road that led us to Bagan wasn't the easiest. The Burmese engineers there hadn't bothered to build roads that wound around the summit. There, the road went straight, stretching towards the summit instead. The resulting incline gradients of ascent were infernal, even more so with the midday sun hitting our skulls. Each ascent was done in pain and with liters of water. On several occasions, I finished first, far ahead of Khanh Nguyen, left Tank at the top and ran towards her so I could push her at arm's length. The descents, often steep and bumpy, didn't bring any relief.

Two or three days were spent enduring pain, heat, and sweat. But at the end was Bagan, the kingdom of a thousand pagodas. After our long efforts, the kind that must leave traces in your muscle tissues, we finally left the mountains. We reached a large plain that should lead us to the city of Pale, the last step before Bagan. There, the carts were pulled by oxen; the rhythm of life was recalled a time gone by in Europe.

That night, it would be a hotel at twenty thousand kyats[1] a night. We needed to rest, and I didn't feel like playing hide and seek with the police again. It was a small family *guesthouse* with decent rooms. The owner was a plump woman who, despite her omnipresent laughter, was deeply unpleasant. We would sleep on the second floor that night. It was time to take a shower to relieve me of all my dust. I went down a set of small wooden stairs, Khanh Nguyen following close behind. It was dark now, and the light hadn't yet been turned on at the reception where there were two teenagers in charge of room service.

Suddenly, I heard a loud crash and a scream. I turned around, already anticipating what I might see. It was Khanh Nguyen: already on the ground. She had missed the last step of the stairs and was wallowing in self-pity on the floor. I rushed towards her to make sure that everything was okay, but it wasn't. She writhed in pain, clutching her ankle. The two teenagers at the counter were laughing. I glanced at them with a dark look: "She falls down, and you laugh... What is that?" They seemed to apologize and ran for help. I made her sit on the bench. I looked at the step from which she had fallen. It was the same color as the floor! It was the least well-thought-out staircase in the world. While I took off her shoe and sock, a Burmese man also made their way down those perilous steps and missed the final step, catching himself on the railing with a bewildered look. He certainly wouldn't be the last.

Khanh Nguyen's ankle was either broken, cracked, or sprained. I started to project the worst scenarios in my head. What if that was the end of the trip? On the road, anything could have happened... an accident with a car, that guy shooting at us with his Kalashnikov, fatal food poisoning, brakes breaking, but stopping because of a wobbly step would be the most

---

[1] About fifteen dollars USD

anticlimactic end possible! I counterbalanced these fears by presenting my most optimistic self to the world: "It's okay, it's nothing. We'll see... Don't you want to try to walk a little?" Khanh Nguyen also wanted to believe in it. She got up and walked with difficulty: she limped. We ate pasta soup with chicken in a small restaurant ten meters (3 feet) away from the hotel. The situation wasn't really improving: her ankle had swelled. I took her back to our room and went out to buy ice and a topical cream to soothe her injury. When I came back with the precious products, Khanh Nguyen was lying on the bed. I took all the precautions in the world to apply the ice first for a long time, then the cream and bandage.

That night, I slept badly. I looked with concern at Khanh Nguyen sleeping peacefully. The next morning, we anxiously removed the bandage, revealing that her ankle had doubled in size. I went downstairs and asked if one of the teenagers could take her by motorcycle to the small hospital a kilometer away. I followed them by bike. We then rode along the main street of Pale towards the small country hospital. Fortunately, a nurse spoke English and inspected Khanh Nguyen. She immediately proposed to get an x-ray scan. Many Burmese were all around us and must have wondered what we were doing there.

A few minutes later, a doctor with a mouth, red from chewing betel, came towards us with Khanh Nguyen's ankle scan. We listened to him feverishly: "Nothing is broken. It's just sprained. You need to rest for at least ten days." The verdict was in. We were torn between the relief that nothing was broken and the obligation to stop for at least ten days. The Burmese tourist visa only gave us the right to twenty-eight on the territory: we had already burned seven of them. I thanked the doctor and the nurses for their welcome and their care.

Back at the hotel, we decided to take the bus the next morning to Bagan, located one hundred and twenty kilometers (74 miles) away. I did everything I could so that Khanh Nguyen kept off her ankle. As I left, I tried to make the owner understand that she should really change the color of her last step. She giggled haughtily and ignored me.

From the bus window, the landscapes scrolled by. The nature was splendid. There were particularly majestic sugar palms: big stems with multiple inflorescences at the end. And then, very quickly, we crossed the mythical Irrawaddy, which is formed in the Himalayan mountains to water the Burmese plains from North to South of the country. After crossing the long bridge over the Irrawaddy, we finally entered the kingdom of Bagan. Bagan was the capital of the first Burmese empire from the 9th to the 12th centuries and spread throughout the region. It still has thousands of temples and stupas, a large part of which were still remarkably well preserved, over a huge territory. It is also home to some of the most beautiful statues of Buddhas in the world. There were worse places than Bagan for our ten days of forced convalescence!

The bus wasn't allowed to ride into the historic site of Bagan. It left us at the entrance with our bikes and all our material. Khanh Nguyen assured me that she could ride for the two kilometers that we had to do before arriving at the hotel. As often, I admired her perseverance and her resistance to pain and ache. The two kilometers (1.2 miles) were completed in slow motion but fortunately without any cry of pain. The hotel where we were going to stay for a week was run by a large Burmese family where each family member had a very precise task. It was calm and well placed near the most beautiful temples of the site.

A small surprise awaited us in Bagan. It must be said that for several weeks now, our fame had been going into a crescendo, especially in Vietnam. A large national newspaper talked about us and then very quickly many others so that the television also made a small report about us. We were on the news on a channel equivalent to the BBC. The Vietnamese liked our story the more they heard about it: the one of a Franco-Vietnamese couple who were cycling for their honeymoon trip from France to Vietnam wearing two Vietnamese Non-La hats and raising funds for an association here in Vietnam. We were a bowl of cherries to them.

A few weeks before, VTV1, the most-watched channel in Vietnam, had contacted us. They asked us if they could come and meet us somewhere on our journey to make a documentary about us! We said yes immediately. It was a fantastic opportunity to reach a large audience who would significantly increase the fund for the children of *Poussières de Vie*. We proposed Bagan as our meeting spot: the setting had the merit of being superb for beautiful images, and they said yes immediately too!

Before the cameras arrived a few days later, we enjoyed the timeless site of Bagan. The site was so vast that it was easy to find ourselves completely alone among the ruins and feel like one was the first to enter a temple where a centuries-old Buddha was located. The day had to start early, though: before sunrise and the dozens of hot-air balloons that took off with it. It was always a magical moment to see those huge balloons flying over the temples. We let ourselves get lost along the small sandy paths, which snaked around the site, discovering architectural pearls at random, rubbing shoulders with the Burmese themselves, who had also come to discover their heritage. That day passed so quickly among the temples and stupas. In the end, we hurried to find a high point to admire the sunset. Once found, all that was left to do was to let ourselves be carried away in the magic of our surroundings. We admired the beautiful course of the sun reflecting on the domes of the temples, revealing an infinite variety of colors. Herds of cows passed in front of us as nightfall arrived, leaving behind them a beautiful screen of dust which gave the place an even more solemn and majestic dimension.

To be there with Khanh Nguyen was worth all the gold, silver, and copper in the world to me. As with Persepolis in Iran, to have come all the way there by bike gave us a sense of accomplishment that was second to none. Once again, I felt that my life had entered another dimension. I fully accepted the death that awaited me, whether it was tomorrow or in sixty years.

The VTV1 team met us in a small restaurant in Bagan. They had arrived that next morning: first, they would scout a location and the day after, we had the full day to do the report. There were three men: a cameraman, a sound engineer, and Lam, the show's star presenter. Lam, with his round glasses, put us at ease right away with his availability and simplicity. He immediately asked Khanh Nguyen how her ankle was doing and assured her that it was up to her if she wanted to pedal tomorrow or not. If she didn't want to, we would improvise!. After a copious breakfast offered by Lam, we all agreed to meet the next day at five in the morning for the sunrise.

The alarm rang at four. We left on our bikes, wrapped in the silence of the night. Our shadows crept among the temples and stupas of Bagan. The crew was waiting for us, just for us. Khanh Nguyen didn't complain about her painful ankle and moved forward at her own pace. We branched off to take a small path that led to a group of several temples. The TV team arrived about twenty minutes later.

As soon as the first rays of sunshine appeared, we shot as many videos and sequences of us surrounded by the temples as we could together. From right to left and then from left to right. For another shot, the cameraman sat on the back of an electric scooter and filmed us in action on our bicycles. I told myself that they would make beautiful images, a beautiful memory for our children and us... Lam then sat down with us and took the time to ask us many questions, giving the charitable dimension of our project the most attention. We shared our most beautiful memories, our moments of doubt too. I already talked with nostalgia for Iran, Georgia, North-East India. We weren't so far from Vietnam anymore. I contemplated if I really want to arrive at our destination, if I wanted it all to be over. I was starting to worry about the after. How could we get back to a *normal life*, paying rent, earning a salary? How could we not savor new encounters and landscapes daily? How could we stay in the same place for several months, nailed to the ground? I pulled myself together and told myself that I had to go back one day. After having read Ulysses' The Odessey, I knew that journeys only really make sense if they have a destination. Without one, it's little better than aimlessly wandering, and from that would come madness.

I kept all these thoughts and instincts deep inside, keeping them from Lam and Khanh Nguyen. The day with VTV1 went beautifully: they didn't force things and put us in the best condition to obtain beautiful images. "The show will be broadcast in about a month," said Lam as he left us with his two colleagues. Their plane for Rangoon was tomorrow morning. We said goodbye and hoped to see each other again on their TV set in Hanoi.

We took advantage of Bagan for a few more days while Khanh Nguyen recovered properly from her sprained ankle. It would soon be a week since the accident, but we couldn't really hold on anymore. We could've waited at least ten days as recommended by the doctor in Pale, but the call of the road was getting louder and louder. I suggested that we pedal for the day and see how things went. We still had more than eight hundred kilometers (500 miles) left before reaching Thailand.

The first steps were going well. We were now at December's end, and the temperatures were pleasant to pedal in. Let's say that we only sweated after twenty minutes of cycling instead of the usual two minutes... The profile became mountainous again, and the ground dry. There wasn't a drop of water there. We took extra water bottles, just in case, despite the jars full of water along the roads. With clear water inside, these jars were at the disposal of the locals who worked in the fields and of travelers whenever they were needed. With the food poisoning of Khanh Nguyen still in our minds, we avoided putting our lips to them...

Khanh Nguyen's ankle held out. It was only at the end of the day that she began to feel tired, which then faded away during the night. I was hopeful that the injury would soon be a winter memory. We continued to advance south towards Thailand and the border town of Mae Sot.

It was then New Year's Eve. For the night, I spotted a guesthouse in the town of Takton that accepted foreigners. It was the only one in the city we passed through. We dropped our bikes in front of it, and I headed towards the reception while Khanh Nguyen kept an eye on Monster and Tank. I greeted the young woman at the reception and asked her in English:

"How much does a room cost for two people and one night?"

"It's 50,000 kyats[1]..."

"50,000 kyats! But that's almost three times more expensive than elsewhere!"

"We have only a few rooms left, and that's our price for tonight..."

"Is it impossible to make a small discount?"

"No, it's 50,000 kyats."

Faced with this impossibility to negotiate, I mumbled a small goodbye and left. We had experienced the hard law of supply and demand. It was the only hotel within a fifty-kilometer (31 miles) radius, so they could apply the price of their choice. I grumpily informed Khanh Nguyen of the price, and she categorically refused it. What other options did we have, I wondered: ask a pagoda to welcome us? It was already too late, and the chances of it working were so low. We could only sleep in our old tent.

We took our time in Takton until the night was fully restored. We enjoyed a hearty dinner with rice, boiled beef, and large salad leaves. It was time to go. On *Google Maps*, I spotted a large area without houses near Takton. It was worth a try! We pedaled two kilometers (1.2 miles) after leaving the city and took a path that quickly went away from the main road. There were fields all around us and indeed not a house in sight. Rare motorcycles whose headlights illuminated the surroundings ran along the path. So, we waited for the right moment to leave the path and blend in with the scenery. Always in fear of being reported to the local police, we had to be as invisible as possible.

---

[1] About thirty-six dollars USD

Bagan, its cows, sunsets and VTV1, Myanmar

We left the path as soon as possible and sheltered behind a big tree that hid us from the road. The place was certainly not perfect for installing our tent, but it would do the trick while we waited an hour or two to dive into the dark night and make sure the place was safe. We lay Tank and Monster close to us and let the time go by. Our rare whispers broke the silence, which could also be interrupted by an old motorcycle or a tractor returning from the fields.

One or two hours later, I signaled to Khanh Nguyen that we would take refuge behind a large haystack that the farmers must have made that day. It was a good hiding place for that night. We pushed the bikes up to it, unpacked our gear and set up our tent. Everything was ready when a gigantic beam of light appeared in the distance. It reminded me of the blinding lights projected by the watchtowers in some bad escape movies. The beam of light seemed to be looking for something in a field a little further away. It swept the space from right to left... I whispered with a certain fear to Khanh Nguyen: "We have been denounced, and the police are looking for us! They will inevitably find us and see our tent".

One, two, and finally, three lights were constantly crisscrossing the fields. We had to put everything back in the bags and quickly. If they saw our tent, we could end up in jail. We tidied everything up frantically. The night was so dark that I was afraid to lose our things, but in less than three minutes we'd everything was packed up, and we were ready to escape. Khanh Nguyen saw that I was in a state of extreme stress. I was sweating and behaving erratically. She tried to reason with me: "Thibault, take a deep breath. They aren't looking for us. Let's wait here. If they see us, we will tell them that we are lost". She hugged me, and I tried to take a normal breath. The halos of light moved away from us.

We were still waiting, still sheltered behind the haystack. Calm returned; the lights disappeared. It was already so late, and we were both exhausted. For the second time, we unpacked all the luggage and pitched our tent. I was about to slip into it when the halos of light returned. This time they were everywhere: in front, behind and closer and closer to us. I shouted, "Let's pack it all up! Quickly!" I dismantled the tent, Khanh

Nguyen put away all our stuff. The lights continued to sweep the area. As soon as one of them arrived to land on us, I threw myself on the ground or behind the haystack. Everything was ready on the bikes: let's go! We pushed our mounts into the night, taking care that no light went towards us. I knew we were going to run into the police but they wouldn't be able to blame us for anything. I would pretend that we were going to that charming 50,000 kyats a night hotel in Takton.

We reappeared on the path. A light in the distance faced us. We were in the middle of Celine's *Journey to the End of the Night* when the narrator gets lost during the night on a battlefield during World War I. I managed to regain my composure, and Khanh Nguyen followed me. I expected to run into a policeman or an armed soldier, but under the headlamp was a man with his clothes, rain boots, and a net. In a split second, I realized my foolishness, my mistake. Those hadn't been policemen looking for us in the fields those last few hours, but farmers who hunted for pests! They used their headlamps to spot their prey. I felt so stupid and relieved at the same time. Fatigue and paranoia hadn't mixed well together. In any case, we would've had to change location, though. Those farmers would have eventually spotted us.

We were back on the saddle again. When the farmers and their beams of light crossed paths, they looked at us, dazed, as if surprised to see us appearing out of nowhere. The main road was redeployed in front of us, and we followed it for a short kilometer (mile) to find a good place to put our tent for the third time. A little further in the fields was a grove surrounded by tall grass. We did our little choreography a third time. Overwhelmed by tiredness, we slipped into our comforter. We recalled that day's events and twists, and we fell asleep against each other.

I set my alarm a little before sunrise and it played its role perfectly. The night hadn't been restful, and I felt that some of my muscles were a little sore. Khanh Nguyen complained a little about her ankle but, according to her, it was only temporary. It was the last day of the year and we needed to mark the occasion. We had two choices: Naypyidaw and its sixty kilometers (37 miles) or Tangu and its one hundred and forty kilometers (87 miles). Naypyidaw was the recent capital of Myanmar. A city taken from irrelevance and obscurity to become the heart of the Burmese administration. Travelers knew naypyidaw to be a ghost town completely disproportionate with wide highways where nobody traveled. There were also gigantic hotels completely empty. Gloomier places for the evening of December thirty-first would be hard to find! The road was flat. We had some tail wind: We decided to pedal to Tangu, which seemed more desirable. If we arrived there, it would be the longest distance we had covered since the beginning of the trip.

The wind was in our favor, and it was pushing us with all its might. The kilometers (miles) passed quickly. We easily exceeded twenty kilometers (12.5 miles) per hour on average... Before lunchtime, we passed the dreadful Naypyidaw and continued along *road number one* to Tangu. That day went well, and we didn't stop drinking or eating the few fruits we had left. It was about 4 o'clock when we approached Tangu. We had just beaten our record of kilometers (miles)! At one moment, I turned around and saw Khanh Nguyen, who was struggling to continue. She couldn't take it anymore. The day before, the difficult night under the tent and our interminable day consumed her last reserves of energy. There were only a few kilometers (miles) left before Tangu and its hotel. I gave all the energy I had left to push her in her back and accompany her in this final event.

    The hotel was finally in front of us. It was magnificent and its owner offered us a more than reasonable price. Finally, a good place to celebrate the new year with dignity! We were completely exhausted. I took the bags up with difficulty while Khanh Nguyen showered, a shower that she had of course skipped yesterday. I slumped down on the bed. The bathroom door opened. Khanh Nguyen came out with a limp. I looked at her sore ankle: it had tripled in size since that morning! We had been pushing too hard those last few days. We'd been unreasonable and that was the result... I felt so bad for her. I wished I could take all her pain for her. The doubts about the rest of the trip came back to my mind like a boomerang. I helped her lie down on the bed and went to the reception desk to get a big tub of ice. We would go see a doctor in the morning.

It was already five o'clock. I went out to buy out dinner and two large beers. I went back up to the room to celebrate our last dinner of the year, and we fell asleep within the hour! I was revived by sudden cries of joy and fireworks lighting in the sky in huge bangs. It was the restaurant in the hotel celebrating the new year.

It was the first day of the year, and what better way to start it than to visit the doctor? The doctor's verdict in Tangu was the same as the one in Pale: she should rest for at least ten days. We had to start all over again! But this time it was not a suggestion. As our visa was about to expire, we no longer had a choice. We would have to take the bus to the border of Thailand.

The owner of the hotel kindly helped us book a bus for the four of us. Tank and Monster were human beings in their own right by that stage of the trip to us! The trip was made in two stages: Hpa An and its sugar loaves then Mae Sot at the border. The driver of the bus to entertain the passengers broadcast karaoke clips in Burmese and with clips as kitsch as possible. The songs got stuck in my head little by little and wouldn't leave me for several days.

After too long hours on bumpy roads, we finally reached Thailand, leaving Myanmar with grave doubts. Would we be able to start pedaling again someday soon? Myanmar was an exceedingly difficult and tiring part of the trip. Largely because of Khanh Nguyen's sprained ankle but also because of the many nights we spent looking for places to sleep without being evicted by the police. If we were to go back to Myanmar one day, it would certainly not be by bike...

On the way South, Myanmar

I used the last bit of data on my Burmese sim package to view the donations received for Poussières de Vie. We were at $11,300 USD for 12,237 kilometers (7,600 miles) traveled and falling behind our target by a lot. I hoped that our greater exposure in the Vietnamese media would quickly increase those donations. With that my data expired. The driver told us to get off the bus and head towards the border post that would open the doors of the ancient kingdom of Siam.

Chapter 23

Thailand & Laos: so close and so far from the goal

Mileage Meter: 12,237 to 14,010km (7,603 to 8,705 miles)

The border crossing was on a bridge over the Moei River, the natural border between Thailand and Myanmar. There was a special queue for foreigners to which an immigration officer directed us. While we were queuing, another agent arrived and grabbed Khanh Nguyen by the hand, telling her to stand in the other queue... He thought she was Thai and needed to queue with her compatriots. She took out her Vietnamese passport. He apologized and left her alone.

We had to pedal a few kilometers (miles) to reach the town of Mae Sot, and did it slowly; wanting to preserve Khanh Nguyen's ankle. Thailand immediately stood out from Myanmar with its perfectly asphalted roads, its cars whose body shone in the sun and 7 Eleven[1] convenience stores every five hundred meters (0.3 miles). It was surely the most *developed* country that we had crossed since our European kilometers (miles).

At Mae Sot we had Ton, a member of the *Warmshowers* community, waiting for us. I had told him about our situation by mail. Ton showed great hospitality and replied: "Let her rest as many days as she needs". It always filled me with warmth to be welcomed like that in the cities we passed through. Ton was a Dutchman who had moved to Mae Sot several decades ago. He was a big fan of bicycle trips and earned his living as an English teacher. Ton welcomed us into his beautiful colonial-style house and led us to a room just for the two of us. It was cool inside and the surroundings were so quiet. Ton lived alone but liked to accommodate volunteers or travelers.

The days followed one another in Mae Sot in the company of Ton and other travelers he'd welcomed at his home, including Laura and Pierre. They were French, also on bicycles and also traveling the world. We took advantage of that time to call our family and friends. All my family were

---

[1] Convenience store chain with a strong presence in North America and Asia

With Ton, Mae Sot, Thailand *Back on the road, Thailand*

Thousands of pagodas and Buddhas, Thailand

doing well, but I wasn't given reassuring news regarding my maternal grandfather, Bon Papa. His health was deteriorating rapidly, and he could hardly communicate. I felt totally helpless, faced with the reality of his long and difficult descent. Deciding to reach the ends of the world involved those great renunciations, however. Khanh Nguyen reassured me when I shared the news, holding me tight in her arms. I felt a bit better, and Khanh Nguyen's ankle, too. Day by day, her situation improved. The pain soon disappeared completely, and she could quickly move it in all directions without fear. We went every day to a modest vegetarian restaurant that offered varied and often spicy dishes. Ton told us his travel stories, especially in Myanmar. The discussion about the endless quests we'd all experienced finding a place to spend the night in that country was inexhaustible!

Finally came the day when Khanh Nguyen felt ready to leave. We took a long walk in the streets of Mae Sot to make sure that the pain wouldn't come back. The next day, in the early morning, we left Ton and Mae Sot. We felt so indebted to Ton for having welcomed us into his home for so long.

We didn't plan to stay in Thailand for too long. Laos and its capital, Vientiane, were little more than six hundred kilometers away (373 miles). It would take us about a week.

Tank and Monster were as happy as ever to be back in business. They always ran perfectly and were admirable for their endurance. The first climbs arrived quickly, and, as in Myanmar, they were fearsome. The road easily rose to more than 20%, which depleted all our energy and water. During the afternoon, the temperatures were around forty degrees Celsius (104 °F). We made few big and beautiful encounters in Thailand. Other than an English man, Christian, and his Thai wife, Thip, who welcomed us into their home, we had no remarkable encounters. I had the impression that I was passing through regions in Germany or Bulgaria again where nobody seemed willing to talk to us again.

We often passed through very dry, yellowing, and uninhabited landscapes that still bore the scars of major forest fires. One comforting feature of that long, solitary crossing was the Thai temples. Thailand, like Myanmar, is a very Buddhist country. We counted more than three hundred thousand monks and thousands of temples. As soon as the afternoon ended, we went to the first temple on our way. We left our bicycles at the entrance and walked back to the temple grounds. I met the first monk I saw and asked him, via smartphone, if we could spend the night. Over the week, all our requests were positively received!

Each monk welcomed us immediately and indicated a place where we could set up our tent. It was so good to know that we couldn't be evicted by the police like we could have been in Myanmar. We experienced bespoke nights in every monk's home we stayed in. Some of them offered us drinks, cakes or invited us for breakfast. Others only told us where to sleep and then disappeared completely until the next morning. Once a bhikkhuni (a female Thai monk) invited us to sleep near her temple. In Thailand, women have only allowed to become monks since 2003. It was still a very divisive subject in the kingdom of Siam. Some considered it distasteful.

The woman who invited us for the evening, Ratana, was slender with a shaved head. She illuminated the temple with her good mood and laughter. She wore long white clothes and shared the tasks at the temple with other monks, who were men dressed in orange. Before sunset, all the monks follow a special ritornello: the sweeping of dead leaves. Every dead leaf must be meticulously swept over the entire surface of the temple. I joined our guests for an evening and swept with them. I had my own little area to perfect. More than a task, it was a thing to be done and redone. Sweeping the leaves day after day carried a meditative dimension. .

The great Ratana told us that there was a story of a Buddhist master who taught a fundamental truth to his young disciple by making him watch him gather leaves. The young novice ran towards the master:

Master! Master! You shouldn't do that. I will sweep the courtyard tomorrow..."

"You shouldn't say that," replied the master in all simplicity. "If I pick up a dead leaf, then there will be one less on the ground. It will be cleaner than if I do nothing."

"I understand, master. But there are so many leaves falling. The moment you pick one up, a hundred more fall..."

"Leaves don't just fall to the ground. They also fall into our souls. I pick up the ones that are in my soul, and maybe one day I will manage to pick them all up."

On my small scale, I interpreted Ratana's story as the need to work on oneself every day, an effort to ward off the evil of becoming discouraged by the magnitude of the work to be done. You have to start with yourself, to have this rigor within yourself. I saw our great cycling adventure as something similar: we had the rigor to pedal every day, and one day, eventually, we would reach our destination. To this day I thank Ratana for alerting me to that.

More than a safe place to spend the night, sleeping in a temple also gave us the guarantee of being able to shower every night. Each temple had a water point. Showering after a long day of sweating and fighting against the humidity was the greatest of luxuries. After sunset, the monks were usually back in their rooms. So, we often stayed alone for long periods of time to contemplate the temple and its surroundings. Each temple had its own architecture and composition. Our tent waited for us patiently until fatigue took over. We then fell asleep among a sky composed of the most beautiful stars.

This is what I remember about Thailand: temples, monks and Ratana's story. You have to make an effort to see each day as an opportunity for improvement. Even if your environment and the people surrounding you don't resonate with you, you mustn't get passive in that task. Khanh Nguyen no longer felt any pain in her ankle, even so, as soon as a doubtful set of stairs came up, I made sure to half-joke: "be careful."

Thailand and its Buddhist monks

We left Thailand to enter Laos, our final and seventeenth country before Vietnam. I happily returned to the Mekong, the mythical river of Southeast Asia that originates in the Tibetan plateau and flows through Laos, Cambodia, and Vietnam. Khanh Nguyen aptly said to me: "If we let ourselves flow along the Mekong we would arrive directly in Vietnam!"

We soon crossed the endless bridge of friendship between Thailand and Laos. Many signs indicated that it was forbidden to ride a bike on that route. However, no policeman signaled for us to stop, so we continued to cycle instead of walking those several kilometers. Getting our passports stamped was a short formality. We had just done our very first kilometers (miles) in Laos when Khanh Nguyen shouted at me, "Thibault! I can't change gears anymore...". I waited for her for a few seconds then got on her brave bike, Monster, to find out what was going on. Indeed, her gear shifter was broken inside. Impossible to repair. She found herself forced to pedal on the lowest gear without being able to change it. If there had been even a little bit of a relief, she would have been done for, but fortunately, the few kilometers (miles) to reach Vientiane were as flat as Belgium.

Vientiane, the capital city of Laos, soon presented itself in front of us. We were once again lucky to be welcomed. That time it was Mayr and Marie-Do, a couple who had settled in Laos a long time ago. Their children lived in a beautiful house in Vientiane, where they left a guest room at our disposal. Marie-Do was an artist and produced sumptuous lacquers. Mayr was unfortunately not there. He was also on a bicycle trip in the west of Laos. We took advantage of Vientiane to recharge our batteries, changed the gear shifter of Monster, and planned the final parts of our trip. The goal would be to join first Louang Prabang in the mountains in the North, then return to Vietnam by the border at Dien Bien Phu. A little more than eight hundred kilometers (500 miles) and big climbs awaited us. It would be one of the most physical parts of the trip, but we were ready.

During those few nights in Vientiane, it was also the time of the Lunar New Year celebrations: the Tết! It was the first Tết that Khanh Nguyen hadn't spent with her family, so, to mark the occasion, she dressed in the

Áo Dài that she had carried all the way in her saddlebags from France. She was gorgeous, with a natural class that had always set her apart from the other girls to me. But during those celebrations, a mysterious virus was beginning to be reported in the Wuhan region of China. The now infamous *Coronavirus*. Cases seemed to be spreading rapidly. Laos had a large common border with China, and it raised concerns.

Khanh Nguyen quickly got scared by the news. I was calmer. I told her not to worry, remembering the SARS virus in the early 2000s with less than a thousand people in the world dying from it. We would see what would happen. A lot of Chinese people were in Laos for the holiday. Most of the cars on the roads had Chinese license plates. It must also be said that Laos was strongly Chinese influenced, both economically and politically. We would have the confirmation during the next few weeks.

Ready to take on the Laotian mountains, we left Marie-Do, her children, and Vientiane early in the morning. We immortalized the 13,000 kilometers (8,077 miles) crossed in front of the Patxuai, Vientiane's triumphal arch.

The few days that we had to pedal to reach the first difficulties, north of Vang Vieng, were of no real interest. We were quickly disappointed by the Laotian food: often not very tasty and quite expensive for the very small quantities we got. Along the road, there were regular works for a new high-speed train line financed by China. All the signs were written in Chinese, and so were all the employees we met. We were fortunate to be accepted for the night in several Buddhist temples with the same hospitality level as our beloved Thai temples. We were progressing well. One day, while we rested along a river, we saw a couple of long-distance travelers passing by on their bikes. They were going in the same direction as us but much faster. I didn't even have time to shout 'Stop!' at them. They were already out of reach of my voice.

Little interest, as I said: Vang Vieng, for example, was more a hangout for alcoholic backpackers than a quiet and peaceful place. The sugar loaves that surrounded it, however, fortunately made it a little less superficial. We decided not to stop at Vang Vieng and to continue towards the North of Laos by following *road number thirteen*. The landscapes began to become quite sumptuous as we gained altitude. The mountains rose quite steeply, and large rivers flowed here and there. Our legs got hot as we climbed. At the top of a climb, we took the opportunity to buy a bag of oranges. The two cyclists from the day before made their appearance! I waved at them, and they finally stopped at our level. Their names were Steven and Annie: a couple of Parisians who had left at about the same time as us to reach Southeast Asia. Steven had a long traveler's beard and a fine body; Annie was obviously of Asian origin and had a beautiful and frank smile. The current passed well between our spirits, and we decided to pedal for the next few days together.

The road meandered elegantly along the imposing massifs, and its incline gradients were therefore acceptable. Climbing the passes was done without much pain and at our own pace. Steven had the best performing member of the group and traveled lightly: he flew far ahead until we lost sight of him completely. We formed a small peloton with Annie and Khanh Nguyen while chatting in his absence:

"You left at the same time as us... It's funny to meet up here almost a year later," I said to start a conversation with Annie.

"Yes, we may have taken different paths. We went through Turkey, Iran, Oman..." Annie answered between breaths.

"And what do you think about Iran? For us, it's our favorite country," Khanh Nguyen said.

"It was nice, but the Iranians are too... clingy. Always following us, sticking with us, inviting us. We preferred Turkey! People are adorable there."

"Clingy, the Iranians? They are just super welcoming and respectful, I think. If you want clingy locals, I advise you to go to Northern India", I said, concluding the conversation while accelerating, giving some quick pedal strokes.

The impression of a country compared to another varies so much according to the traveler's personality, their age, and the experiences and random encounters they make. I still didn't like my dear Iranian friends being criticized, though. The Mustafa in me re-awakened at that challenge to my adopted compatriots!

The afternoon was coming to an end as we approached the village of Kasi and its mountainous regions. Northern Laos was home to many ethnic minorities with their own language and customs. Their small villages were all along the road, and there were mostly young children greeting us and shouting all together "Bye-bye!" We passed through locals in a village showering together out in the open! Each member of the village went to the village fountain with their towel, flip-flops, and soap. I saw an opportunity to shower before setting up camp and going to bed, but Annie didn't seem interested and had to find Steven anyway. Before leaving us behind, Steven had given us the GPS coordinates of where we'd camp that night. Annie proposed to meet back up there before setting off in search of Steven.

We stopped near a fountain where the whole village was showering one by one. We took out our towel, soap, and clean clothes for the night. The children and women around us didn't seem intimidated by our presence. They were more amused by the situation than anything else. A woman had just finished washing her hair, and it was finally my turn. I undressed as fast as possible and was in my underwear in front of the whole village! People chuckled good-naturedly here and there. The water was cool, so I soaped, shampooed, and rinsed myself as fast as possible. It was Khanh Nguyen's turn, who had to wash her hair! The operation took a few minutes. Several young mothers waited patiently for their turn, then Khanh Nguyen was done! We dried ourselves as fast as we could before we caught a cold, and we left again because it was almost dark.

The feeling of riding my bike again, clean and beautiful, hair in the wind, in sumptuous landscapes with the woman of my dreams was enlivening, to say the least. The last rays of sunshine illuminated the Laotian sugar loaves and then silence. Just the wind, the sound of our wheels on the asphalt, and that was it. The meeting point with Steven and Annie would be in front of us soon if I trusted my phone. We arrived at the exact point and looked around. There was no trace of our two companions. There was no network, and it was impossible to reach them. We continued to go down along the mountain. Still no Steven and Annie. I lost hope and told Khanh Nguyen: "We should stop, I think, there is a kind of wooden refuge there, behind, it is perfect for tonight".

A classic evening and night would then take place: rice and vegetables cooked with our stove, teeth brushing, and restful sleep in our tent. And silence, always silence and its few birds.

We woke up in the morning mist and set off again to conquer the Laotian summits. Nobody on the road. We took advantage of the first village we passed to have breakfast and stock up on provisions for the next one. While I drank a truly disgusting canned coffee, I saw Steven appearing on the road we had just taken. He was happy to find us again and asked us:

"Where did you end up sleeping?"

"We looked for you for a long time! We shouted your names all over the mountain..."

"We didn't hear you! The site was located a little higher than the road. It was near a school under construction. Not bad to sleep, but in the morning, there was a guy with a rifle... He was just guarding the construction site."

"We slept a little lower... Not very far from you! And Annie?"

"She's coming!"

I realized that there wasn't only one way to cycle the world as a couple. I didn't see myself letting Khanh Nguyen out of my sight for more than a minute. If anything happened, I had to be able to intervene, like a

Sugar Loaves, Vang Vieng, Laos

Breaktime, Laos

good bodyguard. But Steven and Annie both seemed more independent: Steven went solo in front and often left Annie far behind. Annie pedaled at her own pace, with music or a radio show in her ears. Steven then waited for her, sometimes for an hour at the top of a mountain. I worried for him what could happen to Annie in that meantime without his help.

Our little quartet got back together for the day. There were still so many children and their vibrant "bye-bye"s by the side of the road. We didn't fail to answer every time. Another important fact to mention: we met many long-distance cyclists arriving in front of us: French, Dutch, and Chinese. We met more cyclists in Laos in two days than we did in almost a year on the roads! Each meeting was an opportunity to take a break to discuss where we came from and where we were going. At the end of the day, we decided to stop in a small guesthouse for ten US dollars a night. Steven and Annie wanted to reach Luang Prabang faster and left us to continue pedaling a little longer. We promised to meet there, in one of the most beautiful places in the world.

Our room for the night was built in a kind of precast without any insulation in the rooms next door. The slightest movement or whisper could be heard. Three or four girls shared a room to the left of ours. The Chinese owner allowed us to bring in Tank and Monster.

The sheets were dirty. Luckily, we had our comforters and pillows... I watched the news for the day: the coronavirus continued to spread. There was talk of new cases in other countries but not yet in Laos. Was it a good idea to sleep where we were? Guests - all men - arrived, who were also Chinese. After a quick dinner, we went back to our room. The men were with the women from earlier, in short outfits, in a large room next to the reception. We looked at each other and laughed our heads off. The night was likely to be messy, but after all our experiences, sleeping in all conditions, we were ready to face it. For several long hours, they screamed, yelled, laughed, and spilled. I oscillated between sleep and wakefulness, between fatigue and total irritation, Khanh Nguyen too. The only positive point: the act of flesh wouldn't be committed in the room next to ours, which saved us from unbearable sounds. Midnight passed, and the noises stopped. It was a matter of falling asleep before it started again.

We needed two more days to reach Luang Prabang. The mountains were still beautiful, and the children still numerous. It was relatively cool, and each pass was crossed without too much sweat and tears. The only black point: my rear tire started to weaken on the side: there was a one-centimeter (0.4 inches) wide hole that I sealed from the inside with a piece of rubber to protect the inner tube. We still had a little less than three thousand kilometers (1.864 miles) to go. Would we be able to do it?

A little before noon, there we were: Luang Prabang! The jewel of Laos. It was the ancient capital of the kings of Laos and their elephants. Located on the banks of the Mekong, its legend had been built over the centuries by traveler's tales. Thanks to a remarkable work of UNESCO, the jewel had kept all its former glory and its special atmosphere. Persepolis, Bagan, and finally Luang Prabang by bike: what more could you ask for?

We were also lucky to be welcomed by the family of Tamim, a friend of mine who lives in Vientiane. They ran a small hotel in the center of Luang Prabang and had kept a room available for us. It was Vanh, a former French teacher, who managed that little world with mastery. In French, which was, of course, perfect, she congratulated us for having come so far and invited us to stay as long as we wished. It would take us about a week to get my visa for Vietnam at the consulate in Luang Prabang.

The news wasn't good on the coronavirus front however. The first cases had appeared in Vietnam and we were beginning to fear that the borders would close right under our noses. It would be a real disaster... to travel the world and be denied passage at the very last border point. We went early in the morning to the Consulate to get my visa. The immigration staff recognized us immediately: "Oh, you are *Non-La Project*! We saw you on television!". A couple of Belgians who were also doing their visa for Vietnam came and greeted us. Eef, the girl of the couple, began:

"Hi, I'm Eef, and he's Stef. We've been following you on Instagram for a long time. We started in Belgium and we would like to reach... Bali!"

"Bali! You still have a long way to go! My name is Thibault, and this is Khanh Nguyen. What is your road?"

"We will leave Luang Prabang by the North and enter Vietnam by Dien Bien Phu ... For the rest, we will see ... Surely Sapa!"

"We will enter Vietnam by Dien Bien Phu too! We have to cycle together!"

"Oh yes! It would be great..."

Eef was gigantic, at least one meter ninety (6.2 feet). Stef was slightly shorter and wore round glasses. They both spoke Flemish and English. Their route was slightly different from ours: they would take *road number 13*

Conquering together the Laotian summits, Kasi, Laos

to Muang Xay. On the advice of the French cyclists we had met on the road a few days earlier, we would ride up the Mekong by boat to the village of Pak Beng. We would then take the *2W road,* which also went up to Muang Xay, where we wanted to meet our two Belgian friends! The *2W* road was more beautiful and much wilder than the *13* and then to go up the Mekong by boat was something to do to boot!

It took five days to get my visa. We spent unforgettable moments enjoying the streets of Luang Prabang, its colonial architecture and Buddhist temples. The Vat Xien Thong stood out. Built in the 16th century, it was remarkable for its beauty with its seven cascading roofs and the richness of its facades in the colorful and sumptuous style of Louang Prabang. One could stay there for hours at the Vat Xien Thong without taking your eyes off of it. Every evening, we walked along the Mekong River to observe the slightest nuances of the sun setting over the reflections of the waters of the great river. Five days felt like five long years. The humble traveler loses their fragile notion of time while in Luang Prabang. We also met Steve and Annie for a last dinner together before they left for the South of Laos.

The following evening, we met Stef and Eef again, who would leave one or two days after us. We promised to meet again in Muang Xay to enter Vietnam together. We were almost there. It was a small matter of only three hundred kilometers (186 miles). I had difficulty realizing how it would go. What would my emotions be and those of Khanh Nguyen? I preferred not to anticipate anything, as usual, leaving myself the right to be surprised.
In the afternoon, we went to the Vietnamese Consulate to get my visa, the final visa that gave us the right to end the trip in beauty. The visa was finally there, well stuck and stamped on a page right in the middle of my passport.

Early in the morning, we left Luang Prabang as well as Vanh and her family who had welcomed us so kindly for the week. Luang Prabang was still

The Vat Xien Thong, Luang Prabang, Laos

Sunset over the Mekong River, Luang Prabang, Laos

sleeping as we drove through its small streets and temples. We had to drive about ten kilometers (6 miles) north to reach the pier

The boats were already waiting down there. It was necessary to go down quite steep stairs to be able to embark. Our boat to go up the Mekong was built all the way up with its tables, wooden seats, and kitchen. We relieved Tank and Monster of all their equipment. Two employees installed them on the roof of the boat. They were held by a few ropes, which, I hoped, would be enough to keep them on board with us. They were lucky, Tank and Monster, that is. They had traveled by plane, bus and car. They'd crossed the Black Sea by boat, and now they were going up the Mekong river! Few bikes could say the same.

The trip took almost a day against the current. During long hours we admired the beauty of the Mekong and the region. The environment was quite hostile with its mountains and jungle. Few houses could be seen certainly. We also passed a few boats. I let myself, little by little, be absorbed by things. Khanh Nguyen was sitting right next to me, her head on my shoulder. Time expanded again as the sun set, just before we arrived in Pak Beng. The mountains were glowing red. The evening birds started to sing. The boat docked, and everything stopped. Tank and Monster were still there. The village of Pak Beng was located a good fifty meters (150 feet) higher than the Mekong River. We would have to push everything on a slope as steep as Cleopatra's nose. It would take several round trips and a lot of sweat to reach the entrance of the village. For that night, there were plenty of choices to find a room. We took a 10 USD room for the night.

With a big smile and a lot of strength, we started our last three hundred kilometers (186 miles) before Vietnam. It would take us two days to reach Muang Xay, where we were supposed to meet our two Belgian friends: Eef and Stef. *Road 2E* was incredibly calm and peaceful. At the maximum, we passed by a car every hour. Lost between Thailand, China, and Vietnam we swallowed the kilometers (miles) easily. There were regular wooden shelters where we could rest for a nap or lunch. The rivers were numerous, and several times, we bathed with the people of the village. The children were always amused to see us share their daily ritual. There was curiosity but still a distance which they kept between us. We rubbed shoulders without really meeting each other.

After one hundred and forty kilometers (86 miles), we finally arrived in Muang Xay. We could hardly do worse in terms of the city. It was a road junction that led to nearby China. Muang Xay was concrete, industrialized, and absolutely everything was written in Chinese. During those last days, the Coronavirus occupied all the media space, and the city was as if depopulated. A few Chinese people ran their stores as best they could, but the majority of the shops were closed with their large iron curtains rolled down to the bottom. I called Eef and Stef to find out where they were: they were one day behind schedule. We didn't see ourselves spending more than one night in this horror of a city, and I suggested joining them a little further on the road: in Muang Khua. That night we stayed in a quite sordid hotel, often found in secondary Chinese cities. We hardly dared to take off our clothes before slipping under the sheets.

―᠊᠊᠊᠊᠊

Leaving Muang Xay was a real relief. In addition to the sordid aspect of this city, the threat of Coronavirus was growing. It was best not to stay there too long, knowing that ninety percent of the city was made up of Chinese people who regularly transited and traded with the nearby Chinese provinces.

At the exit of Muang Xay, the road became calm and serene again. Mountains and rivers took back their right. All the children continued to greet us with their famous "bye-bye"s. I felt better. We spent one night under the tent along the calm Nam Phak river before arriving in Muang Khua. Muang Khua was a small sleepy village located at the meeting of the Nam Ou and Nam Phak rivers. An impressive suspension bridge connected the two parts of the village. On the other side, we found a room for the night with a breathtaking view of the bridge and the river. Eef and Stef finally arrived one day later and met us on the other side of the bridge. They both seemed to be in great shape. We all agreed to leave the next morning for Vietnam. There were still one hundred kilometers (62 miles) to go before we arrived at the border.

The last hundred kilometers (62 miles) for Vietnam weren't the easiest, with important climbs to cross. We also met our first cars with Vietnamese plates! Another clue stood on our road: a red and white bollard on which was written: "HANOI", the capital of Vietnam! Above was written "512 KM" (318 miles). We were not far anymore. Eef and Stef drove at our pace, climbing and descending the mountains with us. We could have crossed the border today, but our Vietnamese visas were valid only from the next day. We would have to spend the night somewhere close to the border.

Finding a place for the night was difficult. We were high in altitude, and the steep cliffs left little room for a good place to set up our tent. After long kilometers (miles) of surveyance, I located a ladder that led to a place where it was impossible to see what happened from the road. I shouted to Khanh Nguyen, Eef, and Stef to stop, and I scouted ahead to see if the place would be suitable. I climbed the wooden ladder and discovered a perfect place to camp: it was flat, there were few stones and bushes that sheltered us from the road. Nobody would be able to spot us there.

With our two Belgian friends: we swapped stories, travel anecdotes, life before, and of future possibilities. The sun was almost down when each of us headed with our partners to our respective tents. I lay down next to Khanh Nguyen, my wife, my beautiful half with whom I was living my dream with. I whispered to her:

"How do you feel deep down inside? Tomorrow we'll be in Vietnam!"

"I don't know. I have the impression that with all our appearances in the media, in the newspapers, on TV, that we won't be able to cycle quietly... That our trip won't really be one anymore. And then my family is still far from us... We have to cycle for almost two thousand kilometers

With Eef and Stef before crossing the border, Laos

(1,240 miles) to reach Saigon. It's still far..." said Khanh Nguyen, avoiding meeting my eye.

"But it's just great that many people are waiting for us all along our journey from North to South Vietnam!" I answered, taking her hand in mine. "There will be many beautiful people to meet, I'm sure. It means that we did something different, something out of the ordinary... And you'll see, very soon, we'll be back to your family."

"I preferred to cycle anonymously, just the two of us. We don't need to shout from the rooftops what we're doing..."

"I agree with you. But it's also what kept us going all along. Without social media, without the media, we wouldn't have met Amin in Iran, for example. We wouldn't have received all these messages of support that did us so much good in such difficult times.

We would have been able to stop anonymously, without anyone knowing, but then how could we have collected donations? Without Facebook, Instagram, and the media, the pool would have remained at zero."

"It's true... I know... It's just that I'd like to keep that intimacy that we both have. Let's go back to being private people."

"The journey will end, and we'll be completely anonymous again, you'll see. There will only remain these memories. These great memories spent together from France to Vietnam. From my home to yours."

After those few words were exchanged, we fell asleep quickly

Our mileage meter was at 14,000 kilometers (8,700 miles) for 13,384 US dollars collected. The donation counter started to rise on the mileage counter. I hoped more than anything that we would be able to reach the 16,000 US dollars for the children of *Poussières de Vie*.

Chapter 24

Northern Vietnam: back among the rice fields and Covid-19

Mileage Meter: 14,010 to 15,013km (8,705 to 9,328 miles)

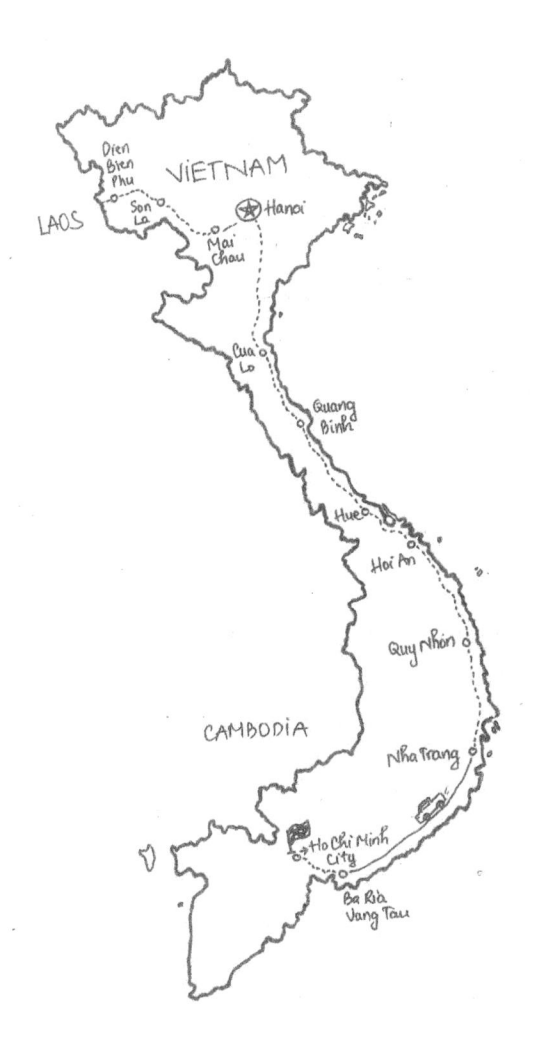

The day dawned one last time for us outside of Vietnam. Every night I slept in that tent, it was a relief to wake up alive next to Khanh Nguyen. I could see that everything was still there: the bikes, our bags, my wallet... Nothing had moved. Eef and Stef were already awake and were starting to put away their equipment. I gave Khanh Nguyen time to emerge then started preparing breakfast: oatmeal, mangoes, and bananas. Stef made coffee.

It was soon time to leave. After a few more kilometers, the border finally appeared. A large blue sign indicated the boundary to Vietnam, and we immediately posed in front of it to immortalize the moment. I placed the camera, set the timer, and there we were, the four of us. The Laotian officer quickly stamped our passports, and then there was a long buffer zone to cross to reach the Vietnamese border. Large displays alerted us about the coronavirus. An officer took our temperature, and we had to precisely indicate our course over the last few days. A Vietnamese immigration officer came to speak to Khanh Nguyen: "Oh, but you are Non-La Project! I saw you on TV. I'm so surprised to see you crossing this border. I really thought you would enter Vietnam from somewhere else..."

After a discussion with the immigration officer, it seemed that the situation was under control in Vietnam. The few cases of people who had contracted the nasty virus had been quarantined along with their entire neighborhood. Nevertheless, we had received many messages from friends and family who warned us or urged us to put on masks. The situation was getting a little more difficult right away, but I knew that, as usual, we would deal with it.

The road was in poor condition on the way to Dien Bien Phu. It was not maintained, dented, and dusty. Everyone covered their mouth to not inhale that dust, but as we lost altitude, the beautiful rice fields, so characteristic of Vietnam, revealed themselves to us. Arranged by the hand of men in terraces, they were of a beautiful and lively green that accompanied the movement of the wind. Non-La hats were now everywhere. Every farmer wore one. The two we had carried all the way from France must have felt overjoyed!

We would spend the night in Dien Bien Phu. Dien Bien Phu sounds like a bad memory for a Frenchman and a great victory for a Vietnamese. A dirty war between 1953 and 1954 rang the death bell for the French presence in Indochina. We didn't always realize it as strongly, but all the territories we had crossed were littered with death, war, murder, and violence. In our modern societies, death is something we dare not face. We must quickly mourn it, cultivate our eternal youth. As we pedaled in front of the gigantic monument to the dead of Dien Bien Phu, I thought back to the Maxims of La Rochefoucauld:

"Neither the sun nor death can be looked at with a steady eye."

For a few days, we would play tourist and culinary guides for Eef and Stef. It was a pleasure to find Vietnamese cuisine with all its diversity and freshness but also to enjoy a ca phê sua da[1]. Our two Belgian friends were very quickly impressed by the Vietnamese flavors and for a more than reasonable price. In Vietnam, dong is the currency. On all the bills, the face of the father of the nation: uncle Ho Chi Minh. A US dollar is worth about 23,000 dong... I felt like I was back in Iran with its insane exchange rate. A bowl of Vietnamese Pho[2] costs about 30,000 dong or... a little more than a US dollar. A full meal! Delicious food can be found anywhere, which was

---

[1] Vietnamese coffee with condensed milk and ice cream
[2] Vietnamese noodle soup with beef

Vietnamese rice fields, Dien Bien Phu, Vietnam

Ascent of the Pha Din Pass, Vietnam

perfect for us.

We took to the road again through the mountains of North-West Vietnam. The majority of the Thai ethnic minority group live there. The women are easily recognizable: when they are married, they wear an imposing bun that thrones well above their head. Not exactly practical when it comes to putting on a motorcycle helmet however... The Thai generally have large houses made of wood and bamboo. In the region of Dien Bien Phu they cultivate rice a lot. All day long, we met large groups of people who were busy maintaining their rice fields. I often saw high buns emerging among the rice shoots.

The temperatures were around twenty degrees Celsius (68°F), which was perfect to face all the passes we had to cross. Khanh Nguyen now climbed every pass with pleasure. What a metamorphosis compared to our first climbs in France! Eef and Stef were perfect fellow travelers and always ready to discuss anything and everything during those long days of always moving forward. It was easy to stop whenever we wanted to have lunch, buy fruits, or bread. It must be said that in Vietnam, there are people everywhere, even in the mountains. That contrasts sharply with Laos where we met few people during the day. It would be more difficult for us to camp in nature, and we already knew some of the bad sides of Vietnam. While most of the population is honest and lovable, a small minority of thieves were remarkably good at stealing belongings, especially at night. I'd heard too many stories of cyclists who'd had their stuff, or even their bikes, stolen during the night while they slept peacefully in their tents. With Khanh Nguyen, we decided not to camp unless we had no choice.

The road continued to climb, but the good mood of our brief small group of four and the sumptuous landscapes almost completely erased the fatigue. After a long day, we arrived in the city of Tuan Giao. It was there that our path separated from our two Belgian friends. They would continue north to Sapa while we would head east to Hanoi. We found two rooms in a nice communist style hotel in the center of the city. A last ca phê sua da with all four of us in the morning, and then it was time to say goodbye.

We hugged each other and I told them that they were welcome when they arrived in Saigon. They planned to be there a few weeks after our arrival.

The two Belgians towards the North, the two Franco-Vietnamese towards the East. We found ourselves alone, once again. Eef and Stef were our last travel companions. No sooner had we left them behind than we started the last big pass above 1,500 meters (4,920 feet) of our adventure. That was the famous Pha Din Pass with its 1,648 meters (5,407 feet) of altitude. The road was deserted. The wind and clouds started to accumulate, but fortunately, the rain wasn't there. I surprised myself, feeling cold at that altitude. It was indeed the first time since North-East India. The locals weren't very friendly with us. A guy on a motorcycle even made fun of Khanh Nguyen by shouting to her in Vietnamese, "You are too slow, go faster. Come on!"; easily said from a motorcycle with a beer belly

After a good hour of climbing, we reached the top of the pass and found ourselves among the clouds. The wind still blew as strongly as ever. The descent finally began: the cold and humidity made me shiver. For the night, we would stop at a motel for 10 US dollars a night. We were the only customers that evening. The room was damp but clean. For dinner, we had a bowl of Pho Ga[1]. The hot soup gave me strength and motivation; I saw that for Khanh Nguyen too. Before going to bed, I checked our messages: there were many requests from journalists for interviews and TV shows. I discussed all the offers with Khanh Nguyen, and we decided to only do one TV show and another small event in a coffee shop with those who had followed us regularly on *Facebook* and *Instagram* on our journey, both in the capital Hanoi. We chose the TV show "Talk Vietnam", which had the merit of being a forty-five-minute-long format and in English. The TV team would be waiting for us on our return to Hanoi. We turned off our phones and snuggled up tightly against each other to face the night in all its freshness.

---

1 Noodle soup with chicken

Breakfast, Moc Chau, Vietnam

Khanh Nguyen and the Vietnamese rice fields, Moc Chau, Vietnam

Cities and villages followed one another: Son La, Moc Chau then Mai Chau. We were surprised by the very low number of visitors or tourists in these places that were usually so popular. The Coronavirus was scary at that moment, and many travelers had canceled or postponed their trips. Therefore, we enjoyed the endless tea plantations of Moc Chau and the green rice fields of Mai Chau alone. Several times, passers-by who recognized us stopped to greet us and take pictures. The road continued: Muong Khen, then Hoa Binh. We weren't far from Hanoi anymore.

For breakfast: it was Banh Mi[1] or Xôi[2] and always with a Vietnamese coffee! It was very easy for us to find fruits on the road: pineapples, bananas, grapefruits, oranges. We bought a nice grapefruit before getting into Hanoi. With its 8 million inhabitants, we had to avoid the rush hour so we wouldn't get stuck in a traffic jam. We made our entrance in the suburbs of Hanoi after ten in the morning instead. The traffic was reasonable, but we had to be careful with the big trucks, whales for whom we were but parasites. I always tried to get as far away from them as possible.

We finally reached central Hanoi and followed its main avenue, Nguyen Trai. The motorcycles were present by the thousands, but we kept our pre-trip driver reflexes. I loved this little game which consisted of sneaking among cars and scooters to choose the most efficient trajectory. I got a call from the director of the show "Talk Vietnam". Her name was Trang, and she spoke a little French: "We are waiting for you in front of the Hanoi Opera. We will get some shots of you in Hanoi and also a short interview before our on-set show in three days". The district of Hanoi still has some very beautiful French colonial buildings, including an Opera house. Trang and her entire team welcomed us warmly. We were asked to put on our famous Non-La and cycle around the Hanoi Opera. Then a cameraman followed us for a few kilometers (miles) until we reached Tay Ho lake. I saw that Khanh Nguyen was tired and not happy with the extra kilometers (miles) just for a TV show. I felt sorry for not having clarified beforehand. I

---

[1] Vietnamese Sandwich
[2] Sticky rice sprinkled with fried onions and chicken

tried as much as I could to convince Khanh Nguyen and assure her that it would soon be over and that it would make beautiful memories for us! She pouted a bit less. The TV team multiplied the shots with us, asking us many questions about Tank and Monster, about our adventure. This took a good two hours and ended before Khanh Nguyen completely cracked. Trang gave us an appointment on their set in a few days. There would be no audience for the recording because of the Coronavirus.

We spent a few days in Hanoi, an ideal time to have Tank and Monster repaired for the last part of the trip. What endurance! We were hosted for the duration of our stay by Kien, a young engineer who had followed us for a long time on *Facebook*. He had an apartment in the center of Hanoi in which he welcomed us with pleasure. We were really lucky to have been welcomed in almost all the major cities we passed through during the year on the roads. Adorable people like Kien were inspired by our adventure together and wanted to make a difference. It was a great lesson we learned from our adventure: following your great passion and helping others creates a kind of virtuous circle where many people, even complete strangers, are ready to support you on their own scale and without limits. We had been the great witnesses of this in every single country we had crossed.

Before going to bed that night, I watched the news: all coronavirus cases in Vietnam had been identified and isolated. There hadn't been any contagion for the last few days. That was a good sign for the rest of the trip.

It was finally the day of the *Talk Vietnam* recording. We had an appointment at nine o'clock at the headquarters of VTV. The guards let us enter with Tank and Monster, who would be with us on the set of *Talk Vietnam*. Khanh Nguyen had her make-up session, but not me, no need apparently! The show was taped, so we didn't have to worry about the stress of the live show. The host took the time to understand our trajectories and what had gotten us to leave for so long and to travel so far.

The ninety minutes of the interview went by quickly. I had the feeling that the show would be of quality: we had time to share our state of mind and the moments that mattered so much to us. We talked at length about Reza, Zara, and the Qashqai in Iran. Those memories were still so vivid within us that it was easy to unfold them and express them to others in the right words. After we concluded the interview, the host thanked us. We, in turn, warmly thanked Trang and the whole team for devoting an entire program to us and for the quality of their questions. The program would be broadcast after we arrived in Saigon

We crossed Hanoi again with Tank and Monster to reach a local coffee shop where we had planned a presentation in front of about 30 social media fans. We were limited in number because of the Coronavirus. Meeting them, however, was a highlight for us. The virtual finally materialized into the real: we were no longer pseudonyms or images. For one hour, we presented the images and videos of the highlights of the trip. I also spent time on the terrible experience in Iran with the military man and his Kalashnikov as well as the pervert and his sexual harassment. As I told the story, I saw some faces filled with fear. I quickly explained that it hadn't represented the full journey at all. The journey had so far proved how one could receive many kindnesses and travel the world in relative safety. There was laughter when we told the story of the stormy night in the tent in Bulgaria and when the little donkey, Eeyore, followed us for miles in the Iranian mountains.

Some came up to the front to see us at the end and told us that they also wanted to go on the roads one day: by motorcycle, by bike, or by hitchhiking. It is an extremely rewarding feeling when someone comes to you to tell you that you have inspired them, that you have given them the strength to follow their own dreams. Ten o'clock had passed, and it was time for everyone to go home. The departure for us was scheduled for tomorrow at six in the morning, heading south. We planned to cycle along the coast to Saigon. We would have a few climbs on the menu, many beaches..

Recording of the Talk Vietnam program, Hanoi, Vietnam

Meeting our "fans" in Hanoi, Vietnam

From My Home To Yours

We left Hanoi early Sunday morning in the direction of Ninh Binh. I love Hanoi with its big alleys lined with tall trees. There is something special and singular that emerges from this city with all its street vendors carrying their flowers, vegetables, and fruits. Leaving on Sunday was a good choice: there was barely any traffic. After a few hours, instead of following the main road, we followed secondary roads that followed the canals. Ducks were the kings there. They were everywhere in their tens of thousands, buffalos too.

We had a small level of notoriety in Vietnam. Every time we stopped to stock up on fruit and water, the vendors recognized us: "We saw you on TV yesterday!" On the road, several times during the day, motorcycles rode next to us, then the driver addressed Khanh Nguyen: "You are the Non-La! It's incredible, from France to Vietnam by bike?! How is it possible?"

Everything went well until we reached Cua Lo, located 280 kilometers (87 miles) south of Hanoi. The weather was gloomy, the sea grey. In Cua Lo, Danh and his family welcomed us. Danh followed us on *Facebook*, and his dream was to travel the world one day by bicycle. When he had heard we would be passing through Cua Lo, he invited us to his house to spend the night. A few kilometers (miles) passed before we entered Cua Lo. I cycled ahead two hundred meters (650 feet) and a really weird guy on a motorcycle arrived in front of us. He wasn't driving straight and didn't seem to know where he wanted to go. He saw me and once he passed me, decided to drive back. I started to worry: would he try to attack me or steal something? I saw Khanh Nguyen in the distance who was not yet in danger. I accelerated frantically and tried to put some distance between the biker and me. He made big signs of stopping me and shouted incomprehensible things. The biker with his motorcycle was now on the right side of the road, so that he blocked me against the metal railing. There was no way out: I looked at him, suddenly realizing he was completely drunk. He could barely stay on his motorcycle. I made sure he had no weapon in his hands and got off Tank to use it as a barrier between us. He must have gone too hard on the rice wine

340

for lunch. I waved to Khanh Nguyen to tell him in Vietnamese to leave me alone. Once he was next to me, the guy calmed down a bit. He shook my hand quickly, then went full speed in the other direction. My pulse was still on the roller coaster. I just hoped for his sake that he got home safe and

Duel of Titans, Vinh, Vietnam

sound. I came to my senses while trying to explain to Khanh Nguyen what had just happened. After a few minutes, we took the road again towards Cua Lo and Danh's house.

Danh lived with his parents. They were a catholic family, a common occurrence in the Nghê An area, where Cua Lo is located. Their house was near a church and its statue of the Virgin Mary. I called Danh to tell him that we had arrived. The door opened, and Danh came out to meet us. He was shy and discreet by nature. I noticed that he had a bone deformity which made him stand awkwardly. He was rather thin and had long hair tied up with a catogan. Danh spoke in a low voice and you had to listen carefully to hear him. I tried to give him confidence, show him warmth, and make a few jokes. In the house were his parents and his big brother who worked as cook in a restaurant by the sea. Because of the Coronavirus, there were no more tourists, so everyone was at home waiting. We spent a day with Danh and his family. Danh was fragile, but he impressed me with his determination and willingness to explore the world. He had several bike trips in Southeast Asia under his belt. Danh's family were very conservative, and he had never told them about his great passion for cycling. Therefore, they were clueless that he had traveled all over Southeast Asia, and they certainly wouldn't know when he decided to travel the world one day.

That day, we shared our experiences, advice about roads to take, and getting the visas. He only nodded his head in response. He seemed to want to keep a low budget. He scared me a little bit when he suddenly said he would want to leave with a gun. In a way, Danh forced respect in me. So many variables had played against him in his life, but he had tried to overcome them by his own sheer iron will.

The road resumed for Tank, Monster, Khanh Nguyen and I. The climate that day was thick and sticky, the clouds were low, and the sky as threatening as before. Things weren't going well: many people avoided crossing paths with us, even putting both hands in front of their mouths. While we were taking a well-deserved break for lunch, the customers at a table right next to ours suddenly changed places to move further away. Glancing from them back Khanh Nguyen opposite me, I told her wryly:

"Do they think I have Coronavirus, or is it my sweaty smell?"

"Stop being paranoid... It's nothing against you, I think. Maybe they have something confidential to tell each other."

"Then why go to a restaurant?"

The kilometers (miles) followed one another. We cycled eighty-four kilometers (40 miles) to reach the seaside town of Thiên Câm, located in the province of Ha Tinh. The place wasn't very interesting but had several small hotels. Khanh Nguyen suggested asking several to make sure we got a fair price. Each time, I waited in front of the hotel with the bikes while Khanh Nguyen asked what the price was for a night, preventing the owner from seeing who was accompanying her. The first hotel offered 300,000 dong[1], the second 200,000, and the third 150,000 dong. We decided to go back to the second one and its 200,000 dong to book a room. That time, the owner saw me and said to Khanh Nguyen with unnerving confidence: "I'm sorry, I don't have any rooms anymore... The last one has just been booked". This seemed rather suspicious because his hotel was completely empty. We left the hotel grumbling and went back to the first one at 300,000 dong per night. Same answer from the boss: no more rooms available. We were left with the third one at 150,000 dong, which we really didn't like, but it was the last choice available. Its owner walked up to Khanh Nguyen and gave her the world's most bogus excuse: "We have a wedding this weekend, and unfortunately no rooms are available. I'm really sorry".

The message was clear. We weren't welcome in Thiên Câm. The information of our presence in the city had circulated quickly. It didn't matter if we explained that we had returned to Vietnam more than three weeks ago and that we had thus exceeded the fifteen-day incubation period of the Coronavirus. Nobody wanted to listen. The psychosis had contaminated the country. The news constantly alerted the population about new cases, especially the thousands of cases and deaths in Europe. The prejudicial equation was now becoming clear: a European = the coronavirus. In less than forty-eight hours we went from being small local celebrities on TV to the slightly less enviable status of plague victims.

[1] About thirteen dollars

Mandatory night under the tent, Thiên Câm, Vietnam

From the Atlantic to the Pacific, Ha Tinh, Vietnam

We decided to go to the nearest police station to report our situation. A young police officer in his twenties asked us for our passports and verified our entry date into the territory. Khanh Nguyen explained that we had nowhere to sleep. We asked him if we could set up our tent for tonight in the courtyard next to the police building. He laughed. "Don't think about it for a second! I will find you a hotel without any problem. Follow me!" He straddled his Honda, and we followed him for a few meters to arrive...at the same hotel whose owner had no more rooms because of the wedding that weekend. He seemed perplexed why we would return with a policeman. The policeman talked to him for a few seconds, and then the owner conceded: "Ha... maybe I finally have a room free. Let me check it out." I was relieved and saw that Khanh Nguyen was also relieved, but our joy was short-lived. The young policeman had just received a call, talked for a few moments, and then hung up. He walked towards us with a grim face saying:

"I just received a call from my superiors. You can't stay in our city tonight..."

"But it's already dark! And the nearest town is thirty kilometers (18.5 miles) away. Can't you help us?" I answer him in an angrily.

"No, I'm sorry. We can't do anything for you."

This was the first time that a police officer had categorically refused to help us throughout our entire trip. No choice: we would have to camp. Before arriving in Thiên Câm, I remembered seeing a kind of sandy ground with a few trees to hide behind. I signaled to Khanh Nguyen to go with me and quickly. Time was running out, and it would soon be dark. We crossed the city at full speed. As we passed by, children shouted and threw "Corona! Corona!" at us. It was a strange atmosphere to travel in.

In a few minutes, we left the city and stopped near the area I had spotted. There were still some cars and motorcycles circulating. When the street was clear of people, I signaled to Khanh Nguyen, and we rushed towards the bushes. Nobody seemed to have seen us. We hid behind the trees and waited a few minutes to catch our breath. The situation we were in had been unthinkable before we arrived. Coming back to Vietnam was supposed to be synonymous with going back home. Instead, I had the impression that we were now fugitives on the run: *Bonnie and Clyde* on a bicycle.

We set up the tent and all our equipment in silence. I waited a good hour outside the tent to ensure that nobody was lurking around our little home. Giving in to fatigue, I entered the tent and lay down next to Khanh Nguyen. She decided not to warn her parents about what was happening to us to not worry them. They wouldn't sleep if they knew that we were sleeping in a tent in Vietnam.

─────

In the early morning, it was time to leave. The night was surprisingly peaceful. Once our saddlebags were installed on Tank and Monster, we left again. Just a few pedal strokes, and I had a strange feeling: I had a puncture in the back. The day started well! It took me five minutes to take off the tire, change the inner tube, put the tire back on, and inflate it.

I felt like I was cycling with a big knot in my stomach. I even lost the pleasure of cycling. Khanh Nguyen was in better spirits. From now on, as soon as it was time to buy something: fruit, cookies, water... she was the one who went alone. I stayed at a good distance so as not to frighten the locals. It was completely absurd. I now wore a cloth mask to try to reduce fear in others. A little old lady in pajamas walking on the sidewalk arrived in front of me. It was only when she was a meter away that she realized I was a foreigner. She rushed to put her two hands on her mouth and made a ridiculous detour to avoid the encounter. All I could do was imitate her, place both hands on my mouth, and move my head from left to right.

I kept pedaling all day long with the same big knot, growing tighter and tighter as I went. The same evening, hell started again. We continued to go around the hotels that refused us one by one. Several times, we were yelled at through the window to go away. We finally found a hotel that accepted us but whose manager asked me not to leave the room before tomorrow morning so as not to frighten the other customers. We yielded to his requests and thanked our lucky stars that we at least had a roof for that evening.

We had crossed the 15,000 km (9.320 miles) mark, but our hearts weren't really up to the celebrations. We still had a little more than 1,000 kilometers (620 miles) to go before finally arriving in Saigon. The only small relief of the day was the increasing donations. We were at 15,080 US dollars, which means that the donations had finally passed in front of the kilometers again! Finally, a small light in the darkness.

I turned off my phone and closed my eyes. I wondered if it was really worth continuing as everyone we encountered saw me as a giant walking virus. I didn't dare talk openly about it to Khanh Nguyen.

Chapter 25

Central & South Vietnam: the end, what end?

Mileage Meter: 15,013 to 15,950km (9,329 to 9.910 miles)

March in the province of Ha Tinh was hot, and I wondered which sauce we would be served that day: chili or nuoc mam[1]? In the morning, Khanh Nguyen called several hotels for the coming night to see if they would accept a Frenchman who had been in Vietnam for more than three weeks. We only received negative answers. We asked ourselves why we were persisting in pedaling. We had received several messages from Khanh Nguyen's family asking us to stop, saying it was already very good to have arrived in Vietnam and that we had nothing left to prove.

It was becoming less and less socially acceptable to be traveling so much across such a distance. People were being told to stay at home, to limit their movements. If we caught the Coronavirus, we would contaminate all the people we met. It would be an awful scandal. I could already see us on the TV news. I felt the forces of despair in me take over, and I emptied my bag in front of Khanh Nguyen:

"Come on, let's stop."

"What? How?"

---

[1] Vietnamese fish sauce

"You heard me. We have no interest in continuing. To continue can bring us only negative things: the Vietnamese people would reproach us for being stubborn, and if we catch the Coronavirus, it would be a catastrophe..."

"Are you sure about what you're saying, what you want?"

"We could leave Tank and Monster in this hotel, take the bus to Saigon and come back once everything is over."

"But the risk is the same! Taking the bus is the best way to catch the virus. And we aren't so far from the goal anymore. In ten days maximum, if we pedal more than one hundred kilometers (62 miles) per day, we will arrive in Saigon."

"Think about all the consequences this could have..."

"I want to continue. We aren't going to stop here after all this way. We have been through many more difficult things, and we continued... To stop here would be a failure. I don't want to look back and dwell on this trip as an unfinished business".

I was taken aback. I had thought, wrongly, that Khanh Nguyen would have also wanted to stop, even more than I did. I couldn't believe that she was the one trying to convince me to continue. Our exchange had the effect of a large icy bucket of water being thrown over my head. It revitalized me. It put my internal forces of despair back in their place. I looked her straight in the eyes:

"We will finish this."

∽

For the next ten days, we needed to activate our internal survival modes. First, we posted a message on our Facebook and Instagram pages asking for help from all those who had followed us. We indicated our route for the next few days and asked who might welcome us: Dong Hoi, Dong Ha, Huê, Hoi An, Tam Ky, Quang Ngai, Quy Nhon, Tuy Hoa, Nha Trang.

We received dozens of responses within a few hours from friends and

The mythical Cloud Pass (Hai Vân), Thua Thiên Huê, Vietnam

even strangers. Among them, hotels even offered to host us for free. They understood our situation, sympathized with us, and hadn't fallen into the blanked fear regarding the Coronavirus. Our hearts were overcome with gratitude for those in such solidarity with us. We could still do it. For almost ten days, we pedaled non-stop. Yes, people continued to avoid us, to put their hands on their mouths when they realized that we were travelers, but most nights, we knew that someone would be waiting to welcome us in. That changed everything for me psychologically. Cycling every day came with a goal, a mission, and all our energy to channel. I would like to take this opportunity to warmly thank all of our benefactors.

Excluding one night in our tent in the jungle north of Quy Nhon, we always had a place to stay. Whether it was a friend of Khanh Nguyen's big sister or a couple who had been following us for a long time on *Facebook*, they were there for us. We knew that we were in a race against time before Vietnam got locked down. I pedaled hard. A potential encounter with an overzealous local police officer was a constant fear for me.

When we were north of the ancient imperial city of Huê, it happened. We were riding towards our destination of the day when a policeman with his green uniform whizzed past us on his motorcycle. I saw him register who he had passed before he stopped dead. He turned around and started to follow us. I thought anxiously, "It's all over. He's going to quarantine us". He continued following us for a few hundred meters, at our speed. I began to prepare my speech and my list of arguments. Out of the corner of my eye, I saw that he had stopped again, however, consulting his cell phone. That enabled us to leave him behind. We arrived at a hotel run by Catholic sisters for the night. I was sure that the police would be waiting, in the Burmese way, but nothing happened. False alarm..

We left early, drinking a lot of water, and taking long breaks, negating the effects of the heat of the day. There were some small passes to cross along the coast, including the mythical pass of the clouds: the Hai Vân pass. With all the mountains and passes we'd overcome in the last year, it didn't represent a big challenge. We didn't really have time to enjoy the landscapes, but they were there: the sea, the dunes, and sometimes the rice fields. They accompanied us as if they were in the background.

In one week, we pedaled more than nine hundred (560 miles) to reach the North of Nha Trang, one of the biggest cities in central Vietnam. We were almost there! Only a few hundred kilometers (miles) remained before we would arrive in Saigon! Once again, the manager of a hotel offered to welcome us. The only condition was that we register with the local police and have our temperatures taken. The manager, let's call him Tuân for discretion's sake, told us: "Fifteen kilometers (9 miles) from Nha Trang, call me. I will contact the police". We waited patiently for the arrival of the police on a parking lot, in the shade of some tall tree, for a long time. Suddenly an ambulance arrived and stopped in front of the parking lot. They got out of the ambulance wearing masks, all in white, pushing a stretcher. Khanh Nguyen whispered to me: "Thibault, is this really for us?"

What was quite strange was that the nurses weren't coming towards us. They entered one of the modest houses in front of the parking lot. I certainly didn't dare to go up to them to inquire. Ten minutes later, they left the house pushing a little old lady on their stretcher! They were not there for us! Tuân chose then to call, explaining that a policeman would be waiting for us in the hall of his hotel. We laughed with relief at the misunderstanding.

It took us less than an hour to reach Nha Trang with its tall buildings standing along the beach. We arrived at the hotel of Tuân, where a policeman and a nurse were waiting for us as stipulated. It was our moment of truth: our temperature had to be below 37.5 °C (99.5 °F). The nurse started with Khanh Nguyen: 37.3°C (99.14°F). She was all clear. My turn: 37.1°C (98.78°F). We were safe! I had never been so happy to have a nurse tell me my temperature! We then had to fill in some papers concerning our health and our travels before the policeman and nurse left. We thanked Tuân as much as we could for welcoming us under those conditions and for taking the risk for us. He only replied that we needed to rest well for the rest of the journey. .

From My Home To Yours

◦∽◦

The cases of Coronavirus were rapidly multiplying, and soon the entirety of Vietnam would find itself confined. There were new cases in two provinces we had to cross: Ninh Thuan and Binh Thuan. Any movement from foreigners was completely forbidden there. The task seemed impossible. I was turning the problem upside down. Like fugitives on probation, I had the unpleasant feeling that our time was coming to an end. What to do?

Khanh Nguyen was sitting on the bed in our room with a magnificent view of Nha Trang and the sea framing her from behind. We both looked at each other, and without saying a word, understood what we had to do. It was time to stop. No more bullshit. There were too many headwinds. It was time to stop confusing panache with blind obstinacy. I hugged her silently. After a long and beautiful moment, I whispered to her, "We've given it our all. It's time to be reasonable now. I love you." Tears ran down her cheeks, and with that, the *Non-La Project* stopped.

A few minutes later, we received a call from Khanh Nguyen's parents. They were keeping up to date with the Coronavirus evolution and without even consulting us they had rented a car from their village located in Ba Ria, three hundred and fifty kilometers (217 miles) from Nha Trang to come to get us, Tank, and Monster.

◦∽◦

For the last time after almost a year on the road, I folded up my clothes one by one and placed them into my saddlebags. Everything was in its place. I emptied my two water bottles, filling them with fresh water. I put my camera and my phone in the bag attached to my handlebars. I checked the tire pressure of Tank and then Monster, giving them a little pump just in case. We said goodbye to Tuân, who held out his hand poignantly, wishing us the best.

We had planned to join Khanh Nguyen's parents on the outskirts

The big reunion, Nha Trang, Vietnam

of the city. We set off along the sea. I knew I would miss those moments: the first pedal strokes carrying so much promise, the innocent freshness of the first lights of the day. After a few kilometers (miles), we arrived at the meeting point. Khanh Nguyen's parents weren't there yet. We didn't speak much, doing everything we could to keep our composure. A few minutes passed, and a car appeared in the distance: it was them! One year and almost sixteen thousand kilometers (10,000 miles), and there we were, finally reunited! We hugged each other, cried, laughed.

EPILOGUE

Mileage Meter: 15,950 to 16,025km (9,910 to 10,000 miles)

When I wrote the tale of our adventure that you just read, I was still in the Ba Ria region, in the shadow of the house in which we isolated ourselves from society along with Khanh Nguyen's parents. Two weeks of voluntary isolation - so as not to pose a risk to Khanh Nguyen's grandparents - were extended by two weeks of national confinement. But you will be pleased to know that our adventure didn't stop there, Saigon was impatiently waiting for us!

Travel restrictions were soon lifted, and after more than a month of not moving, we could finally reacquire our freedom to cycle Vietnam's roads. We still had twenty-five kilometers (15 miles) to go before reaching the promised 16,000 kilometers (10,000 miles) and fulfilled our contract. Only seventy-five flat kilometers (47 miles) separated us from Saigon. Like two birds held for too long in a cage with too tightly closed bars, regaining joy and the freedom to cycle made us go in all directions. With our masks tightly installed on our faces, it only took us a few hours to reach Saigon. A year before, we had left the city where this had all started for us, and now we were back! Saigon is a city in constant flux: new neighborhoods, high towers, and roads spring up in such short time. Our lives were nothing in the shadows of those steel, concrete, and glass giants. Who had changed more that year we thought: Saigon or us?

We had an appointment at the French Consulate in Saigon where a reception would be held in our honor. At the Consulate, the members of the *Poussières de Vie* NGO, the Press, and the Consul General were there. A large panel had been set up in our honor with the names of all the donors. I felt emotional seeing those names. How much had we collected after 16,000 kilometers (10,000 miles)? 17,395 US dollars! The goal was more than fulfilled thanks to all our donors and benefactors who came from Vietnam, France, the

United States, Australia, Iran, Austria, and more! We had done it! I must admit that I sometimes had great moments of doubt in our ability to raise that amount of money, especially when the kilometers (miles) we were traveling accumulated faster than the donations. Hope gradually surfaced, thanks to the media exposure we had gotten closer to our goal.

Now, dear reader, it is time for me to try to put an ephemeral end to this tale. Through all these pages and my words, I hope that I have been able to convey to you a bit of the very substance of the longest journey of my life.

Become what you are is the injunction that can summarize all my lines best. This injunction is also reflected in Pindar and then Nietzsche. The notion is paradoxical: *Become what you are.* How can you try to become what is there all along? In essence, the idea is that we all have forces within us that are just waiting to be expressed. For me, those were the forces of travel, adventure, and the attraction of the unknown. For you, it's perhaps something else. There are forces within us that want us and that lead us. Believing that we are masters of ourselves, of our destiny, and our actions is perhaps the most damaging illusion of humankind in my view. For the more you try to ignore your inner forces, the more you will pursue more conservative ghosts, leading you away from yourself. The more you test the forces within you, and the more you try to embrace them, the more you will become what you are.

    This is what happened during one year on the roads of the world. I became what I was. I had the best reasons in the world not to make this trip: a good financial situation, a career to follow, and a family to start with Khanh Nguyen. But I listened to the beautiful little siren of adventure inside me and trusted my deepest instincts. The result was my completely jubilant joy, cycling every day, camping in the middle of nature, and meeting all those great souls who had strewn our journey from France to Vietnam. *Become what you are* is something dynamic. It's dynamite. I questioned and imploded many of my certainties to discover magnificent little truths. There will be a before and after this trip. I know that it will take the rest of my life to really understand how this bike trip has turned my whole physical and psychic ecosystem upside down.

But the real hero of our adventure was certainly not me: it was Khanh Nguyen. She was the real heroine. She was the one who, without any certainty, without any cycling experience, without any adventurous background, accepted to go with me and without any reservation. It was the omnipotence of love that expressed itself in her, a great Nietzschean 'Yes!'. Her endurance, determination, and beauty were admirable during those thousands of kilometers (miles). She took up an enormous physical challenge, but above all, a gigantic moral test. Several times she could have stopped, as in Azerbaijan, Iran, India, Myanmar, or even Vietnam, but each time she found the inexhaustible resources within her to continue. It was her on the second part of our trip that was the more solid of the two, the more serene, the one who reassured me and gave me back my confidence in times of difficulty. I would like to show her through these lines all my admiration and infinite love for her. The trip was beautiful because it was the experience of a lifetime together.

That's also the last little truth I have to share with you. We are nothing without those we love and without others. *Become what you are with and thanks to others.* We are the fruit of a long legacy. For me, it was my parents and grandparents who were the solid foundation on which I was able to begin the never-ending journey to *Become what you are.* My mother, my father, and the constellation woven by my ancestors and grandparents showed me the way. It remained for me to have the strength and courage to follow it or not. We are the fruit of our encounters, and in the end, we aren't much without the others. Nothing comes absolutely from oneself. How could we have made those sixteen thousand kilometers (10,000 miles) without the help of the hundreds of people who welcomed us with open arms along the way? I sometimes have flashes of happiness thinking back to the divine Maria and Vojtech who had welcomed us to their home in the Czech Republic, to Amin, Assieh and Hussein in Astara, Iran, to Reza and Zara in Aspas, still in Iran, and to the thousands of hugs received by all these students in uniforms from North-East India. I relive those moments spent in Georgia with the incredible Fanny we had spent days woven of light and happiness to experience freedom and true freedom. Those moments of life made me dizzy and were an inexhaustible well of joy and happiness. I even came to accept the idea of death, to get used to it. I know I have experienced the most beautiful things in life, and I can leave it when it wants me to. When it feels it's the right time.

Finally, our adventure was rich in meaning because it showed us the meaning of solidarity. It wasn't entirely centered on us but also on those who needed help, that little nudge that can, sometimes, change a life. Having been able to set up this pool for the street children of Saigon who are helped by *Poussières de Vie* invested us with a kind of mission. We couldn't give up for their sakes and for all the donors who believed in us. It was them too that I particularly want to thank. They don't know how much their gifts, small or large, meant and how much incredible strength they gave us to continue again and again towards Vietnam.

It's up to you, dear readers, to begin this magnificent adventure of Become what you are. If you have opened this book, it's because, maybe without knowing it, you surely have within you all the resources and strengths to do it.

The Non La Project gear list

Thibault's bicycle ("Tank"):

- 1 x Bicycle Patria Terra 2014 (second hand), steel frame, handlebar with three different hands positions
- 1 x Shimano SLX groupset (3x9 speeds)
- 2 x Sputnik 26" Rim
- 2 x Tire 26" x 2.00 Schwalbe Marathon Plus
- 2 x Mudguard
- 1 x Brooks Saddles B17 - Black leather - Man version
- 1 x Tubbus front rack
- 1 x Tubbus back rack
- 2 x Ortlieb Sport Roller Classic - 25L - Grey
- 2 x Ortlieb Sport Roller Classic - 40L - Grey
- 1 x Ortlieb Rack Back - 31L - Grey
- 1 x Ortlieb Handlebar Pannier - 7L - Grey
- 1 x Bell
- 1 x Front light
- 1 x Front wheel Dynamo - Shimano
- 1 x Back light (battery)
- 2 x Water bottles

Khanh Nguyen's bicycle ("Monster")

- 1 x Giant 1997 steel frame (second hand), tailor-made handlebar with four different hands positions
- 1 x Shimano Deore groupset (3x9 speeds)
- 2 x Sputnik 26 Rim
- 2 x Tire 26" x 2.00 Schwalbe Balloon
- 2 x Mudguard
- 1 x Brooks Saddles B17 - Black leather - Woman version
- 1 x Tubbus front rack
- 1 x Tubbus back rack
- 2 x Ortlieb Sport Roller City - 25L - Black
- 2 x Ortlieb Sport Roller Classic - 40L - Black
- 1 x Ortlieb Rack Back - 31L - Black

- 1 x Bell
- 1 x Front light (battery)
- 1 x Back light (battery)
- 1 x Lock (integrated to lock the back wheel)
- 3 x Water bottles

Camping, shower & laundry gear:

- 1 x Tent- 2 persons - Hubba Hubba NX (Grey color)
- 1 x Footprint - Quechua
- 2 x Silk inner sleeping bag - Cocoon
- 2 x Sleeping bag - Sea to Summit Micro Series II
- 2 x Ultra-sil compression sack - Sea to Summit
- 2 x Sleeping mattress -Therm-a-Rest ProLite
- 2 x Airpillow case - Exped
- 1 x Lightbulb – Quechua
- 2 x Headlights – Quechua
- 2 x Compact Towel, Quechua
- 2 x Small bottle for soap and shampoo
- 2 x Toothbrush
- 1 x Toothpaste
- 1 x Electric Shaver
- 1 x Small bottle of detergent
- 1 x Foldable Sink – Sea to Summit – 10L
- 1 x Laundry bag
- 14 x Clothespin
- 1 x Clothesline

Cooking gear:

- 1 x Cooking stove - MSR Dragonfly
- 1 x Fuel bottle - 590ml - MSR
- 1 x Cutting board
- 1 x Cooking pan – Quechua
- 2 x Plates mug, fork, spoon
- 1 x Pocket knife
- 1 x Water filter - Sawyer
- 2 x Water bag – 10 liters

- 6 x Containers for salt, pepper and spices
- 1 x Bag for vegetables and fruits

Clothes (for one person):

- 1 x Buff
- 1 x Helmet – Decathlon
- 1 x Beanie
- 1 x Winter scarf
- 1 x Long sleeves shirt – Icebreaker 200 Oasis
- 2 x T-shirts
- 1 x Shirt
- 1 x Jumper
- 1 x Winter Jacket
- 1 x Rain Jacket – Quechua
- 1 x Legging – Icebreaker 200 Oasis
- 1 x Pair of Jeans
- 1 x Short pants
- 2 x Pair of Socks- Icebreaker
- 4 x Underwear
- 3 x Bras (for Khanh Nguyen!)
- 1 x Pair of cycling gloves
- 1 x Pair of Winter Gloves – Quechua
- 3 x Pair of shoes (one for cycling / one for walking around/ flipflops)
- 2 x Shoe cover for rain – Vaude
- 1 x Pair of Sunglasses

Repair gear:

- 3 x Spare tubes
- 6 x Extra spokes
- 1 x Spoke wrench
- 8 x spare brake pads
- 1 x Patch kit (punctures)
- 1 x Pump
- 1 x Multi-tool
- 2 x Quick link (for the chain)
- 1 x Chain lube

- 1 x Repair/Duct tape
- 20 x Rilsan type collars
- Spare nuts, bolts, and washers

Electronics:

- 2 x Mobile Phone and charger
- 1 x Computer – MacBook Air and charger
- 1 x GPS – Garmin Inreach
- 1 x Camera – Canon EOS 6D, two batteries and charger
- 2 x Lens (50mm and 70-200mm) – Canon
- 1 x Gorilla pod
- 1 x Intervalometer
- 1 x Power bank (10,000 mAh)
- 1 x Hard Disk – 1 TB

Miscellaneous:

- 2 x Non La hats (!)
- 1 x Bike Lock
- 2 x Pepper spray
- 1 x Sunscreen Lotion
- 1 x Roll of Toilet paper/tissue
- 1 x Mooncup (for menstruations)
- Documents (passports, photocopies, emergency letter, travel insurance card)
- Basic first aid kit
- Paper books

ACKNOWLEDGMENT

I would like to thank EVERYONE for their support, their messages, gifts and/or for welcoming us into their homes throughout our long journey. To list your names would require another book!

I would also like to thank all the donors who participated in the fundraising for *Poussières de Vie*.

Finally, I would like to address a special thanks to Francis Murphy-Thomas for editing the English translation of this book.

AUTHOR'S NOTE

First, I would like to deeply thank you for having read this book.

If you have enjoyed it and want to make the book known, leave a comment on the platform page where you purchased it or tell your friends and family about it! Recommendations are the key to success for self-published authors!

If you want to contact us or if you have noticed any grammar or printing mistake inside the book, we would really appreciate it if you could send us an email to the following address:

nonlaproject.adventure@gmail.com

We invite you to follow our Instagram
and Facebook pages too:

Instagram : @nonlaproject

Facebook: nonlaproject

Best,

Thibault Clemenceau